Praise for The Battle for Brazil

"Suzanne Litrel's *The Battle for Brazil* offers insight into the inter-Iberian tensions that existed before the Luso–Dutch War and the strains it placed on Spain and Portugal's awkwardly interwoven colonial systems and economies in sugar, silver, and slavery. Although her work offers an important and original view of European and colonial war, global early modern empire, and colonial economies, the most groundbreaking aspect of Litrel's contribution is the immaculately researched analysis of the impact of Dutch occupation on Brazil's marginalized populations. She succeeds in finding the human voice in the various colonial archives; and with exceptional clarity narrates how Indigenous, Africans and Afro-Brazilians, Jewish and New Christians, and women negotiated and re-negotiated alliances with one, or both, sides involved in the conflict. They challenged the racial, religious, and gender hierarchies entrenched in the Iberian colonial empires. Litrel introduces her reader to an emergent Brazilian people—not Portuguese—who shaped the resistance to, and the expulsion of, the Dutch occupiers. In their decades-long challenge to colonial structures, the author is arguing for a new understanding of the very origin of Brazil."—Zachary R. Morgan, author of *Legacy of the Lash: Race and Corporal Punishment in the Brazilian Navy and the Atlantic World*

"Portuguese King Sebastian's legendary demise at the Battle of Alcácer-Quibir in 1578 and the challenges of Spanish rule and Dutch occupation immediately following profoundly shaped the Luso-Brazilian world. Suzanne Litrel confronts the mythologized narratives that sprang out of these critical years, showing how men and women from diverse backgrounds in Portugal, Brazil, and beyond navigated the tempestuous currents of this era—ultimately transcending the very myths that their stories would beget."—Erik Lars Myrup, author of *Power and Corruption in the Early Modern Portuguese World*

"Suzanne Litrel brings the seventeenth-century Atlantic world to life, showing how Brazil's fate was forged not only by empires but by diverse people whose struggles and alliances changed history. Enriched by original findings from the archives, it is a narrative that stands alongside, and pushes beyond, the classic works of Boxer, Russell-Wood, and Alencastro."—Ian Read, author of *The Hierarchies of Slavery in Santos, Brazil, 1822–1888*

"For a long time, historians of colonial Brazil and early modern Portugal downplayed the importance of breaking down the Dutch dominance in northeastern Brazil, seeing it as a failed attempt by European invaders to establish an enclave in South America. Recently, groundbreaking research projects are contesting this perspective, and following that lead, Suzanne Litrel's *The Battle for Brazil* highlights the extreme challenge, the strategy, and the Portuguese willpower in fighting an Atlantic war on two fronts for its survival as a nation and a worldwide empire. This included maintaining Brazil at all costs. Myriad sources, used with fluid and impressive dexterity and sensibility, from different languages, geographies, and backgrounds, make this work a major contribution to Portuguese, American, Atlantic, and colonial History. *The Battle for Brazil* shall remain a milestone and a standard work in those fields for many years to come."—Rodrigo da Costa Dominguez, author of *Fiscal Policy in Early Modern Europe: Portugal in Comparative Context* and coeditor of *Portugal in a European Context: Essays on Taxation and Fiscal Policies in Late Medieval and Early Modern Western Europe, 1100–1700*

The Battle for Brazil

The Americas in the World
JÜRGEN BUCHENAU, SERIES EDITOR

The Americas in the World series publishes cutting-edge scholarship about the Americas in global and transnational history, politics, society, and culture as well as about the impact of global and transnational actors and processes on the hemisphere. The series includes both works on specialized topics as well as broad syntheses. All titles aim at a wide audience.

Also available in the Americas in the World Series:

Transnational Humans and Transnationalisms in the Humanities: Crossing Boundaries in the Americas edited by Max Paul Friedman, Stefan Rinke, and Núria Vilanova
Cocaine: Criminals, Routes, and Markets edited by Sebastián A. Cutrona and Jonathan D. Rosen
Embracing Autonomy: Latin American–US Relations in the Twenty-First Century by Gregory Weeks
The Dollar: How the US Dollar Became a Popular Currency in Argentina by Ariel Wilkis and Mariana Luzzi
North American Regionalism: Stagnation, Decline, or Renewal? edited by Eric Hershberg and Tom Long

THE BATTLE FOR BRAZIL

Resistance, Renewal, and the War Against the Dutch, 1580–1654

SUZANNE M. LITREL

UNIVERSITY OF NEW MEXICO PRESS | ALBUQUERQUE

© 2026 by the University of New Mexico Press
All rights reserved. Published 2026
Printed in the United States of America

Library of Congress Cataloging-in-Publication Data
Names: Litrel, Suzanne author
Title: The battle for Brazil : resistance, renewal, and the war against the
    Dutch, 1580–1654 / Suzanne M. Litrel.
Other titles: Americas in the world
Description: Albuquerque : University of New Mexico Press, 2026. |
    Series: The Americas in the world | Includes bibliographical references
    and index.
Identifiers: LCCN 2025035796 | ISBN 9780826369055 paperback |
    ISBN 9780826369048 hardcover | ISBN 9780826369062 epub
Subjects: LCSH: Brazilians—Race identity | Brazil—History—Dutch
    Conquest, 1624–1654
Classification: LCC F2532 .L57 2026 | DDC 981.032—dc23/eng/20250815
LC record available at https://lccn.loc.gov/2025035796

Founded in 1889, the University of New Mexico sits on the traditional homelands of the Pueblo of Sandia. The original peoples of New Mexico—Pueblo, Navajo, and Apache—since time immemorial have deep connections to the land and have made significant contributions to the broader community statewide. We honor the land itself and those who remain stewards of this land throughout the generations and also acknowledge our committed relationship to Indigenous peoples. We gratefully recognize our history.

Cover illustration: Tereza Costa Rêgo, detail of *Women of Tejucupapo*.
Collection of the family, Recife, PE, Brazil.
Designed by Felicia Cedillos
Composed in Adobe Garamond Pro

For Chris

Contents

Acknowledgments ix

INTRODUCTION 1

CHAPTER ONE. The Return of the King: Prophecy, Imagination, and Memory 11

CHAPTER TWO. Journey of the Vassals: *Plus Ultra* Salvador 35

CHAPTER THREE. "Wild Nations of People": Rendering Faith, Collaboration, and Resistance 57

CHAPTER FOUR. Mistress, Mother, Soldier, Spy: Luso-Brazilian Women of Dutch-Contested Brazil 81

CHAPTER FIVE. "Hunger, the Biggest Battle": Finding an Army, Fueling Resistance 103

CHAPTER SIX. "All Men Have Death in Common": Restoration, Coordination, and Conflict 129

CHAPTER SEVEN. Discourse, Diplomacy, and the Commercialization of War 149

Epilogue 169

Notes 173
Bibliography 211
Index 231

Acknowledgments

Perhaps it's fitting that a history that begins with high hopes, an enduring dream, and unexpected challenges began to take shape during a global pandemic. By March 2020, with university access shuttered to the unaffiliated, social media (at the time, Twitter) alerted me to networking and grant opportunities, online discussion and writing groups, and more. But for the encouragement and good cheer from family, friends, and fellow scholars—as well as generous funding that once again afforded me access to library and archival collections—*The Battle for Brazil* would have occurred only in my imagination.

This work was envisioned early on in my return—after two decades!—to graduate school. My professor, adviser, and dissertation chair extraordinaire, J. T. Way, took me from almost no historical training to the completion of my doctoral work—and by extension this book. In my first semester at Georgia State University, as I flailed around for a topic on early sugar-producing Brazil, he suggested I "take a look at [the artist] Frans Post"; somehow he intuited my interdisciplinary approach to research and learning. Later he and fellow committee members Ghulam Nadri and Jake Selwood helped me envision additional chapters "for the book." Thanks go as well to Denise Davidson and David McCreery, both of whom read parts of this work in the choppiest of draft stages for my dissertation. I remain deeply grateful to the late Denis Gainty, who believed that a nonspecialist could take on a completely new discipline, field, and topic.

Scholarly generosity beyond Georgia State coaxed this book into existence. In 2021 an online Omohundro Institute "coffeeshop" on the Dutch Atlantic enabled me to workshop a new chapter on provisioning. Many thanks to Deborah Hamer for allowing me to crash the Dutch Atlantic party, to Joris van der Tol for his deep dive into and analysis of the chapter—and to all participants in that wonderful discussion group. Erica Heinsen-Roach and Sylvia Mitchell afforded me the opportunity to deepen this work, first at an American

Historical Association (AHA) conference panel sponsored by the Forum for Early Modern and Global Interactions (FEEGI) and then at Purdue University during its wonderful symposium on Ibero–Dutch entanglements. Lauren Benton encouraged this project early on and sharpened my focus. She listened to me muddle through how Sebastianism fit into the story of Dutch Brazil, helped hone my research question, and encouraged me to "just follow the evidence." I also appreciated her incisive comments on a new chapter at the 2023 Dartmouth History Institute. It was there that Ellen Nye and Paul Musselwhite offered keen critiques, which—along with the lively discussion that followed—helped bring the chapter into focus. Online or in person, *meus amigos brasilieros e portugueses* deserve a special mention: Hugo Araújo, Rodrigo Dominguez, Thiago Groh, Thiago Krause, Nelson Marques, and Bruno Miranda have been generous in sharing their expertise and materials.

I best imagine history when I can catch a "glimpse"; art has always been my starting point. Seventeenth-century images of the Dutch in Brazil first captured my attention, while recent creations helped round out the work. Many thanks to the wonderful staff at the Ricardo Brennand Institute, who facilitated permission to use an image of Frans Post's 1642 painting *Fort Frederick Hendrick* (chapter 3). I'm so thankful to Thiago Groh for connecting me directly to the family of Tereza Costa Rêgo. A detail of the late artist's astounding *Mulheres do Tejucupapo* graces the cover of this book, and an image of the full mural can be found in chapter 4. I am eternally grateful for her family's permission to use the image for the book. For me, her work captures the spirit and essence of the *Battle for Brazil*.

Early modern documents are increasingly available online, but research grants at institutions broadened possibilities for this work. During my dissertating days, a travel and research grant from Indiana University's Lilly Library afforded me time to sift through Charles Boxer's voluminous notes and correspondence. These opened up unexpected avenues for investigation. Funds from Georgia State University also helped research during my doctoral studies; several grants sent me to Portugal and Spain. But post-graduation and well into the pandemic, university libraries and archives remained off-limits to independent researchers. A short-term postdoctoral fellowship from the Omohundro Institute opened up time and space to return to this work. What a joy to return to the stacks and read deeply, this time for the book! Many thanks to Carol Gilmer and Martha Howard for helping me set up writing space. I'm grateful too for lovely conversations with Joshua Piker and Catherine Kelly, both of whom made me feel right at home. A short-term fellowship from the John Carter Brown Library and direct access to the JCB's rich collection proved invaluable. I remain thankful for Karin Wulf's warm welcome, as well as great conversations with José Monteluongo, Bertie Mandleblatt, Pedro Germano Leal, and Gabriel Rochas. Valerie Andrews and Kimberly Nusco provided critical help as I navigated the collections, and Allison Conroy coordinated fellowship logistics, including housing. Thanks as well to all my Fiering House fellows, especially and including Michelle McKinley and Shai Zamir. The summer of 2022, marked by friendship, camaraderie, and great scholarly exchange, remains a cherished memory.

Trying out new work in public settings has always helped me sort through material. My students at Georgia State and Kennesaw State helped shape my global approach to the Dutch challenge for Brazil. World History Association (WHA) friends have also encouraged this work over the past decade at the annual conference—and beyond! Thanks especially to Jack Bouchard, Sharon Cohen, Candice Goucher, Alan Karras, Laura Mitchell, Ian Read, Rick Warner, and Merry Wiesner-Hanks.

I am deeply appreciative of the whole University of New Mexico (UNM) Press team for their unwavering support. Jurgen Buchenau was unstintingly generous with his time, attention, and expertise, and he and Michael Millman—dream editors!—helped usher this work into existence. It was an absolute pleasure to work with the entire UNM Press production team—such a perfect blend of professionalism and deep care. I am also thankful to the press for arranging blind peer review of the book. The anonymous reviewers offered detailed and thoughtful comments, suggestions, and critique—all of which deepened this work and for which I remain grateful.

My family has marked this work through their own example and encouragement. My late parents, Judith and Sandro Segalini, bibliophiles and adventurers, introduced me to Brazil when Dad's work took us to São Paulo. There we stayed for eight formative years, until my senior year in high school; working on this book has taken me back "home." Thanks go as well to my sisters Deb and Carolyn for their good cheer and support. For the past decade, Julia and Alec have endured their distracted mother's musings on the Dutch challenge for Brazil, ordering me to "stop talking" and just write. Finally, I thank Chris, to whom this book is dedicated, for his love and support since our undergraduate days in Ann Arbor.

Introduction

Men invented books to preserve the memory of things past,
against the tyranny of the times, and against the forgetting of men . . .
which is an even greater tyranny.

—ANTÓNIO VIEIRA,
"SERMÃO DE NOSSA SENHORA DE PENHA DE FRANÇA"

IN THE EPIC POEM *Caramaru: poema épico do descubrimento da Bahia*, an Indigenous woman has a vision of a terrible future. From the sixteenth century, Paraguaçu predicts the arrival of plundering Dutch and an ensuing war.[1] Her story turns to triumph, however, as she foresees new alliances and a bold resistance by the men who lead the war. They included Henrique Dias, "captain of the brave Ethiopians," and "strong" Felipe Camarão, commander of Indigenous troops, both of whom steered the Portuguese to victory against the Dutch in 1654.[2]

While Frei José de Santa Rita Durão's 1781 poem, written for the "love of his homeland," is largely fictitious, the protracted struggle against the Dutch in Brazil was not.[3] The Dutch, like the English and French, had long threatened the Brazilian northeast for opportunity and plunder. But only the Netherlanders had seized a large chunk of the South Atlantic colony, first its administrative capital of Salvador (1624–1625) and then the northeastern half of Brazil (1630–1654). By highlighting participants of African and Indigenous descent as loyal Portuguese subjects in Brazil, *Caramaru* evokes the memory of an astounding victory against the Netherlanders.

The global Dutch threat to Portuguese colonies and posts had emerged, for all intents and purposes, when Portugal was subsumed by Spain in the union of the two crowns (1580–1640), but an upstart Luso-Brazilian resistance ended the Dutch Atlantic threat to Portugal in three decades. Written just over a century after the ouster of the Dutch from Brazil, *Caramaru* wed this victory to the national narrative—and with it an emergent, celebratory Brazilian trope of a multi-ethnic, heroic, and imaginative people. This was new: a mixed-descent guerrilla force defeated the mighty Dutch, and the colony of Brazil saved the metropole.

The Dutch occupation of northeastern Brazil (1624–1625, 1630–1654) prompted Portuguese Atlantic action. Prophecy, tradition, and opportunity galvanized *o povo* (the people). As the Dutch assaulted northeastern Brazil, aid from the metropole—whether Spanish-directed, to 1640, or Portuguese-driven, from 1641—proved inconsistent at best. Marginalized men and women maneuvered socioeconomic openings at this moment of profound crisis and made a difference. Far across the Atlantic, they demonstrated time-honored notions of loyalty but with a twist: they negotiated survival and status by drawing from prophecy, breaking social mores, and proving loyal to and betraying God and Portugal. The trauma of Dutch conquest served, then, as a crucible for both elite and popular Portuguese self-understanding—to enduring effect.

The Luso–Dutch struggle for Brazil begins not with seventeenth-century skirmishes on the beaches of Bahia, nor in competition wrought by early modern colonial ventures, but with a young Portuguese sovereign and his ill-executed plan to "be the lord of all of Africa."[4] As a tiny West Atlantic kingdom, Portugal had, until the 1580s, steered largely clear of wide-scale European religious conflict. This included the Dutch war for independence against the Spanish Habsburg Empire (1568–1648).[5] The untimely death of childless Dom Sebastião in 1578, however, sparked a succession crisis, partially resolved by Philip II of Spain's claim and ascension to the Portuguese throne in 1580. This meant that Portugal's participation in Spain's wars—and as a result, engagement with its enemies—now included conflict with the Dutch.[6]

As a result of the union of Spanish and Portuguese crowns, situational and juridical Dutch notions of "just war" led to Netherlandish claims on Portugal's far-flung possessions. The commercial-military Dutch East India Company (VOC), formed in 1602, took the now dual crown as open season on Portugal's "seaborne empire," to most profitable results. The newly chartered company hired Dutch legal jurist Hugo Grotius to defend the spectacular haul of the

Portuguese carrack *Santa Catarina* (1603); his *Mare Liberum* fueled moral justification for Dutch seizure of persons and property.⁷

From Amboina to Cochin, Portuguese *feitorias* (trading posts) fell to the Dutch East India Company's relentless assault. The Netherlanders then turned west. The Twelve-Year Truce (1609–1621) between Spain and the United Provinces afforded both the opportunity to shore up capital and arms, but the interlude only stoked Dutch enthusiasm for war profit. With its expiration, and with the support of the Reformed Church, the Netherlanders went into immediate and overtly belligerent action. In 1621 the Dutch States General authorized the charter of the West India Company (WIC). Like the VOC, its successful counterpart to the east, this new enterprise manifested secular and spiritual ambition.⁸ Now the Netherlanders launched a westerly attack on Brazil, aiming to rake in "white gold," extend Calvinist reach, and—from Salvador—build a South Atlantic empire.⁹ With hopes for a "fruitful harvest of souls" linked to commercial vision, the West India Company targeted Brazil's richest sugar-producing captaincies—first Bahia (1624–1625) and then Pernambuco (1630–1654).¹⁰

Early modern crises shook Portuguese faith through global Luso–Dutch wars. Domestic and continental conflict, the proliferation of print culture, and expanded, creative access to capital manifested in an enduring trial that would begin and end with the lost King Sebastian. Iberian baroque culture reflected crisis peculiar to this era through an awareness of societal restructuring; in the long arc of history, such shifts are not unusual.¹¹ But for Luso-Brazilians, the Dutch episode proved a crystallizing moment in Brazil's historical trajectory. Most notable among such documents, and from which this project amply draws, are Father Manuel Calado's *O valeroso Lucideno e o triunfo do liberdade* (1648), Duarte Coelho de Albuquerque's *Memórias diárias de la guerra del Brasil por discurso de nueve años* (1654), and Father António Vieira's "Carta Ânua" (1626). In their respective accounting of quotidian life during the ongoing battle for Brazil, these and other works indicate not only Luso-Brazilian resourcefulness and ingenuity but also a keen awareness of the historical moment that was Dutch Brazil.

Both in Brazil and in the metropole, history and remembering converged in sacral and prophetic realms, rooted in the very origin myth of Portugal. For instance, Jesuit António Vieira would rouse Portuguese parishioners as the enemy drew near, railing against God for handing the "whole world" over to the Dutch.[12] Vieira drew from his own experience of having fled the Dutch invasion of Bahia in 1624, when he was just a teen. Through him and others, we see an evolution in self-understanding sparked by the trauma of Dutch invasions. Like many Portuguese, Vieira turned to old, prophetic poems to explain the meaning of the Dutch occupation. The sixteenth-century *Trovas do Bandarra* (Ballads of Bandarra), created by shoemaker António Gonçalves de Bandarra, heralded the near ruin of Portugal and the return of a king who would lead it back to glory. For literati and spiritual leaders such as Vieira, such tales provided moral setting and context that gave Portuguese struggles greater meaning in times of crisis.

The effects of this early modern trial manifested across race and class in a reflection of what it meant to be Portuguese. In Brazil, reactions to Dutch challenge gave rise to new articulations of loyalty as Afro-descended and Indigenous residents not only pledged fealty to the Luso (Portuguese) cause but were also rewarded for their traditional expressions of valor, most notably on the battlefield. As a result, when the doubly subsumed kingdom was on the verge of collapse, what it meant to be an acknowledged subject of Portugal expanded to include non-white men and even women who negotiated for survival. The collective memory of Luso-Brazilian victory over the Dutch, including heroic depictions of Afro-Brazilian Henrique Dias and Indigenous Felipe Camarão, manifested in chronicles and now classic poems such as *Caramaru*—remembered, shared, and repeated for centuries to come.

This is a story of how a colony saved the metropole, an episode that endures beyond the end of the Luso–Dutch wars. Contested Dutch Brazil has been described as an "imperial moment" for the United Provinces."[13] This is also true for the Portuguese, who retained control of their prized colony. Brazil's sugar industry may not have regained its prewar production heights, but not long after the Dutch defeat, miners in Brazil literally struck gold. By 1808 Brazil would be the only European colony ever to house its ruling family, sheltering the Braganza royal family from Napoleonic wars and control. Brazil restored the kingdom of Portugal, supporting a waning maritime empire beyond the seventeenth century—and would become a mighty empire in its own right.

This book is also—though indirectly—about *saudade*, that melancholy borne of nostalgia and the people, places, and events that it evokes. It is about unearthing "sites of memory," material, symbolic, and functional spaces where history and memory converge in a collective remembering.[14] Both in Brazil and in the metropole, longing and remembering were rooted in the very origin myth of Portugal. For the seventeenth-century Portuguese, these sites were remembered, articulated, and given new life in discursive, performative, and violent gestures on and off the battlefield. The collective remembering of Luso-Brazilian victory over the Netherlanders helped shaped notions of what it meant to be Portuguese during and beyond the time of the Dutch.[15]

Atlantic Recollection and Renewal

The Battle for Brazil examines the Portuguese Atlantic reaction to the Dutch in Brazil. It takes this turning-point episode out of various scholarly *wunderkammern*, or cabinets of curiosity, and sets it in the currents of an Atlantic history crowded by narratives of Spanish, English, and Dutch empire.[16] Finally, this history suggests that the Dutch episode offers an opportunity to better engage Latin America, and specifically Portuguese America, in world history. For it is from the crucible of this war that nascent, coalescing Luso-Brazilian networks not only helped free Portugal from the Spanish and the Dutch but also—at the very least culturally—began to distinguish the colony from the metropole it rescued.

Remembering the battle for Brazil had once meant tracing Dutch effort, ascendance, and legacy in the northeast—a narrative now darkened with quotidian realities of transatlantic war. Twentieth-century English and Portuguese language surveys of Dutch Brazil have made ample use of a well-ordered Dutch record; this accounts, perhaps, for the enduring legacy of Dutch Brazil and its "humanist prince," West India Company governor-general Johan Maurits van Nassau-Siegen. Here, Dutch Brazil is described in terms of religious tolerance as well as aesthetic and cultural achievement: the aristocratic Maurits brought order and progress to long-neglected Brazil.[17] More recent histories of the Luso–Dutch battle for Brazil and the Atlantic world have homed in on the trials of West India Company efforts, including the ordeal of foot soldiers as they managed waning support and confronted unrelenting resistance. Shifting, opaque alliances with settlers and Indigenous peoples dampened soldierly morale; hunger and disease also took their toll.[18]

The Battle for Brazil builds on and synthesizes the rich work of Brazilian scholars, in particular those hailing from the northeast—for whom the Dutch episode is personal. Soon after Brazil's independence from Portugal in 1822, scholars traveled to the Netherlands to translate and transcribe critical Dutch documents, part of a broader effort to build a national narrative.[19]

Such effort picked up pace into the next century.[20] The resulting collections of Dutch-derived work helped foster the work of Recife-born José Antônio Gonsalves de Mello, whose *Tempo dos flamengos* (1947) offers an enduring examination of the sociocultural effects of Dutch occupation.[21] While he highlighted Maurits's administration (1637–1644), he also noted the failure of the West India Company to acknowledge local concerns and customs.[22] Three decades later, Brazilian diplomat Evaldo Cabral de Mello delved more deeply into dynamics of the conflict-ridden colony. Influenced by the Annales school and in particular the work of Fernand Braudel, his *Olinda restaurada* situated Dutch Brazil in the context of wider European continental conflict.[23] The prolific Pernambucan later investigated how the struggle shaped Luso-Brazilian memory of Dutch occupation from the seventeenth through nineteenth centuries—and with it, the influence of Maurits and the West India Company on the "local imagination."[24]

Brazilian scholars continue to draw from the rich, contemporary Portuguese record, creating fine-grained histories that have guided this work. Ronaldo Vainfas, for example, investigates overlooked "anti-heroes" during the time of the Dutch, considering the choices and impulses that drove double-crossing Portuguese to action.[25] Their evolving status—from sidelined troublemakers to key players in the war against the Dutch—reveals as much about the opportunities they negotiated as it does about the evolution of Luso-Brazilian "identity" during this time. For it was during the time of the Dutch in Brazil that notions of what it meant to be Portuguese far from the metropole appear to have emerged.

Negotiating Dutch Brazil

In explicating the *longue durée* evolution of Portuguese self-understanding and reaction to the Dutch in Brazil, the first chapter of this work opens with the story of Portugal's founding and considerations of Portuguese identity from the twelfth century. The death of heirless King Sebastian in 1578, Philip II's 1580 ascension to Portugal's throne, and the Dutch global attack on Portuguese claims tapped into enduring, discursive notions of Portugal's once-expansive identity and fate. Circulating works such as *Trovas do Bandarra* and *Os Lusíadas* prophesied dark times followed by a glorious era in which Portugal would come to reign as God's kingdom on earth. This chapter traces the collision of Sebastianism, rooted in Portuguese mythological and prophetic tradition, with Dutch military–backed notions of "free seas" and "just war." This meant Dutch conquest of Portuguese overseas posts and enduring attacks in the east and then—with the creation of the Dutch West India Company—in the South Atlantic with the 1624 seizure of Bahia.

Chapter 2 examines the Portuguese reaction to Dutch and Spanish "captivity" through the Iberian reconquest of Bahia. This episode led to the emergence of a transatlantic Lusophone consciousness that cut across occupation, rank, and class. The primary Portuguese account of the 1624 Dutch conquest of Salvador, Jesuit novice António Vieira's report to Rome, sheds light on the coordination of Jesuits and their Indigenous troops. From the backlands, and with the aid of men from neighboring captaincies, they pinned the Dutch fast to Salvador—until the arrival of the largest armada to ever cross the Atlantic. The "voyage of the vassals" by Luso–Spanish loyalists then helped defeat the enemy. Post-celebratory Spanish and Portuguese depictions of the reconquest reveal tension between the groups and how a dissolution of the crowns might affect the ground war in Brazil.

The third and fourth chapters subvert textual and visual renderings of Dutch-held Brazil to examine how, from 1630, marginalized subjects of Portugal negotiated Netherlandish presence in Pernambuco. Indigenous, Afro-descended, and mixed-descent men willingly participated in cross-cultural alliances for the Portuguese cause, exemplified by the actions of Afro-descended Henrique Dias and Indigenous leader Felipe Camarão. Luso-Brazilian and Indigenous women also engaged with and against the Dutch; the most martial of them were celebrated in their time and are remembered to this day. Marginalized subjects in Portugal and Brazil engaged in demonstrations of loyalty and in some cases earned public acknowledgement not afforded prior to the Dutch episode.

On the ground, cross-captaincy coordination sustained the Luso-Brazilian resistance through and after the restoration of Portugal. How did the dissolution of the dual Iberian crown manifest in recruitment, provisioning, and decision-making? Chapters 5 and 6 consider growing coordination—apart from the metropole—within the Portuguese Atlantic world. Despite administrative restructuring that led to the creation of the Overseas Council and a streamlined approach to colonial governance, direct financial and material help was not readily forthcoming. Examining the on-the-ground realities of support for war efforts, the fifth chapter traces waning Crown efforts as Portugal confronted the Spanish threat on the border. Luso-Brazilian coordination coalesced in mustering local men and foodstuff, most notably manioc. Chapter 6 examines the impact of the 1640 restoration of Portugal across Portuguese and Spanish America, forcing Luso loyalists back to Brazil as the trans-American borders closed. Through the 1640s, the resistance coordinated restoration from Rio de Janeiro and Bahia to regain Portuguese rule in the Brazilian northeast and West Africa.

From Brazil, colonialist victories forced metropole action. The final chapter of *The Battle for Brazil* examines how continental efforts to contain the conflict—through negotiation, diplomacy, and literary legitimizing measures—fell short and how local, sustained defiance to the Dutch in Brazil influenced outcomes. Post-restoration, a depleted treasury and no end to the Luso–Dutch war in sight prompted Dom João IV to consider selling Brazil to the Dutch. The surprising success of the "Divine War of Liberation" (1645–1654) ended such talk: Luso-Brazilian resistance forces successfully coordinated and pushed pack against the Dutch, with relatively minimal support from the metropole. This marked an agentic shift as colonialists forced the hand of the Crown. By 1648, clear Luso-Brazilian victories had revived support for a sugar fleet convoy to protect the colony's "white gold." The Brazil General Company, as this armed convoy was known, offered aid by way of munitions and materiel and would replenish treasury funds drained by fighting a multi-front war.

Throughout the long period of suppression—at home by the Spanish and abroad by the Dutch—the Portuguese rallied on the one hand by tapping into prophecy and myth and on the other by demonstrating loyalty, honor, and valor. Emergent, layered discourses regarding sovereign and subject identity, sparked by the Luso–Dutch wars, led to unexpected alliances as marginalized actors negotiated openings in the protracted Atlantic struggle. This cross-class and inter-ethnic coordination of Portuguese men and women coalesced under Spanish rule (1580–1640) but intensified and took on new meaning with Portugal's independence from Spain in 1640.

The Dutch West India Company withdrew from Portuguese America in 1654 and—bankrupted by the end of the seventeenth century—from nearly the entire Western Hemisphere. One enduring legacy of the chronically troubled enterprise manifested where the WIC sought control: on-the-ground resistance led to an emerging Luso-Brazilian identity. This consciousness translated into action, sparking the restoration of Portuguese Brazil and, by extension, the material and spiritual salvation of the kingdom of Portugal.

CHAPTER ONE

The Return of the King

Prophecy, Imagination, and Memory

THE DESERT MARCH FROM Arzila to the Battle of Alcácer-Quibir was one of the few significant decisions King Sebastian of Portugal would make in his young, short life. The other was to retake the North African port of Larache in the first place.[1] In 1578 the Jesuit-raised Dom Sebastião, as he was known, had challenged the sultan of Morocco to reclaim what he believed was rightfully Portuguese; in so doing, he would avenge his family name—and God.[2] And so thousands of Portuguese loyal to O Desejado, the Desired One, the only son of an only son, followed the childless twenty-four-year-old sovereign to their death.

The succession crisis that followed, and with it Spain's subsumption of Portugal (1580–1640), nearly destroyed the tiny kingdom and its global maritime empire.[3] The Portuguese were soon dragged into continental conflict, and Portugal's eastern outposts came under attack. In 1583 Philip II of Spain invaded England with the help of the Portuguese, now his vassals—to disastrous effect. All twelve ships and five thousand men out of Lisbon were lost. Beyond that, Portugal's "Babylonian captivity," as the Iberian Union came to be known, also damaged long-enjoyed trade relations with the Dutch. The Netherlanders had been in revolt against the Habsburg Empire since 1568; the Spanish now embargoed their ships in the port of Lisbon.[4] The Dutch retaliated with a vengeance. Emboldened by an excuse to seize Portuguese-turned-Spanish claims abroad, their military-commercial companies encroached on the far-flung Lusophone world.

The Castilian advance and the 1580 installation of Philip I (Philip II of Spain) to the Portuguese throne also sparked millenarian hope of King Sebastian's return. Now, so the story went, after years of suffering, the king would reappear to lead Portugal as God's sovereign on earth. The Portuguese spoke of "Sebastian sightings," and indeed, more than a few imposters claimed the throne. These included a baker and a Calabrian who spoke no Portuguese.[5] Perhaps the "sleeping king"—a riff on Arthurian lore—had returned.[6] After all, as Sebastianist writer Dom João de Castro reminded his readers in 1603, God had worked miracles for his people before—beginning with the very founding of Portugal in 1139.[7]

What accounted for the pull of messianic thinking in early modern Portugal? If later in this history it would be crisis—the Spanish captivity, the Dutch occupation of Brazil—at the beginning, it was rapid territorial expansion that kept the myths alive. Lusitanian myth, faith, and messianism evolved with early formation of the Portuguese maritime empire, but this dialogic of expansion was rooted in the mythical twelfth-century founding of Portugal. In the early modern era, a trope of exceptionalism iterated in major events: Portugal's early settlement of Brazil, the maturation of the India trade, and the rise of slave-fueled sugar production, with all the wealth that it engendered. Enduring discourse of prophecy connected to Portuguese political ambition, which by the sixteenth century was now global in scope.[8] During the trauma of Dutch global aggression, this narrative took on new meaning in literature and religious texts. Through continued crisis, the death and the memory of King Sebastian sparked prophetic notions. Hinted at in the *Trovas do Bandarra*, they were rooted in enduring moral narratives, particularly in the Old Testament concept of the "return of the king."

The eschatological articulation of the Luso–Dutch conflict drove Portuguese action at home and abroad.[9] This, then, was more than a reflex response to the trauma of Alcácer-Quiber and a king-less Portugal: in the context of the global Dutch threat, Sebastianism also drew from and transformed long-held notions of what it meant to be Portuguese. Such visions collided with and were realized by Dutch action and articulation of free seas and "just" appropriation of land, people, and goods.[10] But the Portuguese millenarian reaction to this crisis—the conflict-ridden first half of the seventeenth-century—reveals that resurrected sentiment, rooted in the very founding of Portugal, mitigated the realities of a kingdom under siege.

Envisioning Portugal: 1139–1603 CE

The founding miracle of Portugal was in its twelfth-century formation as an independent kingdom, free from Galician suzerainty and the more serious Muslim threat.[11] Two years after negotiating the Treaty of Tui in 1137, Afonso Henriques of Portugal curtailed his excursions into Galicia (present-day northern Spain).[12] He turned his attention instead to an immediate and very real concern: an enormous army of Almoravids had crossed the Mandego River, overrun the castle at Leira, and now descended on the town of Tomar.[13] Afonso prepared to meet them on a wide plain. This site would become known as the battlefield at Ourique. According to his chroniclers, the future first king of Portugal gathered his army and swung south. Then he prayed, so the story went, for divine reward.

The night before the battle, Afonso saw a crucified Christ in the sky and a message that his Christian army would defeat the Muslims—or so he claimed. "I will establish a kingdom," he then pronounced, "by whose actions my name will be known to strange peoples."[14] His vision proved prophetic. Badly outnumbered but armed with faith, O Fundador (the Founder) confronted the enemy. Five Muslim kings may have led an army against the Portuguese, but the divinely inspired Afonso emerged victorious:

> Here, upon his own white shield,
> Triumphantly he drew,
> Five blue buckles, clearly rendered
> Five kings defeated, thusly remembered.[15]

Having delivered the Portuguese from the enemy, Afonso now set about memorializing the event and his own role in it. Following the battle, Afonso sought and obtained acclamation from the clergy, nobles, and commoners at the nearby town of Lamego. Legitimized by spiritual visions and secular support, Afonso Henriques became the first king of Portugal. He threw off the Almoravid armies once and for all and permanently secured freedom from his overlord, the Galician King Alfonso of León.[16] Afonso's peers were little more than lukewarm at his acclamation; he had already earned a reputation for restless energy and insolence. But during the course of his long reign (1139–1185),

Figure 1. António Soares de Albergaria, *Miracle at Ourique*. Originally published in Albergaria 1632. Courtesy of Biblioteca Nacional de Portugal via Wikimedia Commons. Licensed under CC BY 4.0. https://creativecommons.org/licenses/by/4.0.

artists and scholars ingrained the victory of Ourique in Portuguese memory; images of the battle-ready king kneeling before a vision of Christ would be reproduced for public consumption in the decades to follow, especially during times of crisis (Figure 1). Within a decade of his victory, King Afonso's army recaptured Lisbon, held by Muslims since 716 CE. One hundred years later, the Portuguese *reconquista* was complete.

In the centuries to follow, spurred by a Christianizing, expansionist vision, Atlantic-facing Portugal would lead the world in global exploration.[17] From the fourteenth century, Portuguese portolan charts, a vast improvement over medieval *mappa mundiae*, directed sailors down the west coast of Africa and, by the end of the fifteenth century, across the Indian Ocean. With their frightening renditions of lurking maritime monsters and other dangers, mappa mundiae were meant as warnings for sinners rather than for practical use by navigators.[18] The rhumb lines of portolan maps, on the other hand, were meant to guide ships from known port to port. Cartographic and other navigational improvements—the caravel, the carrack, the mariner's astrolabe, for example—point to how exploration and expansion were changing Portugal. The incorporation of such East Asian and Islamic navigational technologies enabled the Portuguese to bridge the gap between astronomers and navigators, both of whom had turned to celestial understanding. Now Portuguese pilots moved farther from the coastline altogether—until they sailed in open water and out of land's sight.[19]

Portuguese mythological discourse evolved as well. Since Ourique, prophecy and myth had served as the guiding call to exploration. For example, Dom João II (1455–1495) was determined to track down the mythical Christian king Prester John, whose lost realm, it was rumored, lay behind Muslim lines. By land and by sea, Dom João II sought to find and free him. He dispatched the Arabic-speaking Pero de Covilha, who sent back word of Prester John, as well as Bartholomeu Dias, whose quest resulted in his rounding the Cape of Good Hope in 1488.[20] Spiritual motivation for exploration continued in the years ahead.

The Portuguese, like the Spanish, now assumed rights to and fought over territorial claims far beyond imagined lost kingdoms. The first phase of exploration, confirmed through a succession of papal bulls, envisioned one global ocean but no clear cartographic understanding of what that meant.[21] For instance, with the Indian Ocean not yet on the horizon and the Spanish to contend with, the Portuguese were granted, by the 1479 Treaty of Alcaçovas, all Atlantic islands save the Canaries, as well as monopoly rights to the west coast of Africa.[22] The Spanish claimed—and the Pope accepted—territory north of and including the Canary Islands. And so the Portuguese and the Spanish staked global, if tenuous, claims with the Treaty of Tordesillas (1494), which created an arbitrary line that ran through South America.[23] The Portuguese would push the line of demarcation farther west than originally imagined, but the shifting boundaries indicate a general desire between Portugal and Spain to maintain peace as they divided the world up for Christendom.[24]

Portugal and Spain still sought papal dispensation for their conquests, but beyond religious blessing, economic concerns also drove and justified the exploratory impulse toward expansion.[25] Prolific returns on spices helped fuel this drive. For Portugal, the outward route of what would become the Carreira da Índia, or India trade from Lisbon to Goa, took Portuguese explorers and merchants south from Lisbon to Cabo Verde, skirting the South Atlantic gyre to the Cape of Good Hope—and on to Indian Ocean destinations such as Goa and Cochin. They would create and connect coastal feitorias, forming an expansive—if uneven—maritime empire.

On April 1, 1500, just two years after Vasco da Gama opened a southeastern route out of Portugal, Pedro Cabral made unexpected landfall on the Brazilian northeast. This was not his original destination; he headed east from this "minor diversion," following Vasco da Gama's route to Calicut. Indeed, Crown attention remained fixed on the Indian subcontinent. King Manuel, advised in 1504 of possible attacks on Portuguese there by the Ottomans, Mamluks, and Venetians, intended to create "a whole new state in the Indian Ocean."[26] This led to the creation, by 1515, of the Estado da India, an audacious attempt at Portuguese political and religious oversight over whole South and Southeast Asian worlds. Portuguese missionaries accompanied merchants in the crusade for spices and souls; the king would keep Ottomans at bay even as his subjects traded with non-Christians in pepper, spice, and more. For at least a few decades, then, what would become Brazil was passed over by ambitious Portuguese for far greater reward.

Westward, no such Portuguese equivalent existed—no "state of the Atlantic Ocean." But through the course of the sixteenth century, as Brazil's potential became apparent to the Crown, the actions of settlers and competitors warranted greater administrative control. The Portuguese elite, following Vasco da Gama, generally neglected the Ilha da Santa Cruz, as Brazil was first named, for their commercial crusade to the east. For those seeking noble status and privilege, however, opportunities that were scarce in Portugal could be had in Brazil. Titles and land grants were open to those who could prove—in carefully crafted letters and petitions—loyalty and service via expansionary efforts. Whereas shorter-term Indian Ocean ventures encouraged merchants to handle business and return home, explorers in Brazil settled down and fanned out from Salvador, Rio de Janeiro, and Recife. Brazil also proved fortuitous—a solution of sorts, at least in the short run—for Portuguese New Christians and Jews. After financing an expedition of the northern coast of Brazil, Fernão de Loronha, factor of German Jewish investor Jakob Fugger, headed a consortium of New Christian investors and gained hereditary captaincy of the island archipelago that would be known as Fernando de Noronha. The captaincy, leased out for three years, served as a haven for several hundred Jews and New Christians and turned a nice profit in brazilwood for investors.[27]

Western European challengers followed in Cabral's South Atlantic wake. His brief stop in Porto Seguro had yielded fair returns from Indigenous *pau-brasil* (brazilwood), for instance, as the plant's red dye produced a royal hue coveted by the French and across the European continent. Within three decades, the Spanish, en route to de Rio de la Plata, and the French, hovering off the coast, presented a real nuisance. Along with the English, Irish, and Dutch, they sought treasure beyond brazilwood, pursuing legendary tales of an Emerald Mountain. They also imagined silver mines in the *sertão* (the backlands)—what they hoped would be their own equivalent of Potosí.[28]

As the lure of Brazil's promise attracted unwelcome competitors, the Crown shifted the costly burden of defense to private individuals. They—as with Fernão de Loronha—would be held responsible for transporting goods and labor.[29] By 1530 Portugal had taken steps to administer the colony more formally, but it did so by proxy. The king awarded large land grants to nobles who had demonstrated fealty, practicality, and a religious sensibility, and he gave these *donatários* (lord-proprietors) broad juridical, fiscal, and political powers.[30]

The donatários and those who followed them soon brought Brazil's sugar industry to prominence, ushering in great fortune, new worries, and no end of discourse on decadence. The conflict between divine purpose and worldly wealth played out in public—notably the royal theater. Poet and playwright Gil Vicente (1465–1536) presented his *Auto da Lusitânia* to King João III in 1532. This allegorical drama touched on the mythological origins of Portugal and confronted moral issues of the day—most notably the quest for riches.

As in the contemporaneous English morality play *Everyman*, Vicente's dramatis personae faced judgement for their actions.[31] In a key episode of the two-part drama, he presented two familiar characters, Todo o Mundo (Everyone or Everyman) and Ninguém (No One). Todo o Mundo presents himself as a rich merchant, but he is looking about for something. The shabbily dressed Ninguém asks what he is doing, to which Todo o Mundo answers that, as ever, he is searching for money. No One responds that he is a nobody but that he is searching for conscience.[32] In the piece, two devils, named Dinato and Berzebu (Beelzebub) pose as chaplains; they listen in so they can relate all to Lucifer. Berzebu takes notes on Everyone and No One, and concludes that "Every One is a flatterer/And No One is fooled."[33]

Early modern Portuguese playwrights were not alone in issuing allegorical or other warnings on corruption from riches, but Portuguese identity, in legend and in letters, had long linked expansion to spiritual purpose.[34] As moral and material challenges of Portugal's seaborne empire played out in trading posts and the court stage, Jesuits fanned out across the Indian and Atlantic Oceans, sending reports of their efforts back to Rome and Lisbon. Their goal was to save souls and win converts, and this included reminding the Portuguese of their sacred duties in global expansion.[35] At every level, Portuguese historical actors linked their overseas expansion, driven by the pursuit of wealth derived of spices and sugar, to their understanding of their kingdom's divine purpose.

Making such direct connections between the economic and the spiritual became more difficult by the late 1500s, by which time another treasure beckoned: "white gold," or sugar. The entrenchment of the sugar economy was due in large part to a staggeringly high return on investment. For this reason as well, the Crown paid new attention to the colony after most of the first captaincies failed; of the fifteen original such grants in Brazil, only Pernambuco and São Vicente had survived. Both had been directly run by experienced, hands-on lord-proprietors, a fact not lost on the Crown.[36] In 1549 King Sebastian's father, Dom João III, approved of a single governor-general to consolidate rule from Bahia.[37] This led to thriving *engenhos* (sugar mills), which increased in number in the decades ahead. From 1570, Bahia and Pernambuco accounted for the majority of all engenhos in Brazil, to great results for those directly involved in the sweet business of sugar. Indeed, given the rising demand all across Europe and excellent returns on related investments, revenue from Brazil was more than 50 percent of its cost to the Crown.[38] From 1570 to 1584, Pernambuco led the way with an annual rate of growth at 8.4 percent; Bahia was a close second at 5.4 percent.[39] By the end of the sixteenth century, Brazil's white gold had proved profitable for Portugal.

Brazil's sugar trade sparked new challenges within and beyond the Portuguese Atlantic world. For instance, in 1595 the privateer James Lancaster captured the northeast port town of Recife for a month and loaded his ships with fifty thousand pounds sterling worth of sugar.[40] The rich trade also prompted an expansion of the elite class and considerations of their decadent behavior. Now white gold gave rise to a new nobility, the *açucarocracia*, or "sugarocracy," whose fortunes far outstripped those of the Old World nobility and whose crass behavior invited spiritual reproach.[41] This was a far cry from the times of King

Afonso the Conqueror, who had received divine inspiration and blessing at the Battle of Ourique to protect Portugal's borders against the Moors. Portugal's history had incorporated *his* vision, which had—according to legend—spurred him to claim land in the name of God and Portugal, and not material wealth.

The spiritual dimensions of Portugal's quest for wealth were less apparent to the impoverished and enslaved workers who were forced to produce it, although the conditions in which they toiled were also the subject of moralizing discourses. Securing a stable workforce for the labor-intensive sugar economy proved an enduring problem for planters. To the south, engenhos in São Vicente and Rio de Janeiro began to thrive; *bandeirantes* (backwoodsmen from São Paulo) went deep into the interior to enslave Indigenous people for field and other work. Disease reduced the use of their labor to a temporary solution, and the Crown legislated against enslavement of those it had a "moral imperative" to Christianize. By the late 1550s, Jesuits had obtained permission to herd Indigenous peoples into *aldeias*, carefully ordered and controlled agricultural villages, ostensibly for their own protection and salvation but also to grow sugar cane and much-needed (for the settler Europeans) food crops.[42] By the early 1600s, forced African labor and modifications to the extraction process had vaulted Brazil to the top of all exporters; in terms of output, the captaincies of Pernambuco and Bahia were most prolific.[43]

The demand for labor only increased.[44] By the seventeenth century, the Portuguese had seized and converted the fortress of Elmina on the West African coast for the purpose of slaving. Elmina, originally erected to trade African gold, was now transformed into holding pens for Africans shipped across the Atlantic to work the fields. By 1630, when the Dutch invaded Pernambuco, African labor stoked the roughly 350 engenhos in full operation in Brazil.

From its twelfth-century founding at the Battle of Ourique to full reconquista, Portugal's banner unfurled east and west from Melaka to Bahia. As they led the way in navigational advances, scouring for commercial and religious opportunities, the Portuguese corralled people and goods, connecting Lusophone Atlantic and Indian Ocean worlds. The age-old nuisance of piracy notwithstanding, the Portuguese founded feitorias and claimed territory along the African, Indian, and Southeast Asian coastline. In Brazil, Portuguese demand for forced labor led, by the mid-1500s, to a developing transatlantic slave trade, ratcheting up sugar production in Brazil. Now the once-neglected colony proved its worth. Despite moral concerns regarding material riches, it seemed that by the late sixteenth century, Afonso's vision for a triumphant, expansive kingdom was finally realized. The Portuguese did not predict, however, a Dutch run on their global claims.

Sebastianism: An Early Appeal

The expansion and global reach of Portugal from Galician suzerainty to seaborne empire made real the promise of Ourique: faith-driven action would be rewarded. Navigational advances led to eastern treasure—spice, silk, and jewels—which in turn fueled more exploration. But sixteenth-century literary and religious writings reflected concerns of overreach, a squandering of the spiritual and, with it, the future of Portugal.

Such considerations would take new form in a most unlikely place: a cobbler's shop in northern Portugal. The seeds of Sebastianism, the hope of the returned ill-fated Dom Sebastião—and by extension Portugal and its overseas possessions—took root in the workshop of shoemaker António Gonçalves de Bandarra (1500–1556). Decades ahead of the arrival of Dom Sebastião O Desejado, the erstwhile poet of Trancoso, a mostly New Christian town, stitched together what would become known as the *Trovas do Bandarra*. In the next century, the ballads, drawing from Judaic messianic thought, would reverberate across the Atlantic. Bandarras's work would come to contextualize for the Portuguese the Dutch and Spanish challenge for their "chosen" kingdom.

The *Trovas*, first shared around 1530, begin with the mythical revival of Portugal at the 1139 Battle of Ourique and tells of the kingdom's glorious future. Bandarra tells of a hard-charging new sovereign who would forge the way for God's kingdom on earth while other weak and fearful nations fell in line.[45] This king would have a new name—one unheard of throughout Catholic and indeed Protestant Europe. He would usher in a challenging new age: "This King who is yet born/will roam from land to land/Many people will die."[46]

Portuguese cultural tradition had long been influenced by messianic inspiration, beginning with the origin myth of Portugal and King Afonso's deliverance of the kingdom from the infidels. But Bandarra's work, in its acknowledgement of suffering, reflected challenges revealed in the Old Testament's Book of

Daniel. In its prediction of trials before glory, the work held special appeal for persecuted New Christians.⁴⁷ Like Gil Vicente's *Auto da Lusitânia*, Bandarra's verses took hold in the Portuguese imagination. But while the work of the former played out on the royal stage, the poet-cobbler was hauled before the Inquisition and forced to explain his vision; the church approved of moral warnings but considered prophecy a serious offense. Predicting suffering borne of a yet unnamed Portuguese king smacked of heresy, but after his 1541 auto-da-fé, the suspected New Christian was chastised and released.⁴⁸

The public castigation, however, did little to wane enthusiasm for Bandarra's work in the decades to follow. When the sole heir to the Portuguese throne, Prince Dom João Manuel, died in 1554, a few days ahead of his firstborn's arrival, the whispers began: Was this the "yet born" king about which the cobbler wrote? The heir to the kingdom of Portugal would be named Sebastian, for the saint on whose day he was born. It was a new regnal name, as Bandarra had predicted. No king had ever been named Sebastian, "not in England, France, or Scotland."⁴⁹

The birth of Sebastian, sole heir to the throne, from the start had a special significance.⁵⁰ But while the tidings were good, the outcome was terrible. The ideal early modern sovereign "heeded his advisers, studied well, dispensed justice, balanced prudence with bravery, and took care not to put the royal body at risk." He also ensured the continuation of his line.⁵¹ Sebastian did none of these. Raised by Jesuit priests, he shunned women and matrimony to serve, instead, as a soldier of God. This meant reclaiming forts in North Africa for God's chosen kingdom, Portugal. When the shereef of Fez lost his throne to his uncle and reached out to the Portuguese for help, Sebastian took action. Against the wishes of his mother, Juana, her brother Philip II of Spain, and his great uncle confessor and guardian (upon Juana's departure for Spain) Cardinal Henriques, Sebastian was determined to restore North Africa to Portugal—or at least the part of it that had been lost decades earlier. As his council and advisers tried to steer him off course, his plan caught the public imagination.

King Sebastian wanted to be "lord of all Africa."⁵² He seemed destined to lead Portugal to new heights; the *Trovas* had already indicated that a "great lion" would "conquer all" in Africa.⁵³ For some literati, Sebastian *was* that lion, worthy of his own story. In 1572 Luis de Camões presented his epic poem *Os Lusíadas* (The Lusiads) as a gift to the then teenaged Sebastian, which perhaps served as partial incentive for the king to chart his own heroic course.[54] Echoing the old ballad, *Os Lusíadas* marked the memory of King Afonso the Conqueror's 1139 quest to banish infidels from Portuguese Iberia. He would then "establish for myself a kingdom by whose actions my name will be known to strange peoples."[55] Ten cantos of *ottava rima* described Vasco da Gama's journey into unknown waters and to a glorious outcome. As in Greek classics, the gods observed, advised, and impeded the Portuguese; in his Lusitanian quest, the explorer had Venus on his side. Canto I makes clear that his journey—and by extension that of Portugal—eclipsed all other great maritime adventures and victories, from the Greeks to Alexander the Great.[56] King Sebastian was determined to do the same.

The memory of ages past spurred Sebastian to the action that seemed prophesied in the *Trovas*: Indeed, a new king who would "roam from land to land/ [and] many people would die." By July 1578 he had mustered about seventeen thousand noblemen, including untried youths, to crusade across the Mediterranean.[57] In the end, Sebastian's plan to extend Portugal's borders and reign over Africa would and did result, as predicted, in the death of "many people."

While the original goal was to capture Port Larache, Sebastian chose to order a landing at Arzila. After much discussion on whether to continue by sea or on foot to Larache, Sebastian chose the latter, refusing even the option of marching along the shore, with the ships hugging the coast and keeping the soldiers in sight. The more practical options ran "contrary to that of El-Rei, whose warlike and daring disposition loved danger," wrote an eyewitness, "because from these came glory."[58] The army waited eighteen days at the port for supplies before commencing a long march overland in the desert heat. This delay afforded Sultan Abd al-Malik time to gather a force of thirty thousand men.[59] In the ten days that Dom Sebastião's men trod through parched Northeast Africa to challenge the infidels, his opponent amassed an army at least twice that size. But this would be no reenactment of the Luso victory against all odds at Ourique, for "the Christian army lacked supplies and the men marched, afflicted, exhausted by the journey and bothered by the heat, which was insufferable."[60]

This march of folly rendered the Lusitanians no match for Abd al-Malik's men. They surrounded the Portuguese (Figure 2). "O terrible duty!" cried Captain Aldana, when the awful outcome was clear.[61] The final, fatal blunder came

Figure 2. Miguel Leitão de Andrade, *Batalha de Alcácer-Quibir* (Battle of Alcácer-Quiber). Originally published in Andrade 1629. Photographed by Georges Jansoon. Wikimedia Commons. Licensed under CC BY SA-3.0.

on the battlefield. Sebastian had commanded his vastly outnumbered men—many of them inexperienced and in their early teens—to await his direct order to do battle. A fair number dropped their arms and fled, scrambling for their lives. Sebastian forgot his own order as the enemy advanced and swooped on the most loyal as they stood. Nearly half of his army was cut down on the spot. The rest of the cornered, fatigued men could barely hold their own and were captured for a fine ransom. Only one hundred survivors escaped to tell of the horror. Though a naked, possibly royal body was hauled out for identification hours later, it seemed that Dom Sebastian had "disappeared"—at least in 1578.[62]

Was it possible that the confusion wrought by the loss of Sebastian and therefore the Portuguese Empire marked the start of a new era, a universal monarchy, as predicted by Bandarra? For many Portuguese, Bandarra's prophetic *Trovas* evoked the Old Testament's Book of Daniel 7:25 in its description of a long, trial-ridden "time, a times, and a dividing of times."[63] That era had begun. The death of Sebastian marked the beginning of profound humiliation for the Portuguese. The tubercular sixty-seven-year-old Cardinal Henriques, successor to Sebastian, was hardly a replacement for the zealous, if erratic, young king. The scramble to understand how this could have happened to Portugal only added to the appeal of Bandarra's work.

Sebastian's bones would arrive a few years later via Ceuta, but in the popular imagination, his body was never found—giving rise to rumors that he lived still and would return.[64] Ahead of and during Spanish claims, contenders jostled for position, each claiming Lusitanian legitimacy by birth and by right. They included the elderly Cardinal Henrique, son of O Venturoso, King Dom Manuel, who oversaw Portugal's greatest era of expansion; the Duchess Catherine (Catarina), granddaughter of Dom Manuel; and Dom António, unwilling prior of Crato, grandson of Dom Manuel, and illegitimate son of the dead infante Dom Luis. The aged and infirm Cardinal Henrique sought to reverse his vows, marry, and issue progeny; he could likely only hold the title for a few years at best. Dom António was pushed to the side as Cardinal Henrique, who favored Catherine, assumed temporary power. The prior of Crato, definitively excluded from the succession-making process due to his bastard status, spent years insisting on his right to assume the throne.[65] Catherine, the best candidate in terms of lineage and ability, was discounted due to her gender. In the end, a foreigner—Philip II of Spain, whose legitimacy was established through his maternal line—was crowned king of Portugal at the 1581 Cortes summoned in Tomar. The union of the crowns would have a profound influence on the trajectory of the kingdom of Portugal, not the least of which would be the Dutch assault on Brazil.

The "nationalists," those who supported a Portuguese royal on the throne, were not yet finished off, however. They included Dom António and his loyal followers, among them Dom João de Castro, who had fought for the Portuguese hopeful when he proclaimed himself Dom António I of Portugal in June 1580. This Antonist adventure continued for nine years. The would-be king finally lost to Philip's troops at the Battle of Alcântara. He fled to England, the Azores, and France, where he died in 1595. The Philippine era, however, had just begun.

For the Portuguese, the *Trovas* provided a spiritual center and lessons that transcended this time of crisis.[66] One day, in another form, Sebastian would assume his rightful place as sovereign of a fifth and final world monarchy led by the Portuguese after the Assyrian, Persian, Greek, and Roman Empires.[67] Like claimant to the throne Dom António, his frustrated supporter João de Castro departed to France, where he immersed himself in the prophecies of Bandarra. Convinced that the real Sebastian was alive, he met with and next supported the so-called Prisoner of Venice, the Calabrian Marco Tulio Catizone. While he had fought for Dom António as rightful heir over Philip II, he now wielded the pen, writing hundreds of folios justifying why Catizone was the legitimate Sebastian returned to claim the throne. Castro tried to rally support for the prisoner by weaving into his justifications his interpretations of Portuguese prophetic tradition, beginning with the Battle of Ourique, when King Afonso saw a vision of Jesus Christ—a sign of God's grace for the Portuguese.[68]

Catizone was publicly executed in 1603, but by now Castro had immersed himself wholly in his studies, examining Sebastian's life, work, and horoscope.[69] "[At] the same hour that [the Lord] gave Portuguese his only son to save them from the Devils' bondage, He gave them a Prince to save them from that of Castile," he concluded, skirting a dangerously prophetic line to make firm his argument that one day Sebastian would return. From Paris, far beyond the reach of Spanish censors and Holy Offices of the Inquisition, Castro published his own biography of King Sebastian, *Discurso da vida de el rey dom Sebastião de Portugal*.

Castro shored up his work with a wide range of literary and prophetic sources, including Bandarra, Nostradamus, Isadore, and Merlin—and vivid detail.[70] In his tenth chapter, he described how a body with seven wounds was picked out among the corpses at Alcácer Quiber and hauled out for identification; some Portuguese averted their eyes from the gruesome sight. Castro declared in his work that other prisoners who were present and being held for ransom either said nothing or agreed that this was indeed the body of the king, in the hopes that they would be released that much sooner. At the right time, all would recognize the true returned king, and he in turn would reveal a glorious, unsurpassable Portugal: "Hail, hail the always welcome King Sebastian our Lord: he who with the standard of the Holy Cross will extend it across the whole universe, surpassing even Alexander [the Great]."[71]

Also from Paris, Dom João de Castro transcribed and published the first print edition of Bandarra's forbidden *Trovas*.[72] Castro's prolific efforts notwithstanding, the short-term result of Sebastian's death was the continuation, for Portugal, of Philippine rule. The kingdom's vassalage to Spain would only end with a Portuguese coup in 1640. In the next century, what endured, it seemed, was Sebastianism—a hope, fueled by shared verse from the *Trovas*, nurtured by *Os Lusíadas*, for the return of the Portuguese king.

In April 1581, the Spanish king, Philip II, was presented as Philip I of Portugal to the three Portuguese estates at the Cortes meeting at Tomar. Prior to taking up residence in Lisbon for the next few years, he agreed not only to a policy of noninterference in Portuguese custom and tradition in Europe but also to grant Portugal autonomy in government and overseas business.[73] Spain also offered protection for Portuguese territory overseas, and indeed Spanish forces drove the French out of the Azores in 1583.[74] But because they were folded into the Spanish Empire, this meant that the Portuguese were now embroiled in the Habsburg war with the Dutch. This is because the Dutch, sworn enemies of Spain since their revolt in 1569, would see Portugal as aiding the enemy. Portuguese troops were dispatched to whatever front Philip requested—even and especially against the Dutch.

With or without Spanish oversight, demonstrations of loyalty to the Portuguese crown opened the door to staying true to Portuguese roots, even in exile. In spite of upended socioeconomic relations, one boon of the Iberian Union, to the merchants at least, was that *conversos* and *nova cristões* were now connected in a vast trade and finance network.[75] That is, families of converted Spanish and Portuguese of Jewish heritage joined circuits of trade into a route that "girdled the globe"[76] and forged tighter links across the Iberian world.[77] This included ties to Jews outside of Spain and Portugal. For example, Duarte Nunes da Costa and his family, who had fled Lisbon for Hamburg in 1611, dispatched his teenaged son Jerônimo to Amsterdam by the 1620s to expand the family trade; they remained connected to and even recognized by the Portuguese crown during and after the Luso–Dutch conflict.[78] That is, a Jewish supporter of Lisbon, living out his days in Amsterdam, could and did not only help the Portuguese wage war against the Dutch; he would also one day, as in the case of Jerônimo Nunes da Costa, be named an agent of Portugal.[79]

Being Portuguese mattered—in a way that was deeply intertwined with formal declarations of faith. As Portuguese explorers, merchants, and soldiers staked claim around the globe, Bandarra's ballads impinged on local Portuguese. Skirting with prophecy, this work also drew inquisitorial attention. But with the untimely death of King Sebastian and the succession crisis that followed, belief in the king's return—Sebastianism—picked up through the early seventeenth century.

Grotian Interventions and the Dutch Threat to Brazil

As Portugal's crisis deepened, the perseverance and writings of self-exiled believer Dom João de Castro encouraged word of King Sebastian's imminent return.[80] Well into the reign of Philip II, Castro's first major work was printed in 1602, the charter year of the Dutch East India Company. Within the year, the Dutch menaced Portuguese feitorias in their quest to control the lucrative East Indies spice trade. "Where now is the old faith of the Portuguese? The hopes and belief in God?" wrote Castro.[81]

Twenty years after the death of Sebastian, the Dutch United Provinces had achieved, since their initial rebellion in 1568, a modicum of domestic stability. Savings amassed by the waning of sixteenth-century Dutch Protestant sectarian conflict (Holland and Zeeland were predominantly Calvinist by 1572) had encouraged a groundswell of commercial activity and deep interest in overseas potential.[82] Maritime aggression was no small part of the Dutch strategy to take the struggle for independence off Dutch soil and into Habsburg territory. What would become the United Provinces sought to engage in commercial activity as a way to string together the newly created republic or a loose confederation of states. In 1602 the Dutch East India Company was granted a charter by the States General. Part expansionist activity, this was at once an act of rebellion against Spain and an outlet for investors.

In February 1603, two Dutch vessels attacked the *Santa Catarina*—a richly laden Portuguese carrack that had departed from Macau—seized its contents, and put them up for sale.[83] The Melaka-bound carrack, which carried merchants, seven hundred *soldados*, and somewhere between eight and one hundred women and children, never made it to the final destination of Goa. For seasoned Indian Ocean traders, including the Portuguese, the contents of the *Santa Catarina* were nothing out of the ordinary for the place and time. But to the members of the newly formed Dutch East India Company, they represented nothing short of an otherworldly boon.[84] The staggering treasure of raw silk, gold, sugar, spices, and more amazed northern European merchants when the contents were revealed at an Amsterdam auction.[85]

Privateering had long been a common practice, but in an unprecedented move, the Dutch East India Company hired rising Dutch jurist Hugo Grotius to pen an apologia explaining the actions of the VOC.[86] By relying most heavily on the official October 11, 1604, testimony of Captain Heemskerk, who described hostilities of the Portuguese against the Dutch, Grotius argued that absent an independent judge, an individual had the right to take the law into his own hands. In practice, this was nothing new: far from the metropole, individuals took measures they deemed fit. However, Grotius put into writing notions of citizenship and subjecthood on the periphery, with far-reaching consequences for the Portuguese.[87]

In the early seventeenth century, territorial rights and claims proved both fluid and foundational as agents of aspiring empires tied law to geography and the irregular imperial spaces.[88] Through his legal writings, Grotius strove to undermine Iberian claims far from home.[89] An unapologetic agent, in this case of the VOC, he deemed the seizure of the Portuguese ship within Captain Heemskerk's bounds. The Dutch were, after all, at war with the Spanish, and now Portugal was joined with Spain. His main argument for the seizure and sale of the contents of the *Santa Catarina* was that the Dutch engaged in a "just war" against the Spanish.[90] Keen on shaping foreign policy, Grotius wrote for a new world, imagining a sharp break from medieval tradition of securing ecclesiastical approval in the dividing of secular spoils.

Backed by moral arguments, Dutch maritime aspirations took aggressive form—to great damage for the Portuguese. For "why should the Pope . . . make decisions regarding the division of the world between two monarchs, when our lord Christ had rejected all earthly government?" argued Grotius in his *Mare Liberum*.[91] This work would become foundational for international and maritime law. The pope, he wrote, "was not the main ruler of the world."[92] The Dutch East India Company took Portuguese (now Spanish) claims, and one by one the East Indies fell to the Netherlandish invaders.[93] Grotius's influence in the Netherlands was almost immediate. To his great misfortune, Grotius found himself aligned with the losing side in Dutch politics and out of the

Netherlands for the rest of his life. But once safely in exile, he continued his work from France, writing arguments on behalf of the Dutch.[94]

Grotius worked in Paris for the Dutch cause at the same time that Dom João de Castro, in his self-exile from the Iberian Peninsula, churned out pro-Sebastian folios for the Portuguese.[95] They would never connect, of course, neither on the streets of Paris nor in their writings. While Castro's writings reached into the past by remembering Portuguese prophecy, tradition, and Portugal's divine purpose, *Mare Liberum* supported Calvinist aspirations for a global, commercial empire—at the direct expense of the Portuguese. Public and private support for Atlantic expeditions was fomented in part by language that both created a new worldview and recalled epic struggle, leading to private and public support for Atlantic expeditions and sugar from Brazil. "The cause of the Dutch is more than that of a [mere] competitor," wrote Grotius, "inasmuch their own profit is bound up with profit to the entire human race, a universal benefit which the Portuguese are trying to destroy."[96]

When the Dutch threat was made clear, not only the Spanish crown but also wealthy individuals in Brazil, aware of imminent danger, chipped in for defensive purposes. For instance, in 1603, the same year the *Santa Catarina* was seized and all its contents sold off, António Cardoso de Barros reminded King Philip II of Spain of the funds his father had lent him for the fortification of the city of Bahia.[97] It is not known whether Barros received remuneration, but the king decided more work was needed. While his primary concern at the time appeared to have been for the protection of the churches, he had good cause to be concerned about the weak state of Brazil's northeastern coastal defenses. Philip also maintained that the protection and good order of the Catholic Church would ensure divine support. The shoring up of coastal South Atlantic defenses were "necessary," wrote Philip in 1607, for ". . . for the good guarding and defense of their churches."[98] By 1608 Philip II had ordered fortifications for coastal towns in Brazil, from Salvador to Recife. This was also to protect sugar-producing engenhos and to otherwise avoid contraband, on the rise with the continuation of the Spanish–Dutch conflict.[99]

The Twelve-Year Truce between Spain and the Netherlands (1609–1621) restored the above-mentioned Estado da India and Luso–Dutch trade—but not without routine piratical challenges. The Crown, buoyed by sugar production from thriving Pernambuco, encouraged the granting of *sesmarias* for the raising of cattle and even more sugar cultivation.[100] But corsair attacks on the Brazilian northeast continued through the truce and began to interrupt trade. For instance, in 1618, André Lopes Pinto wrote to the king on the challenges of fulfilling brazilwood contracts and the overall difficulty, given continuing corsair threats, of this commerce.[101] That same year, *fidalgo* Martim de Sá wrote to Philip II requesting a ship with soldiers and munitions, the purpose of which was to expel enemies of Portugal from the coast of the captaincies of Rio de Janeiro, São Vicente, and Cabo Frio.[102] Despite the truce, a very real Dutch threat had materialized off the coast of Brazil by 1619. Flemish and Dutch traders were no strangers to Brazil through the interregnum, but now Martim de Sá expressed his written concern to the Crown regarding a Dutch ship that had captured a *galizabra*, an armed vessel meant to bring treasure to Spain independent of the annual sailing fleet.

By 1621 a flourishing Lisbon served as a major trade and naval entrepôt. In the lull of peace, Dutch ships swarmed this port and others for salt, wine, and more. But the cessation of peace meant that Spanish armadas, stationed there, in Cadiz, Flanders, Gibraltar, Valencia, and other Iberian ports, ensured that Dutch ships would be forced out of all Spanish Empire ports in East and North Africa from 1621. This action underpinned Spain's general strategy of deploying trade embargoes to limit land war.[103]

Through the early 1620s, then, as Philip IV's *valido* (favorite, trusted adviser) and minister Count Olivares worked on plans for an Atlantic-Mediterranean fleet to guard against the Dutch threat, "the imperial [Spanish] ship seemed to right itself, plugged the leaks and sailed on."[104] But from Brazil, Captain-General Martim Soares Moreno wrote to King Philip asking for assistance in building a fort—as well as soldiers and officials, weapons and munitions, and gunpowder to protect against attacks by the Dutch and the ever-present French.[105] Three years later, indicating his ongoing concern with a potential invasion, Moreno continued with such requests and asked this time for fifty soldiers to build fortifications.[106]

As the Dutch solidified their position in the East Indies, chipped away at Portugal's overseas kingdom, and prepared to head west, continued Portuguese expansion and fortification of the Brazilian northeast served as partial defense against attack.[107] Such preventative measures proved more than reasonable: at least one ardent advocate of the Dutch military-commercial organization that would become the WIC seized on those points, arguing that "moral duty" merited an attack on Spanish-held territory across the Atlantic—in particular Brazil.[108] Outrage against the Spanish proved a boon for printers, who had produced at least twenty-five Dutch-language editions of Bartolomé de las Casas's *Brevísima relación de la destrucción de las Indias*, by 1648.[109] The Dutch claimed that the Spanish had done "nothing but to abuse our Fatherland as they have done in the New Indies." William of Orange's assertion of "shared anguish" with Indigenous people under Spanish control provided a justification for would-be Atlantic colonialists. His call to arms provided the spark to create a westbound search for gold, glory—and "justice."[110]

Potential for profit trumped moral concerns. A popular 1608 pamphlet had already argued for the creation of a company that would explore the natural riches of Brazil, but by the seventeenth century, the Brazilian sugar trade was the most lucrative trade in the Western Hemisphere. The Dutch, who had established sugar refineries in Amsterdam by 1621, were after the raw source."[111] These prospects lured potential Dutch West India Company investors into the fold.[112] Upon expiration of the truce (1609–1621), the States-General granted a charter for the Dutch West India Company and permission to implement its Grand Design (Groot Desseyn) on Brazil and the South Atlantic world.

Portugal's financial situation declined. East of the Atlantic, the Dutch continued to claim Portuguese possessions, and by 1622 the English had conquered the strategic port of Hormuz. Once again, the Spanish forbade Luso–Dutch trade. This inflicted great pain on Lisbon and Setúbal, but the prevailing thought was to drag out the embargo, engage in short wars, and wear down the Dutch.[113] Spanish officials took a hard line, noting in 1629 that the Orangist Dutch "war party," comprised of military men and hard-line Calvinists, continued to enjoy more popularity than the Republican "peace party."[114] The ensuing damage to the Portuguese economy resulted in a slump that affected the grain and salt trade and lasted to 1641.

The Netherlanders proved a serious threat, given their ambition and militant reach, which now extended across the Atlantic. With the end of the truce and the creation of the West India Company, Brazil was now vulnerable to attack. The Crown was especially mindful of the warnings from Salvador's *engenheiro-mor* Francisco de Fróes de Mesquita, whose post was to shore up defense.[115] One year after the expiration of the Twelve-Year Truce, in 1622, King Philip IV of

Spain (Philip III of Portugal) expressed concern to Diogo de Mendonça Furtado, governor-general of Bahia, regarding potential invasions and urged him to engage in fortifications of Bahia and other strongholds. Salvador, set back but accessible from the Bay of All Saints, was, as the Portuguese administrative center and colonial capital of Brazil, a prime target. The king followed up in the next month with Furtado with further concern regarding the condition of the forts in Bahia and the rest of Brazil.[116] However, armed with material incentive as well as moral and legal justifications, the newly formed Dutch West India Company now focused its attention on Brazil.

Remembering, Forgetting, and Mythologizing

In the context of crisis, the mythological origins of Portugal, combined with visions of a challenging but glorious future, helped forge a new self-understanding of what it meant to be Portuguese. In his epic poem *Os Lusíadas*, gifted to King Sebastian, Luis de Camões had remembered the deeds of the great navigator Vasco da Gama. Like the Jesuits who warned of sin that followed in da Gama's wake, Camões reflected that perhaps Portugal had forgotten its purpose and lost its way. Below, in the closing lines of the poem, Camões begs off the Muse and a dissonant lyre, wondering if his work fell on deaf ears and a hardened people, a country mired in greed.

Nô mais, Musa, nô mais, que a Lira tenho Destemperada e a voz enrouquecida, E não do canto, mas de ver que venho Cantar a gente surda e endurecida.	No more, Muse, no more, for the Lyre is untuned, my voice hoarse Not from song, but from seeing That I've been singing to a deaf and hardened people[117]

His words, like Bandarra's *Trovas*, proved prescient. Camões had presented this poem to King Sebastian just a few years before the sovereign would lead thousands to their death and Portugal to near collapse. As a result, decades after Alcácer-Quibir, the Portuguese, tethered to the Spanish, navigated into an uncharted world of Dutch peril. Yet the demand for *Os Lusíadas*, even in crisis, continued apace. A chorus of printers sounded Portuguese collective remembering of past glory: no fewer than eleven editions of his epic poem were issued during the sixty years the Portuguese endured the time of Spanish "captivity."[118]

From Paris, Dom João de Castro churned out thousands of pages connecting the fallen King Sebastian to O Encoberto, the Hidden One, who would return to restore Portugal's glory. Yet despite the popularity of his *Discurso da vida* (Discourse of Life), this story seemed far from the truth.[119] The Iberian union wrought in the succession crisis that followed the king's death dealt devastating consequences for Portugal, chief among them the Dutch assault on the kingdom's overseas holdings. This ran contrary to visions of Portugal's divinely ordained, global reach. An unwilling participant in the Habsburg conflict, the kingdom suffered from domestic challenges as well as attacks on its overseas holdings.[120] At the height of this trauma, when the Dutch seized Bahia in 1624, Dom João de Castro kept alive the hope of King Sebastian's return. His work indicated that it would take a near-crushing blow to Lusitanian consciousness, and Bandarra's reminder of the kingdom's otherworldly purpose, to revive the glory of Portugal.

Memory—that ephemeral reality—is subject to "permanent evolution, open to the dialectic of remembering and forgetting."[121] Thanks in part to Dom João de Castro, the "Miracle of Ourique," Bandarra's *Trovas*, and Camões's *Os Lusíadas* remained relevant through Portugal's seventeenth-century trials. During the initial round of Dutch attacks on Portuguese possessions abroad, these works served as a reminder that Portugal had liberated itself from captivity and had embarked on a journey of renewal before. For João de Castro and other Sebastianists, the fateful loss in 1578 not only helped contextualize uncertainty and trial but also marked the start of a remarkable new era. It seemed then that Portugal, a biblical David, was pitted against multiple Goliaths. For the Portuguese, this meant that "now the time of God's marvels has arrived," as Dom Castro wrote, and the "Kingdom of Portugal, small, humiliated & captive," would transform into the seat of divine conquest on earth.[122]

CHAPTER TWO

Journey of the Vassals

Plus Ultra *Salvador*

ON MAY 8, 1624, Salvador of Bahia, the heart of Portuguese America, fell to the Dutch in a lightening attack. Despite warnings from Philip III (IV of Spain) and sightings from Cabo Verde of enemy ships en route to Brazil, the town was caught off-guard. Dutch West India Company vessels slipped easily into the Bay of All Saints and dropped anchor. Upon sighting Dutch ships, most residents had fled to the interior; Dutch soldiers found a handful of old men and slaves in an otherwise empty town.[1] They proceeded to secure Salvador, vandalize the church, and empty wine cellars in celebration. In less than twenty-four hours and with relatively few casualties, the Atlantic seat of Iberian power had fallen into "heretic" hands. The Portuguese refugees who had fled to the backlands, however, lay siege on the Netherlanders for a year.[2]

Accounts of Dutch Brazil tend to either skim over the Luso–Dutch battles of Bahia (1624–1625, 1638) for the more extended Dutch presence farther north (1630–1654) or home in on minute details of 1624 and the resounding Iberian restoration the following year.[3] In this telling, the story of Dutch Brazil begins in 1630 and to the north, where the West India Company contested, held, and settled some of the richest sugar-producing lands—and more.[4] At best, the 1625 rescue of Bahia is analyzed in isolation and as an example of waning Luso–Spanish cooperation.[5]

In the context of Dutch and Spanish "captivity," the 1625 restoration of Bahia and subsequent efforts to protect the capital of Portuguese America reveal more than intra-Iberian tension. Saving—and later defending—Salvador sparked a transatlantic Lusophone consciousness that cut across occupation, rank, and class. In Portugal, preparations to outfit a rescue armada in 1624 proceeded apace. With or without the Spanish, Lisboetas and others appeared ready to rescue Brazil. Post-restoration representations of that effort reveal that the intentions of Lisbon's working class and elite were not aligned, due in part to a weakening dual crown. In Brazil, efforts to contain the Dutch foreshadowed a Luso-Brazilian consciousness and cross-class coordination to handle external threats, as well as a self-understanding quite distinct from the metropole. By land and by sea, this first battle for Bahia helps trace not only Portuguese tensions regarding Spanish action to protect Brazil but also a growing Luso–Brazilian coordination.

Non-elite explorers and lesser fidalgos had, since the sixteenth century, appealed to sovereigns to claim rewards for their efforts—a direct line to the metropole for ambitious colonialists.[6] Here, the colonialists were an extension and reflection of the metropole. But it was in this first traumatic "moment" that a distinct Luso–Brazilian identity began to emerge. With the 1624 invasion of Salvador of Bahia, *moradores* (local residents), Jesuit priests, Tupinambá allies, and junior officers and officials coordinated to contain the Dutch threat.

The Dutch Grand Design and 1624 Invasion of Salvador

Luis de Camões may have exalted lush Banda in a celebration of Portuguese maritime expansion, but by the early 1600s, not thirty years after the epic poem's printing, the Dutch had driven out most Lusophone rivals from the East Indies altogether. They then took aim at Brazil.[7] In 1603, the same year the VOC seized the Portuguese carrack *Santa Catarina* off the coast of Melaka, Philip III of Spain warned the governor-general of Brazil, Diogo Botelho, of a possible Dutch attack either on Bahia or Rio de Janeiro.[8] One year later, the king's concerns came to pass: merchant letters out of Flanders alerted the Crown of twelve armed Dutch *urcas* (cargo ships) heading to India to contest Portuguese feitorias. More than thirty such vessels would be sent to the coast of Brazil, São Tomé, and Cabo Verde—and still more to cause damage to the coast of Mina.[9] Governor Botelho proved ready. He mustered a successful defense of Brazil, sending two captured caravels along with his own letter to Philip as proof. The Spanish king noted his swift and efficient response.[10]

Dutch attacks tapered off with the Twelve-Year Truce (1609–1621) between Spain and the seven rebel provinces, but this interregnum marked only the end of the first half of an enduring conflict—what would later be known as the Eighty Years War.[11] During this time, domestic issues roiled the United Provinces, with far-reaching consequences for Spain, Portugal, and Brazil. *Stadhouder* Maurits of Nassau and his "war party" of Zeeland and Amsterdam merchants chafed at the decline in economic and expansionist opportunity; the temporary peace slowed down the plundering of Portuguese possessions abroad. Religious issues also colored the conflict between the "peace" and "war" parties. Arminian (Remonstrant) Johan van Oldebarneveldt secured lasting recognition for the provinces as an independent state. However, orthodox Maurits and his Calvinist "war party" saw the truce as a lost opportunity in the Americas.

Religious and political differences boiled over to tragic consequences. Oldebarneveldt, a staunch believer that salvation was a function of faith rather than partial atonement afforded to a predestined few, was executed in 1618. His protégé, Hugo Grotius, another political casualty by virtue of his Arminian beliefs and association with the "peace party," was sentenced to life imprisonment at Loevenstein Castle. Though Grotius managed to escape, the ardent nationalist and author of *Mare Liberum* spent the rest of his life in exile, trying and failing to write his way back into the good graces of the States General.[12] His work, however, would be used to great effect to claim Portuguese land, people, and property. As a result, the Twelve-Year Truce proved more damaging to the Iberian crown than could have been predicted in 1609.

East and west of the newly recognized republic, the truce did not translate into a complete cessation of Dutch attacks on Portuguese claims. To the east, the Dutch had pushed the Portuguese out of the Spice Islands by 1619; to the west, they captured twenty-eight Portuguese ships off the coast of Brazil in the year 1616 alone, perhaps presaging future invasions.[13] Close to the end of the truce, Amsterdam-based informants leaked to the Spanish crown Dutch plans to seize Brazil and Angola. However, no serious plans to prevent such action were put into effect.[14]

Upon the expiration of the truce in 1621, the States General granted a charter to the West India Company, the main purpose of which was to conquer Brazil.[15] The profit-seeking company, however, appealed for public support along moral lines. Beyond expressing concern for their Indigenous "brethren" across the

South Atlantic, proponents of the Dutch West India Company charter also argued for the importance of obtaining justice for the Portuguese. They would "liberate the Portuguese, having rendered most destitute and in an unchristian way the real master of the Kingdom of Portugal (to which Brazil belongs)."[16] But the "missionary mindset" of the WIC was not imagined; while not in the charter, instructions to colonizing clergy made clear that all under their care—whether of Portuguese, Spanish, Indigenous, or African descent—were to receive Calvinist instruction.[17]

Promises to "liberate" Portuguese and Indigenous people from Spanish rule receded, however, as the Dutch finalized plans and took square aim at the richest sugar-producing captaincy in the Western Hemisphere. In a publication presented to the States General regarding why the Dutch West India Company should conquer Brazil, Jan Andries Moerbeeck floated the likelihood of an unopposed head tax on the Portuguese in Brazil. He argued that the war tax would not be met with much opposition, as locals would now be freed "from the tyranny of Spain."[18] But by 1624 the United Provinces had set in motion the WIC plan to unseat Salvador of Bahia as capital of the Iberian colonial world.[19]

Well into the seventeenth century, Brazil was considered "cow's milk" to the Iberian and, later, Braganza crowns (from 1641). During the time of the union, Spain could depend on the Portuguese colony to operate independently and to supply the Crown with choice exports, not the least of which was sugar.[20] Still, the Spanish considered Portuguese America, with its poorly defended coast, a weak link in Spain's Atlantic imperial system. Salvador de Bahia was at particular risk, constructed as it was for easy access as the colonial capital of Brazil and not at all for defensive purposes.[21] In fact, the town had been assaulted more than once by the French and the Dutch. But by gaining access to Brazil, Moerbeeck calculated that the Dutch could control a thriving internal trade of sugar, ginger, and "other fruit" as well as about sixty thousand chests of sugar for export should Pernambuco fall into Dutch hands.[22]

What would become known as the Dutch Groot Desseyn, or Grand Design, featured a multi-continent approach to sweep Portuguese South Atlantic claims, specifically Brazil, into the Dutch fold.[23] For the first phase of this plan, the West India Company targeted Bahia and Pernambuco as the two most important "places in the country, fortified with competent garrisons . . . if the Dutch took these they could take possession of Brazil."[24] Beyond strident arguments to liberate the Portuguese, a major selling point to investors and the general public was the "great pain" that would be inflicted on the Spanish as the Dutch gained silver and sugar: "West India can become The Netherlands' great source of gain/Diminishing the enemy's power as it garners silver plate."[25]

News of the Grand Design reached Spain, but while Philip IV ordered a general shoring up of defenses, there seemed to exist no other plans to protect Brazil. Exactly one month ahead of the capture of Salvador, former governor-general of Brazil Gaspar de Sousa, now charged with expansionary efforts in the northeast, seemed unaware of Dutch designs on Brazil.[26] Through the first decades of the seventeenth century, as the VOC assumed control of the Spice Islands, the king ordered Sousa to establish residency in Olinda, the seat of Pernambuco. From there, Sousa directed the launching of *sumacas* (coasting boats) from Pernambuco, Bahia, and Paraiba in search of the "lands of the Amazon River." His other charge was to sweep the coast of non-Iberians, including the French and the Dutch, who had long made inroads with local tribes. He remained unaware of the Dutch West India Company plot to conquer Brazil, beginning with the northeastern coast.[27] As late as April 1624, unaware of a Dutch-articulated attack on Portuguese America, he complained instead of the chronic nuisance of lawless heretics, including a "disgrace that happened in Bahia": his military commander (*capitão-mor*), whom he had ordered to pursue "five ships of corsairs," had died, along the "with many nobles who accompanied him." Given the timeline and imminent West India attack on Bahia, the corsairs were likely Dutch. Above all else, Sousa was frustrated by more than the loss of life: the Iberian expansion into and conquest of Maranhão, northwest of Pernambuco, he wrote, were now "impossible." Such concerns, however, were routine.[28]

At the time of Gaspar de Sousa's writing, the Dutch had already set into motion plans to capture Bahia, phase one of the West India Company's Groot Desseyn. Just ahead of the invasion, on April 13, 1624, the Dutch ship *Holandia*, carrying future Dutch governor-general of Bahia Johan van Dorth, was sighted just off the Cabo Verde island of São Vicente. Philip IV sent immediate word via caravel to the new governor-general of Bahia, Diogo de Mendonça Furtado. An alert was sounded along the Portuguese American coast—to little avail.[29] Furtado could hardly muster help to prepare for the defense of the city.[30] For one, Marcos Teixeira, the bishop of Brazil, had ridiculed the governor's earlier actions as alarmist, rendering ineffective the governor's call for help.[31] After all, spies in Amsterdam had alerted Philip IV of Spain to the threat two years earlier, and none had materialized.[32] In addition, most *engenho* (sugar mill) owners proved reluctant to leave their fields with the end of *safra* (harvest) season nearly upon them.[33] Those who did show up hung about for only a few days. Mindful of the bishop's words, the moradores slipped back to their fazendas and other work without permission.[34]

Like Governor Furtado, a few Jesuits had received warnings of impending invasion—but these materialized in the form of visions rather than through official correspondence. A few days prior to the Dutch attack, one priest in the choir saw Jesus Christ threatening Salvador with a sword; another later reported seeing God's son with three lances, which he hurled at their church. Jesuit priests, of course, had long warned that hubris, excess, and straying from Portugal's divine path invited divine retribution: this much was evident from Portugal's rule by the Spanish. Still, while Bishop Teixeira had decided that faith would prevent calamity, the punishment feared by Jesuits materialized on May 8, 1624, when twenty-four Dutch ships appeared in the Bay of All Saints.[35]

Armed with commercial and moral justifications, and secret instructions from the States General, and confident of a lackluster defense, in May 1624 the Dutch cruised into the Bay of All Saints and seized Salvador with ease.[36] In short order, the white flag of surrender appeared over the rampart and a lone resident came down the stairs to assure the enemy the town was deserted. A glance at the open doors indicated that this seemed to be the case.[37] They entered into the Santo Antônio section of the town, where they found, according to Bartolomeu Guerreiro, "only a few negroes and two old men."[38] They then imprisoned Governor Furtado in his own home before shipping him off to Amsterdam as a prisoner. All other residents had escaped into the backlands, an indication that the invasion would not, in fact, lead to enduring—or any—Portuguese gratitude to the Dutch for "salvation" from Spanish rule in Salvador. Neither did Indigenous people greet the West India Company soldiers with open arms; many fought with the Portuguese against the Dutch.[39]

Prior to the Dutch conquest of Salvador, Portuguese and Spanish authorities had coordinated to ward off and handle attacks, however ineffectively, as indicated in Philip IV's warnings to the Portuguese regarding coastal defense. With the conquest of Bahia, the Crown now mustered more direct action, assembling a joint Luso–Spanish armada to liberate Salvador. However, after the initial fear of and flight from the Dutch invaders, an on-the-ground Portuguese guerrilla resistance began to coalesce in Brazilian aldeias (Jesuit-run Indigenous villages). This alliance would prove to be the critical factor in fending off further Dutch attacks.

Visionary Jesuit priests foretold of Salvador's ruin, just days ahead of a Dutch arrival. One priest saw an image of Jesus Christ, unsheathed sword in hand, menacing the city; another saw his savior burning down a church.[40] Absent Iberian reinforcements and an organized defense, a landing party of about fifteen hundred Dutch West India Company soldiers disembarked with minimum effort in the Bay of All Saints island of Itaparica.[41] The Dutch West India Company, "more thieves, & corsairs," as one chronicler cast them, "than traders, & merchants," had arrived "to infest the fourth part of the world, New Spain, Peru, & Brazil." The writer lamented the fact that they followed the advice of a certain "Ioam Andre Mortecan, Olandez"—the same Jans Andries Moerbeeck who had argued that the Dutch should "liberate" the Portuguese from the Spanish.[42] Dutch West India Company ships navigated easily past shots fired from the Forte de Santo Amaro and took position in front of the city of Salvador. The "rebel vassals, insolent corsairs" then opened fire.[43] They then made their way to the Monastery of São Bento, raided the wine cellar, and spent the night drinking as reward and as preparation to take Salvador in the morning. When Dutch troops poured into the city the next day, they found it nearly empty and claimed Bahia as their own. For this reason, until the Iberian reconquest in 1625, the West India Company soldiers called Salvador "Batavian land."[44] In 1580 Salvador of Bahia, the colonial capital of Portuguese America, had been folded into the Spanish Empire; forty-four years later it was now conquered and desecrated by the Dutch.

The sight of the Dutch armada sailing into Bahia's Bay of All Saints (Baia de Todos os Santos) prompted residents' widespread panic, fear, and regret.[45] Refugees streamed out from the city and into the backlands. Among those escaping the invasion was Lisbon-born, Brazil-bred Jesuit novice António Vieira. Vieira, no stranger to travel adventure, had migrated with his parents to Bahia the previous decade. As a youth, he ran away from his Portuguese father and mixed-descent mother to join the Jesuit mission.[46] Now he fled with other displaced residents to a backlands aldeia. The year of the invasion, Vieira's superiors selected the precocious youth and future Sebastianist to write the mission's "Carta Ânua," or annual letter to Rome. This he did in great detail, providing the only Portuguese eyewitness account of the conquest: "But who could ever describe the effort and agony of that night! All that could be head through the dense brush were the wails and moans of fleeing women; children cried out for their mothers, who cried out for the husbands, and each and all, according to his fortune, lamented their miserable luck."[47]

As men, women, and children streamed out of town, some Portuguese improvised in battle, inflicting damage to the Dutch as they were able. Vieira wrote of one sailor who was unable to contain his anger at the "audacity" of a West India Company soldier who tried to hoist the Dutch flag. From one of the boats nearest to the beach, the Portuguese sailor lifted a harquebus, shot the soldier in the face, and managed the same feat with the next two, missing not one shot.[48] On land, Governor Furtado, now proved right for trying to muster a defense ahead of the Dutch invasion, urged all able-bodied men to fight to the death, saying that it was better to "die with honor than live without."[49] But such efforts fell short. "Suddenly," wrote Vieira, "[we] heard through the city (without knowing the source) one voice: 'The enemies have already entered, they've entered, the enemies have entered!'"[50] In the confusion and panic, Bishop Teixeira exhorted the remaining Portuguese to fight to the death for faith and king. He took up a sword to defend himself and set an example by heading out into the streets and into homes. But even as he urged on defenders, wrote Vieira, "with no small care they [the bishop and other men of faith] prepared souls for death and bodies for war."[51] In less than twenty-four hours, the colonial capital was in Dutch hands. Governor Furtado, on the brink of committing suicide, was captured along with the few remaining men and imprisoned.[52] Church bells rang out the next day, calling for the first Calvinist service in Brazil.[53]

Yet stage one of the Dutch Grand Design proved a great blunder. Despite the swift Dutch takeover of Salvador of Bahia, the Portuguese regrouped and mounted a fierce resistance from the countryside. First, and with their Indigenous allies, they confined West India Company soldiers inside Salvador by encircling the town, blocking further advance. The Dutch were thus pinned down, with their only escape through the Bay of All Saints.[54] From the north, governor of Pernambuco Matias de Albuquerque sent word of the invasion to

Lisbon.⁵⁵ He then ordered two caravels laden with men, munitions, and provisions to Bahia.⁵⁶

Refugee fighters and volunteer soldiers from the north picked off the Netherlanders, emerging from surrounding *matos* (thickets) to take down any who dared venture out on reconnaissance missions. In one instance, Portuguese rebels captured a few Dutch and some "Africans from Guinea" just outside of the monastery at São Bento. One of the group—Vieira did not distinguish whether African or Dutch—had his hands cut off and was sent to the city with a message hanging about his neck. The note dared the Dutch to meet them and prove their worth in battle. They accepted and sent out a formation of four hundred men, but in the end they reversed course for the safety of city walls.⁵⁷

Given the lack of trained soldiers and munitions, open battle was not an option for the underequipped Portuguese, but improvised resistance, by any means possible, proved effective. Mixed Indigenous and Portuguese groups took matters into their own hands. Lacking adequate weapons and armed mostly with swords, accompanied by Indigenous archers, about thirty ambush parties spread out around the city and kept the Dutch on edge.⁵⁸ "And what horror they [Indigenous archers] inflict on the enemy, who, upon departing [the city], armed and [marching] in their companies on the most protected and ordered routes under the bright sun and serene sky, quickly find themselves under a cloud of raining arrows," wrote Vieira in his "Carta Ânua." This included the commander of Dutch-held Bahia, Johan van Dorth. Months after he assumed control of Salvador, Indigenous archers took him down as he returned from reconnaissance; Portuguese guerrilla fighters finished him off.⁵⁹

Jesuits, moradores, soldiers from Pernambuco, and Indigenous people from nearby aldeias coordinated in restricting the Dutch to the town. Vieira's annual mission letter to Rome offers more than the state of Jesuit missions in Brazil; it reveals successful, inter-captaincy cooperation in the face of a common enemy. Given the Jesuit mission to win converts and spread the Christian faith, Vieira, in his letter to Rome, stressed the valiant efforts of the Tupinambá, Bishop Teixeira, and nameless moradores as worthy of acknowledgment. The "Carta Ânua" makes clear not only the efforts of faithful Christians but also the grassroots response to the imperial challenge—clear evidence of extra-official coordination against the Dutch. Through the decades, Luso-Brazilians, a group forged first in neglect and then in crisis, became quite distinct from the metropole Portuguese.

"In the Spirit of Good Vassals": Restoration and Reconquest (1625)

With the Dutch conquest of Salvador, alliances between groups—moradores, clergy, Tupinambá and Potiguar peoples—emerged as a matter of course. Portuguese effort was not confined to the immediate area under attack or to the backlands to which refugees escaped; on both sides of the Atlantic, they knew that the battle for Bahia offered a potential route to improved social status and economic gain.

In Portugal, a long tradition of lineage-based "nobility of blood" conferred rank and accompanying honors. Non-Jewish men of full European descent who did not engage in manual labor moved easily up and throughout society. All other subjects were considered defective by virtue of their "tainted" blood.[60] These men toiled away in obscurity: they did not receive honors and were rarely singled out except for Inquisitorial attention. For soldiers and officials of fidalgo status, the route for distinction lay in service overseas; reward for staking and claiming land for the Crown could include land, titles, a general grant, and a lifelong pension.[61] Ambitious men demonstrated loyalty to the sovereign by adding to Portuguese territory and fostering connections between Portugal and its claims, even during the Philippine era. The Dutch invasion proved a springboard for such success and a way to skirt "defects" of heritage.[62] For example, Salvador Correia de Sá e Benevides traversed the Atlantic from Lisbon to Rio de Janeiro at age twelve. He accompanied his father to the gold and silver mines, learned Tupí, and sailed back to Portugal. Upon his later return to Rio de Janeiro, he participated in the recapture of Bahia, in 1625. Despite his background of manual labor (working in the mines) for his efforts against the Dutch, Sá would eventually serve as governor of Rio de Janeiro and as governor of Angola, which, along with São Tomé, he recaptured from the Dutch as well.[63]

While those of "pure blood" received the highest colonial posts of governorship and viceroy, such stringency did not apply to lesser positions, especially during times of conflict.[64] Ahead of a royal response and with it transatlantic aid, the fall of Bahia prompted immediate on-the-ground reaction. With the capture of Furtado, the soldier and administrator of Pernambuco, Matias de Albuquerque accepted the appointment of acting governor of Brazil.[65]

From Pernambuco, Albuquerque issued the orders to recruit experienced soldiers to fight against the Dutch in Bahia. Some of them had served Portugal as far away as India.[66] Upon receiving the news about Bahia, he organized and sent south caravels from Pernambuco containing thirty men, cannons, and other firepower. Storms forced the caravels ashore before they reached Bahia, but the soldiers found their way to guerrilla fighters camped outside the city. Throughout the entire year the Dutch held Bahia, Albuquerque sent south for the war effort military supplies received in Pernambuco from Portugal. For instance, after Dom Francisco de Moura, newly appointed captain-major of the Bay of Bahia, spent a week in Recife to procure aid, Matias de Albuquerque added to de Moura's three caravels, bringing the total to six.[67]

The Portuguese Jesuits in Bahia also suspended regular religious and teaching routines and adapted to life at war.[68] Many not only tended to bodies and souls but also led their own troops in battle. Captain Jerônimo Cavalcante de Albuquerque encountered and engaged a Dutch ship leaving the Bay of All Saints for Pernambuco. Fortunately he had on board one priest who administered spiritual aid and another who performed surgery.[69] Father Manoel de Moraes trained and led into battle his *índios aldeados* (village Indians), including Felipe Camarão, who would rise to become "commander of all Indians in Brazil" during the protracted war in Pernambuco, from the mid-1630s until his death in 1648. From the aldeia Rio Vermelho, Bishop Teixeira waged relentless campaigns against the Dutch. Despite his spiritual training, he "never lost the valor of soldier and captain."[70] Before the year was out, Teixeira collapsed from exhaustion, lingered eight days, and died.[71] Vieira described the Indigenous response: they "cried the most at his passing, because he was their father, defender, and protector."[72] While Vieira presented Teixeira in the best possible light to his Jesuit superiors in Rome, it is likely that the índios aldeados did mourn openly for the bishop, whether due to the loss of a military commander with whom they had fought against the Dutch, fear of what would come next, or both.

Across the Atlantic, the terrible news of the capture of Bahia, when it came, reached Lisbon ahead of Madrid. From there, Portuguese officials sprang into action ahead of orders from Spain. Guerrilla efforts to retake Salvador continued daily even as an alert to the Madeira and Canary Islands warned the captains there of the fall of Bahia.[73] Municipal officials of Lisbon also sent a report on to Madrid. Without waiting for regnal orders, Lisbon provided six thousand cruzados to outfit two caravels to aid the rescue of Bahia.[74] Yet with the Spanish and Portuguese treasuries drained from continental war against the Dutch, it took significant cajoling from Philip IV to the council for the metropole to muster more financial aid to support resistance efforts and retake Bahia.

From the metropole, retaking Bahia meant mobilizing soldiers, funds, and administrators, layered coordination that reflected, in the context of the Iberian union, the complex dynamics between colony and metropole. Writing to Lisbon from Pernambuco, Matias de Albuquerque asked for "practical men of the militia"—in particular, seven to eight thousand harquebusiers—gunpowder, assorted bullets and shells, and sustenance for daily living, including grain, wine, and olives.[75] The Conselho da Fazenda (Portuguese treasury) sent this request on to Philip IV of Spain.[76] August 1624 passed in a flurry of activity as the royal treasury made haste to outfit Portuguese ships with meat, munitions, and other provisions for the journey to rescue Bahia.[77]

As preparations for the rescue armada got under way, the *conselho* then turned to the matter of who should direct Portugal's purchase and furnishing of supplies for the rescue armada. Such discussions included the issue of pay, including funds set aside for the commander of the Portuguese armada, Manuel de Menezes.[78] The Portuguese prepared to stock and send twenty-six vessels; an important part of the preparations included encouraging able-bodied, mostly elite men to join the Portuguese armada and help organize the expedition.[79] The Count of Miranda and governor of Porto, for example, both rounded up supplies and took part in the rescue armada to Brazil.[80] With that, the moradores of Vila Viana in northern Portugal followed suit, and apart from very old men, almost all the noblemen there joined in.[81] Discussion and recommendations (*consultas*) of the royal treasury also named a treasurer of the fleet to Brazil for the specific purpose of guarding dispersal of funds, a plum position indicating Spanish trust in its Portuguese "vassals."[82]

Members of the Portuguese elite saw joining the official ranks of the armada as a prestigious career move, even though they would be under the command of a Spanish-led joint armada headed by Fadrique de Toledo Osorio. Portuguese nobility had little initial interest in Brazil, but this was an opportunity to demonstrate a time-honored fealty—that of vassals serving their (Spanish) lord.[83] After all, most of the Portuguese *fidalgueira* (aristocracy) had prospered since 1580—the beginning of the Philippine era. This was in no small part due to the Spanish crown's dismissal of the Portuguese Lei Mental, which had decreed that members of the court could keep their allowances and resources only through the legitimacy of a viable male heir not in the clergy.[84] The Philippine elimination of the Lei Mental thus consolidated elite Portuguese support and rounded up their help to protect the Spanish Empire at home and abroad. As further incentive to entice Portuguese nobles to the (now) Spanish cause to reconquer Bahia in 1625 and save Brazil, Philip offered choice appointments upon their safe return and guaranteed all nobles joining the mission a *mêrce* (general grant) in the event of death.

Members of the aristocracy prepared to join the most extravagant mission since Sebastian's ill-fated expedition across the Mediterranean, but exactly who would go, and in what capacity, was a matter of much discussion.[85] By citing a catalog of achievements, candidates ensured they would stand out among applicants. For instance, when Manuel Ornella requested to join the venture, he cited his decade of military experience in Pernambuco, Bahia, and Rio de Janeiro.[86] Individuals petitioned on behalf of family members too. For instance, Father João Roda Monteiro solicited the services of his uncle Francisco Pereira de Vargas in one the five Portuguese fleets that would join the restoration effort.[87]

While most of the fidalgueira received appointments or petitioned to join the rescue efforts, some were deemed unworthy or unfit to join in. These men were ordered—or encouraged—to remain behind. Such was the case of António de Ataide. Once a "captain in perpetuity" of the Portuguese royal armada, Ataide had, in 1621, lost an India ship, which was captured and burned by enemies. Thus disgraced, he was not recommended to join the venture to rescue Bahia. His son Jerônimo de Ataide had been named to play an important role in the mission to Bahia, but the younger man elected to stay behind to defend his father and help clear the family name. With the successful rescue of Bahia and return of the joint armada, however, Jerônimo drafted a celebratory monograph on the restoration and later commissioned maps of the invasion—his attempt to participate in the experience.[88] His version of the events would not be printed.[89]

Royal requests for help from the Portuguese extended beyond the fidalgueira and into municipal councils and the working class. The city of Lisbon offered 100,000 cruzados to help support the armada meant to rescue Bahia, but Philip IV petitioned for additional funds.[90] On August 6, 1624, and at the king's request, given his "poor state of treasury," Lisbon's House of Twenty-Four (Casa dos Vinte e Quatro), representing the guilds of the city, also contributed to the cause. Founded in the fourteenth century by Dom João I, this key municipal institution of Lisbon offered delegates representing the city's artisans, shoemakers, pastry makers, bakers, ironworkers, and others an opportunity to participate in the political process and to weigh in on issues of the day.[91] Given their "defect" of manual labor (working with their hands), none of these artisans would ever earn noble status; nor were they expected to join the fleet.

But the Casa dos Vinte e Quatro wielded behind-the-scenes power. Members assisted the rescue effort, demonstrating loyalty to the Crown in their prompt response to his request for funds. The guild set clear boundaries. "In the spirit of good vassals," wrote scribe Valentim de Bobadilha, "[we] will give Your Majesty, for this occasion, only fifty thousand cruzados with the declaration that [we] would not be obligated to give anything more for this occasion."[92] Artisan Lisboetas and delegates to the House of Twenty-Four had, in fact, already been quick to outfit caravels even ahead of their Spanish king's prompting. In the end, the group accepted and fulfilled the king's petition for a full 100,000 cruzados. They too would demonstrate fealty—for now.[93]

As material and logistical preparations for the armada wrapped up in the winter of 1624, the Portuguese also offered up prayers for an uneventful voyage and the successful restoration of Salvador. They then set forth.[94] Daily masses included exhortations that the Portuguese who embarked on the historic voyage across the Atlantic would do so in the name of God, as had their Portuguese ancestors. On November 22, 1624, the Portuguese fleet departed for the voyage and with it, according to one contemporary chronicler, carried "all the nobility of this kingdom."[95] Following orders from Philip IV, the Portuguese first sailed to Cadiz but were turned away because of the "great inconvenience" and sent to Cabo Verde.[96] They then took on the "considerable duty" of a more than monthlong wait for the Spanish there before the armadas set joint sail.[97] In March 1625, the largest armada to sail across the Atlantic Ocean began the journey to rescue Bahia.

On Easter Sunday of that year, Portuguese and Spanish ships sailed into the bay and blocked a Dutch maritime escape from Salvador. Within a month, it seemed that prayers offered at the metropole helped realize a remarkable success. The joint armada surrounded the Dutch ships; on land, Luso-Brazilian guerrillas kept the West India Company soldiers pinned to the town. Unable to execute advances into the Brazilian brush or escape by sea, the Netherlanders held onto their position for less than a few weeks and then surrendered. While they had seized Salvador for nearly a year, Dutch rescue ships arrived too late—after the on-the-ground capitulation to the Iberians. The ships then sailed on to raid other locations rather than engage in what would be a losing battle.[98]

The 1624 invasion had warranted immediate action, however, and this would arrive before the more organized and well-financed Luso–Spanish rescue mission. In the besieged colony and ahead of the armada's arrival, lesser fidalgo and lifelong soldier Matias de Albuquerque stepped up to direct the war effort from Pernambuco. For a short while at least, Bahia was no longer the center of Portuguese America, and the Albuquerque family vaulted to greater prominence.

Help came from other captaincies as well. After Spanish and Portuguese troops landed in Salvador, two canoes of Indigenous archers and two caravels "of white people," totaling 250 armed men, sailed in from the south. This group included the above-mentioned Salvador de Sá, who had once worked in mines alongside his father. Son of the governor of Rio de Janeiro and future governor of Angola, Sá arrived with 150 soldiers and Indigenous fighters.[99] The war against the Dutch presaged opportunity for economic and political men like Sá who rallied against the Dutch. For Luso-Brazilians, it would also lead to an emergent identity quite distinct from that of Portuguese subjects in the metropole.

Saving Salvador After the Fact: Post-Restoration Representations

António Vieira's annual mission letter to Rome offers the only eyewitness account of the Dutch invasion, but post-restoration chronicles celebrating the Luso–Spanish success reveal an understanding of how the reconquest of Salvador unfolded and what that meant for future efforts. A comparison of Portuguese and Spanish records and elite memories of the event indicates a weakening Iberian union. At the same time, a silence regarding pre-rescue efforts by Luso-Brazilian moradores and clergy, as well as those of the Lisbon working class, highlights a growing gap between the colony and the metropole. In other words, chronicles such as Guerreiro's *Journey of the Vassals* described the efforts of elite Iberians, but there was no such celebration of efforts made by non-elite Portuguese.

Tracing this social disconnect requires a close look at Portuguese and Spanish representations of the takeover of Salvador. As an English contemporary who fought for the Dutch noted of the Portuguese, "The Spanish king claims sovereignty, though by some denied, and the rest unwillingly accepted of."[100] The same observer, an English soldier who had sailed with the Dutch to take Salvador, noted that "parties in their owne cases are commonly parshall."[101] While he remarked on events from the losing side, for the Iberians, the glow of victory had barely dimmed when Portuguese and Spanish chroniclers put pen to paper. Competing, circulating Spanish and Portuguese representations of the "voyage of the vassals" and the restoration of Bahia belied a (peaceful) union. Seventeenth-century Spain "was a society almost obsessively dedicated to the written word."[102] Portuguese chroniclers, however, wasted no time in compiling their own version of events. Two years after the restoration of Bahia, the so-called Ink Wars were on.

What got into print—and to what end? Chronicles that were granted all necessary licenses and cleared Spanish censors circulated through the Iberian Peninsula. It is no surprise that dominant versions of the story of the restoration emerged from Madrid. The work of friar Bartolomeu Guerreiro was one of the rare Portuguese documents to clear such hurdles, perhaps due to statements of loyalty "in service and in love" to "Your Majesty of Spain." Guerreiro took pains in his *Jornada dos vassalos* to describe the fine work of "Portuguese vassals who achieved the annihilation . . . of rebel Dutch they dominated there."[103] For additional public proof of service to Spain, he included letters from Philip IV (III of Spain) praising the Portuguese for their loyalty.[104]

Baroque representations of the day reveal concerns wrought in no small part due to inter-group change and conflict.[105] For certain, textual and artistic manifestations of societal tension were not confined to the early modern Spanish and Portuguese. But in the case of the Iberian union, nowhere prior to 1640 restoration of the Portuguese crown was this truer than in conflicting accounts on the restoration of Bahia.[106] Meant to please "most people of Portugal and Castile" who wanted to know of the truth of the Portuguese effort in Bahia, Guerreiro's *Jornada dos vassalos* offers a closer look at the Portuguese perspective on the rescue of Bahia.

Contextualizing the Dutch episode in Bahia proved a sticking point: Spanish chroniclers, including Tamayo de Vargas, Philip's own scribe, cast the Dutch in Bahia as a mere episode in the Eighty Year War and the Portuguese as bit players.[107] He took pains to note, for instance, that the Portuguese armada "followed with difficulty that of Castile." As official chronicler for Spain, he made clear the distinction between the imperial Spanish and bumbling Portuguese. Juan de Valencia y Guzmán wrote that the joint armadas had barely set off when one Portuguese ship was lost, along with 140 men—though the artillery was saved. They then had trouble, according to Spanish chroniclers, keeping apace en route to Brazil.[108] In the end, Philip IV's scribe de Castro attributed the Iberian victory over the Dutch less to a unified Iberian effort than to Spanish demonstrations of faith orations (sermons) and days of prayer and fasting.[109]

For some Portuguese, however, the reconquest of Bahia was part of a larger plan, a route to Portugal's divine destiny, even though the kingdom's fate was tied, at this time, to imperial Spain. José de Medeiros Correa's *Relacam verdadeira de tudo o succedido na restauracao da Bahia de Todos os Sanctos* offered the reconquest of 1625 as an example of the "great glory of God, exaltation of King and Kingdom."[110] Jesuit Bartolomeu Guerreiro described the Portuguese as "vassals of heaven"—doing God's work in Brazil, retaking Bahia for God and king. One image of the rescue is folded into Guerreiro's work, a print of the Luso–Spanish armada surrounding the Dutch ships in the Bay of All Saints. This rendering of Iberian imperial unity evokes a subversion of David and Goliath: a mighty joint armada overpowers a tiny Dutch fleet pressed up against the coast. The title of the scene—directed by the "Lusitanian" monarch Philip of "Africa, Ethiopia, Arabia, India, Persia, India and Brazil"—reflects the earliest expansionary traditions of Portugal. For Guerreiro, this was just one more scene of an enduring conflict that played out well beyond the South Atlantic.[111]

Contemporary accounts skimmed Luso–Spanish tension that surfaced in the official record, but evolving notions of subjecthood included continued demonstrations of faith and allegiance to Portugal's monarch—even if he was not Portuguese. Wide-circulating Spanish and Portuguese descriptions note the auspicious holy days of reconquest. For instance, Luso–Spanish troops disembarked on March 29, 1625, "on the eve of the Resurrection of Christ," in preparation to retake the city.[112] Guerreiro describes the dangerous work of the Portuguese in taking up the vanguard *and* the rear guard, and in protecting the city gates when the Spanish retook the town: "What was certain was that Portuguese militia was not interested in anything but service to Your Majesty [Philip IV of Spain], honor and reputation of the Crown of Portugal." On the first of May, the Day of the Apostles, they reclaimed Salvador as Spanish commander Dom Juan de Orellana and his regiments marched through the city gates while the Portuguese stayed behind.[113] Orellana bade Portuguese troops to wait outside city walls and the Spanish auditor-general to follow and take inventory of the wrought silver, slaves, and artillery, noting damage done by the Spanish troops. A Portuguese eyewitness bemoaned such destruction, as well as the Spanish flag that was first hoisted over Salvador. Such events, he wrote, were destined to "languish in the sepulchre of memory."[114] His observations, for the most part, appear to have been borne out. Salvador city councilman Manoel de Rego Sequeira later complained to Philip IV of the considerable damage cause by the Spanish and asked for a two-year moratorium on taxes.[115] This written disconnect—Guerreiro's careful discussion of the Spanish entrance into the town compared to Sequeira's complaints—highlights a growing gap between Portuguese perceptions of the reconquest from the metropole, as was the case with Guerreiro, and in Brazil.

Six years after the restoration, the Dutch returned to seize Pernambuco in their renewed drive to conquer Brazil and fulfill their Grand Design, but the above-mentioned Portuguese nobleman Jerônimo de Ataide commissioned a major cartographic work indicating Spain's global possessions. He had declined to join the "journey of the vassals" in order to clear his father's name, but he chose to make another contribution to the kingdom instead. For his *Atlas of Brazil*, he had João Teixeira Albernaz, Portugal's most prolific cartographer, create a series of maps, which included the restoration Bahia. The result was a near replica of an image in Guerreiro's work. One distinction is that here, the Portuguese are doing the hard work of keeping the Dutch out. The far lower right of the image (Figure 3), unlike the scene in Guerreiro's work, shows a Dutch fleet arrived too late to the rescue: the Portuguese block their access. Ataide's commissioned work, relative to Guerreiro's image, also scales down the

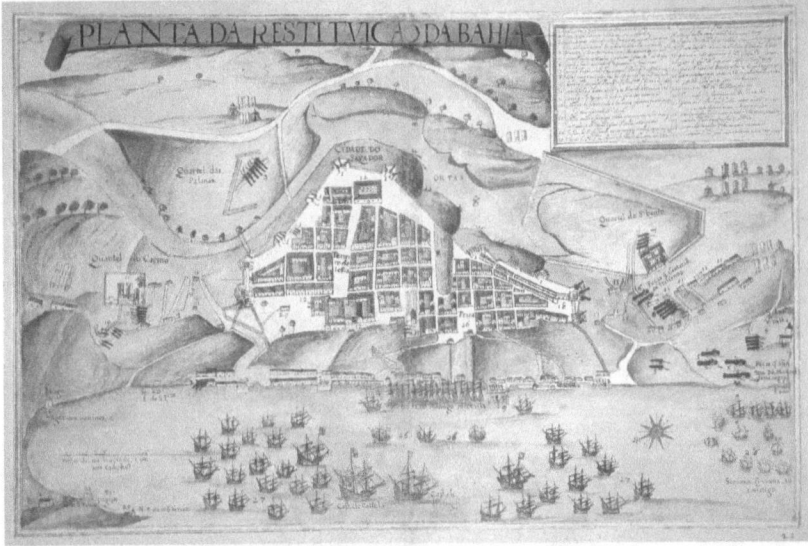

Figure 3. Portuguese perspective: João Teixeira Albernaz, *Restoration of Bahia*, 1631, pen and ink and watercolor. Courtesy of Library of Congress.

size of the joint armada. Six years after a unified Iberian success against the Dutch, this work, part of a survey of Portuguese (and not Spanish) lands, goes further than that of Guerreiro to suggest that the Portuguese were responsible for saving Salvador.

Later Spanish depictions of Bahia's 1625 restoration reduced the Portuguese to passive observers of triumph, an indication of a weakened Iberian union and Spanish disregard for the efforts of Portuguese subjects in Brazil. The 1634 *La Recuperación de Bahía de Todos los Santos*, for example, nearly eliminates the Portuguese from Bahia altogether in its display of Spanish success *plus ultra* (further beyond). This then was the possibility of endless expansion.[116] In Figure 4, the viewer is high above Bahia. Left to right, the gaze is on returning moradores and Philip IV. To the far left, grateful Portuguese subjects make their way back to Salvador. In the center of the painting, a Christ-like fallen soldier, a sacrifice for the cause of restoration, is supported by a comrade and tended by devoted women. In middle ground, to the far right, Spanish commander Fadrique de Toledo Osorio presents the submissive and repentant Dutch with a tapestry of Philip IV flanked by the goddess of war Minerva and his chief

Figure 4. Spanish view: Juan Bautista Maíno, The Recovery of the Bay of All Saints, 1635, oil on canvas, 309 × 381 cm. Courtesy of Museo del Prado, Madrid.

minister Olivares. They had jointly crowned the king with a victor's laurels. The Bay of All Saints, orderly and calm, harbors promise and possibly the adventure of journey as some men launch back to their waiting caravels. Thus this painting, an iconic representation of Spain's transatlantic response to challenges overseas, draws on religious symbolism to make firm the connection between Philip IV and Spain's divine imperial promise.[117]

The promise of Portugal, derived from enduring legends of the kingdom's divinely inspired past success, did not include passive allegiance to the Spanish. Instead, prophecy—years of trials—would be translated into action in both Portugal and its South Atlantic colony. For Luso-Brazilians, this meant resisting the Dutch invaders, either by force or through textual ammunition, such as young Vieira's "Carta Ânua." What started out as a simple mission letter would be translated from Latin into Portuguese and widely circulated as the

Luso–Dutch war endured. Mixed-descent António Vieira, barred from high social standing by virtue of his heritage, nonetheless made an impact as he sought to write the truth of what "really happened." It took him a full two years to write the annual letter "of the terror in all parts of Brazil that has impeded note-taking and has allowed no place to write."[118] But this terror did not prevent him from writing and sending the report on to Rome. Nor did it stop on-the-ground efforts to take down the Dutch through Jesuit-led attacks or intra-captaincy coordination regarding military logistics. The restoration of Bahia foreshadowed the recovery of the kingdom from both the Dutch and the Spanish, an experience that transformed what it meant to be a subject of Portugal—in Brazil.

With the Dutch invasion of Bahia, the Portuguese moved into on-the-ground and transatlantic action to restore the colony. By and large, however, the fidalgueira participated in traditional demonstrations of allegiance by participating in Spanish-led "voyage of the vassals." Still, Luso-Brazilian actions to restore and defend Salvador encouraged evolving notions of subjecthood. António Vieira's eyewitness account of the first Dutch invasion reveals the strength of the Jesuit–Indigenous alliance, in what would be later acknowledged as a hallmark of Portuguese identity.[119] That is, from 1624 to 1625, Jesuit brothers led Indigenous troops from their aldeias against Dutch troops; Luso-Brazilians sent troops and supplies from Pernambuco and other captaincies to Bahia.

Though they would round back to seize Pernambuco, the Netherlanders would never again take Bahia. In the next decade, and thanks to guerrilla forces, Dutch governor-general of Pernambuco Johan Maurits van Nassau-Siegen's planned invasion of 1638 ended, as we shall see, with his damaged ships listing back to Recife. In the end, Dutch failure to secure Bahia meant the slow disintegration of the Grand Design. Saving Bahia, as the Dutch, Portuguese, and Spanish well understood, meant the continued existence of Portugal. Enduring pushback against the Dutch would come from the Portuguese subjects of Brazil, including those overlooked for their "stained" heritage.

The joint Portuguese and Spanish rescue armada, while successful in reconquest of Bahia, engendered the end of a dual crown. The "good vassals" from Portugal (*tão bons vassalos*) made clear that their effort to aid the essentially now Spanish cause of Brazil was also part of a tradition—fealty to the Philippine rule which began in 1580—but their experience uncovered simmering intra-Iberian tension. Subject and self-understanding now transformed to a consciousness that proved distinct from the metropole. For on the ground in Brazil, and across the Atlantic in Portugal, with the initial Dutch invasion of 1624, Luso-Brazilians began to take matters into their own hands.

CHAPTER THREE

"Wild Nations of People"

Rendering Faith, Collaboration, and Resistance

IN APRIL 1640, AS the Dutch sailed into the Bay of All Saints, the moradores of Bahia called upon Santo Antônio (St. Anthony) to protect them once again. By this time, the patron saint of lost causes had been promoted there with full honors to military captain; the city council had decreed that for his "efforts," he well deserved his rank and pay.[1] Their proof included the fact that although Dutch West India Company troops had seized Bahia in 1624, a joint Luso–Spanish force had ousted them within a year. And while the Dutch rounded back to Brazil in 1630 to seize a large chunk of the northeast 1635, Bahia remained intact. Not even a forty-day siege of the town in April 1638 by the governor-general of Dutch Brazil seemed to lift the saint's protection.[2] Prayers to Santo Antônio, it was believed, helped keep safe the richest sugar-producing captaincy in all of Portuguese America.

The Dutch fanned out across the Brazilian northeast, conquering Paraíba (1634), Sergipe (1636), and Ceará (1637), but for the Portuguese, Bahia was no lost cause in 1640—not yet (Map 1).[3] As the enemy prepared to bombard Salvador, the colonial capital of the captaincy and administrative center of Portuguese America, a young Jesuit priest turned to an even higher power than the Lisbon-born saint for help.[4] Padre António Vieira had, after all, already confronted the Dutch threat. In 1624, as a Jesuit novice, he fled inland to an aldeia as the invaders laid claim to Salvador; he also experienced the siege of 1638.[5] Now, as an orator of rising renown, Vieira went on the offense. During the renewed Dutch threat to Bahia, the townspeople attended daily mass and heard

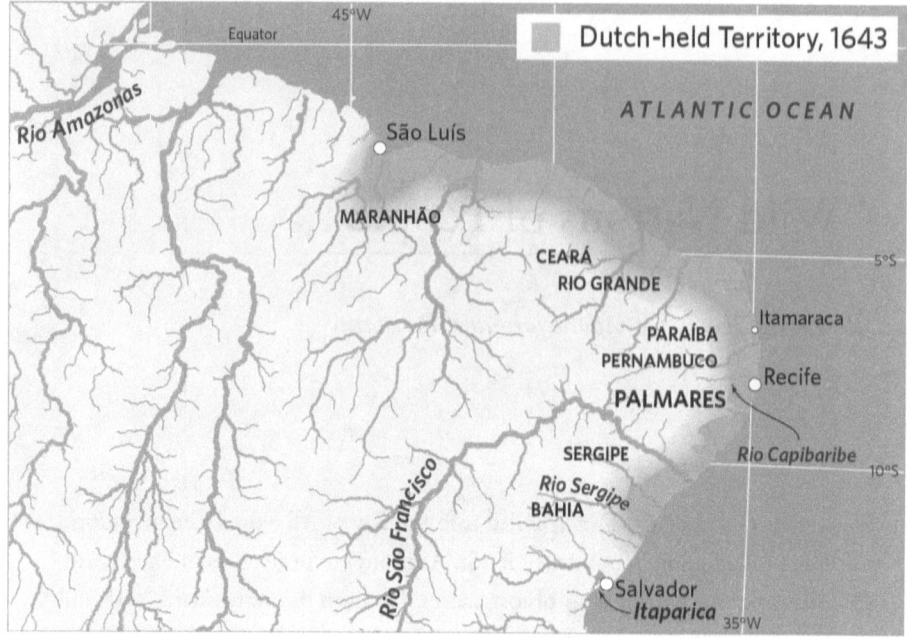

Map 1. Dutch control of Brazil, 1643. By Martin von Wyss, @mvwmaps. © Suzanne Litrel, 2019.

Vieira. Drawing from deep discursive ammunition, the young priest delivered a *conceptismo*-style sermon to rouse his audience to action. Now was the time to recall Portugal's—and by extension, Brazil's—real purpose. He began with God.[6]

"Rouse thyself!" Vieira challenged his heavenly father—or perhaps his listeners. "Why do you sleep?" The Portuguese had sacrificed so much in God's name, railed the priest. Where was he now in the hour of their need? "Consider, my God, and forgive me from speaking out of turn. Consider from whom You take the land of Brazil, and to who You give [it]. For what did we open the seas, never before navigated? If after so many dangers, after some much humiliation, after so many and so grievous deaths, why gain it, if to lose it like this!"[7]

As Dutch ships lingered offshore, Vieira called on God to summon the resolve of his chosen people—in this case the Portuguese. This Old Testament tradition—exhorting the divine to rouse the people—may have seemed to border on blasphemy. The Portuguese had long cast their expansionary mission as divine will manifested on earth. But with the kingdom caving to the Hollanders, Vieira wondered aloud who—if not God—was for the Portuguese.

The liminal space of Dutch Brazil is crowded by biographies of elite actors and narratives of empire. This includes Padre António, who had a seemingly meteoric rise, from runaway to prodigy novice to renowned orator. His powers of persuasion would reach the highest political circles in church and state. Yet the space of conflict also opened opportunity for those previously sidelined from the story—people of African, Indigenous, and mixed descent, as well as Jews and New Christians. They maneuvered for their own survival and in so doing influenced the course of war. Not a few such individuals chose and switched sides, serving the Portuguese or the Dutch at will—and sometimes at the same time. Centuries later, their cross-class, ethnically and culturally diverse alliances, crystallized in the triumph over the Dutch, would be enshrined in Brazilian national consciousness.

The familiar art, cartography, and literature commissioned by the governor-general of Dutch Brazil, Johan Maurits van Nassau-Siegen (1636–1644), renders a far different scene: one of Dutch order, stability, and expansiveness. During the seventeenth-century Dutch Golden Age, the term *landschap*, Dutch for "landscape," meant both "what the surveyor was to measure and the artist to render."[8] Such was the task for Maurits's forty-six carefully selected scholar-aesthetes. Their artistic, naturalist, and cartographic descriptions of the fleeting colony, deployed by Maurits from the mid-seventeenth century on, promoted a "tolerant" and profitable Brazil worth celebrating.[9] But when mapped against on-the-ground sources, the "types of Brazil," imagined by Albert Eckhout and Frans Post, reveal another scene: the breach between the Dutch-commissioned rhetoric of order and progress and the realities of their attempted conquest. When combined with Portuguese language sources, such work points to a Luso-Brazilian identity forged in war.[10]

How and why, from 1630, did marginalized Luso-Brazilians negotiate the Dutch presence and affect the outcome of the war? Regnal Spanish (to 1640) and Portuguese (from 1641) aid to Brazil was inconsistent at best; only the 1625 restoration of Bahia proved successful. Santo Antônio's "promotions," like Vieira's sermons, point to the on-the-ground despair experienced in the absence of assistance from the metropole. They also indicate the importance of unexpected actions taken by local actors in the midst of the protracted war. Through the mid-1640s, the dearth of able-bodied, skilled soldiers for Portugal meant more than just advancement for Indigenous, African, and mixed-descent men who were willing and able to fight for the Crown: some, such as Afro-descended Henrique Dias and Indigenous Felipe Camarão, secured not only their family's sociopolitical status but also a permanent place in Brazilian history.

Dutch Brazil served as a crucible for Luso-Brazilian self-understanding—an experience that manifested not just in conflict but in text and art. Resistance to the Netherlanders also played out, as Padre Vieira well knew, on an Atlantic and world historical scale. The evolution of Saint Anthony from a holy man to a military saint reflected the scales of such improvisation: away from the metropole, Luso-Brazilians refashioned identities that led to survival, breaking social mores and recasting traditional behavior as they shaped the outcome of the war against the Dutch.

"Lessons Learned": the Dutch Conquest of Pernambuco (from 1630)

The short-lived conquest and resounding loss of Bahia in 1625 did not mean the Dutch West India Company gave up piratical practices in the South Atlantic. This instead lent urgency to their quest. Though he failed to seize Salvador in March and June 1627, commander Piet Heyn raided the Bay of All Saints, allowing the company to carry on. Heyn next captured the Spanish silver fleet off the Cuban Bay of Matanzas, and for a short time the Company turned a major profit.[11] The Dutch experience in the Caribbean had, since the late sixteenth century, served as a model for South Atlantic efforts, but this spectacular haul marked the potential for a major Dutch West India Company offensive in Brazil.[12] But by 1629, the Spanish, now on defense across the Americas and on the European continent, engaged in new negotiations for peace with the United Provinces. The West India Company, fueled by commerce and war, mounted vigorous opposition, and the decision to target Brazil was made even prior to the conclusion of the talks.[13] With this resolve came a renewed drive for able-bodied men who would fight for the Dutch cause.[14] Bahia resisted reconquest, so the Dutch aimed farther north, for Pernambuco, the second-richest sugar-producing captaincy in Brazil.

Spain, with Portugal in its possession since 1580, may have braced for a renewed Dutch attack—but those with personal stake made haste when the threat was real. In 1630 Matias de Albuquerque, the governor of Pernambuco, was in Portugal when he received warning from his counterpart in Cabo Verde of an impending Dutch invasion.[15] Albuquerque hurried back to his captaincy and ordered repairs on coastal fortifications. These were not completed, however, when the Dutch began their assault.[16]

On February 14, 1630, five years after the Dutch were expelled from Salvador, their troops poured out onto Pernambucan beaches and marched toward Olinda. Colonel Waerdenburch had prayed hard the night before to "prevent against recklessness" in the conflict.[17] His preparations the next day, however, belied such reflection; he would lead landing troops into battle with almost no defensive gear. His personal chaplain, Johan Baers, begged him to at least wear his breastplate. This he refused, proclaiming that he was "armed with God and a good conscience."[18] Perhaps this show of bravery was meant to boost the confidence of his troops, the majority of whom were raw recruits out of Texel.[19] An experienced military man, Waerdenburch had advance notice of the poorly defended Olinda and its small population, which resided in and made use of two hundred homes, five convents, and six churches.[20] Recife, the captaincy's second-largest town, was at the time populated primarily by sailors and fishermen in 150 homes—hardly a match for Dutch West India company soldiers.[21]

From the beach, Father Manoel Calado watched as Dutch ships drew and returned fire to cover for the landing troops. The assault was nothing short of "divine justice" for the avarice he had observed to that point in Olinda. By his telling, the streets of this "earthly paradise"—set on a hill five miles away from the fishing village of Recife—ran with gold and silver derived from sugar profits. The sin of greed, he thought, had long been on display as elite women paraded about in silk, velvet, and taffeta; they were so bejeweled that it "seemed to rain pearls, rubies, emeralds, and diamonds from their hair."[22] Father Calado was not alone in singling out such feminine excess; an English soldier for the Dutch went further, connecting siren-like women who "spayred noe treasure for apparel to bewitch their loover's harts" to the incestuous ways of the Portuguese he claimed to have observed.[23] For "Padre Óculos" (Father Glasses), however, such wanton displays of excess were but one reason for what he perceived as divine wrath unleashed in the form of the Dutch in Brazil.[24]

Colonel Waerdenburch's men marched in procession up the Pau Amarelo beach toward the hillside town of Olinda; the moradores scrambled after them in defense. The invaders divided into four squadrons, with about four thousand men marching under six flags toward Olinda.[25] By the time his men reached Olinda, the town had nearly emptied out, with refugees fleeing to nearby aldeias. There were few soldiers in Olinda, but a certain Captain Andre Pereira Temudo was shot through even as he wielded his sword. The good captain and his companions, wrote the author of this "true" account, had fought for God and sovereign like "brave and true Portuguese."[26]

Five miles away, the residents of Recife ignored initial volleys of enemy fire. The first shots rang out clearly but were thought to be part of large-scale festivities. Then "the armada from Holland came straight to Recife and commenced firing so much artillery that it seemed the sea rained down upon the land," Calado remembered sixteen years later.[27] Dutch ships sailed past forts guarding the entrance to the harbor and bombarded the beach, diverting attention from Waerdenburch's men, who spilled out onto the beach and started marching toward Recife. Women stumbled and fainted on the roads leading out of town, their children screaming by their side: "In all the tribulation was so great that it is not possible to describe with words; and it is a very different thing to see with one's own eyes than to write about it with pen and ink."[28]

The Dutch attempt to take the Brazilian northeast included fielding far more experienced and disciplined commanders than they had in the first brief attempt, which had hardly secured Bahia from 1624 to 1625.[29] But Dutch strategy was the same: bombard the coast, send in landing troops, and seize towns— in this case, Olinda and Recife. Now the West India Company was also armed with a few translators, thanks to the Poti and other Tupi-speaking Indigenous people the Dutch had taken with them to the United Provinces upon departing the Bay of All Saints in 1625.[30]

As Dutch West India Company troops spilled out onto the beach and marched toward Olinda, all signs initially pointed toward Dutch success. Defending colonists were caught off-guard as troops trudged the steepest approach to the hillside town. The invaders made their way inland, hardly hampered by skirmishes.[31] In their first night in Brazil, the troops fought off the twenty-seven soldiers at the Jesuit convent, helped themselves to the stores, and drank deeply of the "good wine of Spain." According to one Dutch soldier, many passed out from drink and lay sprawling "like irrational brutes" in the streets and abandoned homes.[32]

Yet a few months into the assault, the outlook for the Dutch was grim; up to 40 percent of West India Company men died of disease or hunger.[33] Some Indigenous men and *mouros* (Afro-descended men, possibly of Muslim heritage) crossed over to join West India Company troops, but the Portuguese welcomed the mostly French deserters, who came over in droves in the early months of the campaign.[34] By June 1630, the Dutch invaders were reduced to eating cats, dogs, and rats as two days' worth of rations had to last eight.[35] The following month offered no relief. In the course of one day, for example, two Indigenous men went over to the Dutch—but eight WIC men deserted to the Portuguese side.[36] Most left Dutch forces for lack of food between the fifth and tenth of the month.[37]

Commander Waerdenburch then had the fortune of happening upon Adrian Verdonck, who had lived in the area for the last decade. Though now a resident of Olinda, Verdonck remained while the moradores fled, offering his friendship and help. The Dutch initially welcomed the man's assistance, and he "became beloved by all, especially the Colonel, whose company he kept and whose table he shared."[38] Verdonck, apparently pleased to work with the Dutch, supplied the commander with a fairly detailed assessment of the region. This included a survey of its engenhos, towns, and productive capacities. His report to the West India Company indicated land rich in cattle, sugar, and grain in the various captaincies of the northeast. The captaincy of Pernambuco, he explained, extended as far south as the São Francisco River, some forty miles away, and he noted that silver mines had been discovered there some twelve years earlier.[39] The main city was a thriving center of commerce and trade, he added; mouros came and went selling their wares each day.[40]

In January 1631, Waerdenburch's relationship with Verdonck came to an abrupt end. Accused of treason, the burly Brabander was shackled and dragged into prison.[41] An Indigenous recruit for the Dutch reported that Verdonck's mouro had been seen ferrying letters—"three in three days"—to the Portuguese. It appeared that Verdonck had maintained correspondence with Matias de Albuquerque, the Portuguese governor-general of Pernambuco. Accused of apprising Albuquerque of Dutch plans, Verdonck languished in prison until his torture began in April. He soon tried and failed to commit suicide by jumping out of a small prison window—an attempt to break his own neck.⁴² One unsympathetic eyewitness noted "the astonishment of many as to how such a big, and fat man could have gone through it [the tiny prison window]."⁴³ After a few more days of torture, the Dutch carried out Verdonck's execution, mutilating and then quartering his body. They then posted his head on a spike high outside Fort Brum, had his body parts strewn in front of various Dutch-held forts, and sent the rest to Olinda as a warning to those who collaborated with the Portuguese.

The Dutch earned a reprieve from heavy losses on April 20, 1632, the day Domingo Fernandes Calabar, described in sources as either a *mulato* or a *mameluco*, turned up in their camp.⁴⁴ The so-called first traitor of Brazil and owner of three sugar mills, Calabar offered his services to the demoralized Dutch troops. His action caught both the Portuguese and the Dutch off-guard. He not only had assets but had been injured quite severely by the Dutch the prior year and had sworn revenge.⁴⁵ Yet on the run for criminal acts in Porto Calvo, Calabar soon proved deserving of Dutch protection.⁴⁶ According to one observer, he mastered Dutch in a matter of days.⁴⁷ For Calabar's "advise and meanes" and for being a "polilitique stoute fellow, and knowingge all passages and hye ways the whole land through" Dutch-led forces harried the Portuguese. Fluent in Tupi, Calabar also gained Indigenous allies for the invaders.⁴⁸ He led his own expeditions, nighttime and predawn sorties though secret paths and riverine channels that caught sleeping moradores unaware. By 1635, three years after he joined forces with the West India Company, he was directly responsible for the surrender of Forte Real do Bom Jesus, a major Portuguese stronghold between the towns of Olinda and Recife. This led to the withdrawal of the Luso-Brazilian-Spanish army to Bahia.

As a result of his skill and effort, Calabar received fast promotion, first to captain and then sergeant major, "all this well-deserved, given the considerable damage" he caused the Portuguese.⁴⁹ He made fast friends with fearsome General Sigismond Schkoppe and served on the Dutch West India military council until 1635.⁵⁰ But as one Portuguese eyewitness and high-ranking official noted, after two years of terrible conflict and the "loss and work" that resulted, he was "the first to pass to the adversary."⁵¹ In other words, up until this time, no other Portuguese subject had proven disloyal to the resistance.⁵² It is likely that Calabar was indeed guilty of crimes prior to his defection to the Dutch, but he also received acknowledgement, political status, and honors from his former enemies. Leveraging his mixed-descent identity and his linguistic fluency for the Dutch earned him rewards that were not otherwise easily accessible.

Thanks to Calabar's help, by June 1635 the Portuguese stronghold of Forte Real do Bom Jesus had fallen to the Dutch.[53] This was a major turning point in the war—and for Calabar, whose luck had run out. Thanks to another double-crosser—the spy Sebastião Souto, embedded with the Dutch—the Portuguese came upon a small contingent of West India Company troops en route from the razed fort to another campaign. With them was Calabar. The Portuguese overwhelmed the enemy men, and the French captain for the WIC chose to hand over Calabar to guarantee his life and that of his men.[54] Father Manoel Calado heard Calabar's confession, which he said included weighty concerns.[55] Judgment, when it came, was swift. Calabar was executed without the benefit of last words: garroted, decapitated, and quartered. His body was strewn about Porto Calvo, where he was born. Along with him, Manuel de Castro, a Portuguese Jew, was condemned to death on charges of conspiracy. He was hanged on a cashew tree.[56] Sebastião Souto, the spy for the Portuguese, was promoted to captain on the spot.[57]

Mixed-descent Portuguese subjects crossed over to the Dutch and back again, hindering and helping both sides. Padre Manoel de Moraes, for example, had been a faithful servant of God and Portugal all his life. Originally from the São Paulo area, he had had the option of training to become a Jesuit or joining up with the bandeirantes to drag Indigenous captives into forced labor.[58] He chose the former, and for his overall aptitude as well as his linguistic facility with Tupi, Moraes was sent as an armed Jesuit into service in Pernambuco.[59] There he led his own Indigenous troops into battle against the Dutch from 1630, engaging in battle with perhaps a bit too much relish for his Jesuit superiors. However, a much-impressed Commander Matias de Albuquerque bestowed upon him the formidable title of "Captain-General of the Indians."[60] Like Calabar, this "very dark" priest proved himself in battle and through his fluency in Tupi many times over.[61]

After several years of leading índios aldeados against the Dutch, Manoel de Moraes surrendered quite willingly to West India Company forces at the Battle of Paraiba in 1634.[62] He began working for them at once, betraying the Portuguese and his fellow Jesuits. He passed on valuable information, including the whereabouts of six aldeias. Dressed as a Dutch captain, he communicated with Indigenous chiefs, encouraging them to ally with the Netherlandish invaders. In Recife, the former Jesuit shattered his vows by openly consorting with Dutch prostitutes Cristianaazinha Harmens and Maria "Cabelo de Fogo" (Hair of Fire) Roothaer. Moraes's Jesuit superiors knew he had long broken the sixth Jesuit commandment of abstinence, but he now dropped all pretense. Friar Domingos de Coelho, who had promoted him to govern aldeias in the first place, sent three letters urging him to drop his sinful ways. Moraes declined to respond, and the Company of Jesuits expelled him once and for all.[63]

Besides damaging the Jesuit cause, Manoel de Moraes betrayed his former compatriots in a profoundly personal way. He led the Tupi villagers he had commanded in battle again—only this time against the Portuguese. Like Calabar, he was promoted to captain by the Dutch, but the former priest flaunted his new status on the Calvinist side, taunting Portuguese prisoners, for example for declining to eat meat on Good Friday.[64] In the company of his new compatriots, Manuel de Moraes journeyed to the Netherlands. There he appeared ready to dispense with his wandering eye and soldiering ways as he converted to Calvinism, married, and fathered two children. He proved exceptionally useful to the Dutch cause, developing a Tupi dictionary for the West India Company. This contribution aided Dutch settlement efforts in the next few years.

Upon the dissolution of the Iberian crowns in December 1640 and the restoration of the Portuguese monarchy, Manuel de Moraes abandoned his wife and children in the Netherlands for Maranhão in 1643. His goal was to engage in brazilwood trade, but he was soon captured by the Portuguese resistance. Still, he proved his worth to the Portuguese once again, recanted, and lent his chaplain services at a turning point battle against the Dutch two years later. Ever under suspicion, and never truly forgiven for aiding the Dutch in the first place, he was sent to Lisbon to face the Inquisition.[65]

The examples of mixed-descent Calabar and Moraes highlight opportunities afforded them by the Dutch and what they chose to make of them. Their decisions were a function of not only their position in Portuguese society in Brazil but also their perceived choices given the social landscape. Moraes, for example, chose to return to the Portuguese fold after the restoration of Portugal (1640); Calabar, executed in 1635, of course could not.

"Wild Nations of People": Afro-Brazilian and Indigenous Resistance to the Dutch

The early years of the second Dutch invasion resulted in a stalemate broken only by Luso-Brazilians who crossed over to the enemy, such as Calabar and Moraes. But what of those who remained loyal? By siding with the Dutch, non-elite men, including the above-mentioned "traitors," seemed to earn attention and liberties otherwise not accorded to them by the Portuguese in Brazil. Painter Albert Eckhout's "types of Brazil" indicates freedoms not depicted elsewhere. Yet for their actions, service, and loyalty, Afro-descended Henrique Dias and Felipe Antônio Camarão received unusual recognition—from the Portuguese. A comparison of Governor-General Johan Maurits's commissioned art to on-the-ground actions reveals the evolving possibilities and choices of non-elite actors up until the Pernambucan uprising of 1645.

The 1635 fall of the royal fort of Bom Jesus marked the next phase of the Dutch in the northeast. With much of Pernambuco secured, the Heeren XIX (directors of the Dutch West India Company) turned to the appointment of a long-term governor-general. By 1636 they had decided that Brazilian affairs should be consolidated under a leader, as with the VOC's operation in Batavia. Military commander Crestofle Arciszewsky, singled out for exceptional service and courage during the war, seemed the obvious choice for the post.[66] Instead, the title of governor-general went to the high-born and high-bred Johan Maurits van Nassau-Siegen, a great-nephew of Prince Nassau of Orange.[67] He had military experience, though not quite on par with Arciszewsky; perhaps WIC directors felt that his background would add a certain sheen to the whole enterprise. Certainly in his aesthetic inclinations and fine manners, Maurits seemed to embody the humanist ideals that dominated the aristocratic discourse of the day.[68] He was tasked, however, with solidifying earlier WIC conquests in northeastern Brazil, extending the company's reach, shaking up local government, and streamlining of administrative affairs.[69]

This, then, was a strategic appointment, meant to boost shareholder confidence—and Maurits's prestige. Seventeenth-century Amsterdam and Leiden roiled with domestic and foreign political talk and interest in travel literature, which cut across class lines, given the ready supply of pamphlets, maps, and those willing to hang about Nieuwe Brugh (New Bridge) to watch the ships come in and engage in the latest news from abroad.[70] Such activity transferred well to canvas, as art and empire went hand in hand, for the "aim of [seventeenth-century] Dutch painters" was to capture on a surface a great range of knowledge and information about the world."[71] The aristocratic Maurits, well aware of the influence *his* commissioned images could generate, would handpick "recorders of reality" to voyage with him across the Atlantic and depict a lush, well-ordered Brazil under his rule.[72]

It would be nearly half a year before Maurits would set sail for northeastern Brazil. During that time he carefully selected and commissioned forty-six artists, naturalists, cartographers, and poets for the voyage to Dutch-controlled Brazil. A military man whose familial connections placed him just on the "periphery of the elite," Maurits would extend and solidify Dutch power in northeastern Brazil, but his hired talent was to catalog and collect, to describe and map for the purposes of politics and art.[73]

Loyalty to the Dutch order appears evident in Maurits-commissioned work and is even mapped out on "Brazilian" bodies.[74] For instance, Albert Eckhout, one of the forty-six scholar-aesthetes Maurits plucked out of obscurity to document his tenure in Brazil, created a life-size ethnographic series of the "wild nations of people" the governor-general hoped to "tame" under the his rule.[75] Maurits's aesthetic ambition is displayed in the African, Indigenous, and mixed-descent people depicted as ready to serve him and the Dutch cause. Eckhout rendered a Tupinambá man as a staunch ally; he gazes steadily at the viewer, weapon in hand. He appears calm and ready for battle (Figure 5).[76]

To appreciate the agency, choice, and possibilities of marginalized peoples in Brazil, it is important to note the context in which Indigenous soldiers chose sides. Despite Eckhout's portraits, which render them ready to serve the Dutch, the loyalties of the Potiguar, Tupinambá, and Tapuya people were not readily ascertained. Seventeenth-century colonialists of Dutch Brazil would have most likely encountered the Tupi-speaking Tupinambá or Potiguars, who lived along or near the coastline.[77] These the Dutch termed Brasilianen, as they were most approachable given their long history of interactions with the Portuguese. The Tapuya (or Tapuia) were a non-Tupi-speaking tribe that lived in the Brazilian interior. On the one hand, in the 1624–1625 Dutch invasion of Salvador, then-novice António Vieira reported to the Company of Jesus that the Tupinambá were the "primary weapon" that "dealt horror to the enemy."[78] On the other

Figure 5. Albert Eckhout, *Tupi Man*, 1640–1644, oil on canvas, 272 × 163 cm. Courtesy of the National Museum of Denmark.

hand, after 1630, thousands of Indigenous archers fought with the Dutch *against* the Portuguese. This alliance can be traced from the Dutch expulsion from Bahia in 1625. This is when West India Company officers brought at least twenty Potiguares, including Pieter Poti, to the United Provinces—where they learned Dutch and studied Calvinism—"at great cost" to the company.[79] Such efforts were an important part of preparation for the 1630 Dutch assault on Pernambuco.[80]

Best Dutch efforts notwithstanding, the evidence bears out that neither they nor the Portuguese could claim Indigenous tribes of Brazil as their own. For example, the newly converted (to Calvinism) and now Dutch-speaking Pieter Poti and Antônio Parawba led their own men against the Portuguese upon their return to Brazil. In a letter to his cousin Felipe Camarão, Poti argued that the Portuguese only ever wanted to enslave their people.[81] Though the authenticity of this letter is a matter of debate, Maurits of Nassau had in fact "liberated" them from agricultural and salt farming work. That said, the

Dutch assigned them a deadlier duty instead—to serve as soldiers for the West India Company.

The Tupinambá and Potiguar people may have appeared to favor the Dutch enterprise, but Indigenous loyalty was never certain.[82] Neither was Dutch concern for those they had promised to "liberate" from the yoke of Spanish tyranny. As one West India Company officer noted in 1631, "we especially treated the *brasilienses* the way they treated our own [soldiers]."[83] Throughout one particular battle, the Dutch sliced off ears and noses of the "brasilienses" and brought them to commanding officer Waerdenburch: "In this way Major de Bernsted, like the heroic gentlemen that he was, offered the colonel his sword with half the blade covered with noses and ears and still others offered him the same present." Seeing this, Portuguese commander Matias de Albuquerque sent over a petition to allow both sides to bury their dead without further mutilation to the bodies, as was customary and proper in times of war. The WIC officer noted that the petition was deferred "unless the *brasilienses* were made to do the same."[84]

"Northern [Dutch] images," warns Svetlana Alpers, "show that meaning by its very nature is lodged in what the eye can take in—however deceptive that might be."[85] In Eckhout's ethnographic paintings, Tupinambá and Tapuya men are armed and ready for battle. Indigenous men did indeed at times fight for the Dutch—but they made a real difference for the Portuguese. Felipe Camarão, for instance, had long been trained in Christian ways and in the art of war against the Dutch; his aldea superior was none other than the disgraced Manuel de Moraes.[86] From 1630, Camarão offered his services to ground commander of the Luso-Brazilian troops Matias de Albuquerque, eventually rising to the rank of "Commander of All Indians" when Moraes was stripped of his title.[87] He was singled out by chroniclers as being an exceptionally devout soldier. Fueled by prayer, "Camarão gave infinite thanks to the divine power," one contemporary remarked, "on which depended so much as he was a man fearful of God and a good Christian." According to eyewitnesses, he then took out his relic of the Virgin Mary and kissed it, an example to his men.[88]

In 1638 Johan Maurits ordered an attack on Bahia, a thorn in the Dutch side since their loss in 1625. During what became a monthlong siege of Salvador, the Dutch governor-general offered Camarão and other leaders clemency for resisting the Dutch. The Potiguar leader showed no interest. He replied that he and his men would defend with sword that which the Dutch tried to conquer "with paper." They would never surrender. "And for those who know how to punish, like my soldiers," he scoffed, "your promises and pardons seem ridiculous."[89] Like so many other Potiguari, he would only ever serve the Portuguese, and indeed contemporary chronicles singled out Camarão's valiant and efforts.[90] For this and other actions, he received regnal recognition and a host of honors.

Unlike their Indigenous counterparts, African men rarely if ever served the Dutch in battle against the Portuguese, but they toiled during their rule in ever-increasing numbers on cane fields—or took refuge in runaway slave communities.[91] This gives pause to the loyalty depicted in Eckhout's *African Man* (Figure 6). Here the subject openly wears an Akan sword. This rendition belies his likely status as an enslaved person—an extraordinary leap of the artistic imagination.[92]

Figure 6. Albert Eckhout, *African Man*, 1640–1644, oil on canvas, 273 × 167 cm. Courtesy of the National Museum of Denmark.

The 1630 arrival of the Dutch in Pernambuco marked the start of massive slave flight to the interior as the invaders sacked and pillaged towns to stake claim. While *mocambos,* or settlements of runaway slaves, had developed prior to the arrival of the Dutch in 1630, the one that posed the greatest threat to sugar producers was Palmares.[93] In the chaos that ensued after the first landing of the Dutch in 1630 and the near abandonment of Olinda, about forty African slaves took flight to the interior, where they formed *a palmares* ("the palms") deep in the interior. Palmares swelled as the war dragged on. "During the rule of Count Maurits," wrote one West India Company soldier stationed in Pernambuco at this time, "the Negros of these Palmares wreaked considerable damage, especially on those living in the countryside, in Alagoas, and 300 musketeers, 100 mamelucos and 700 Brazilians were needed to contain them."[94] The Dutch viewed as a menace the "band of thieves and fugitive slaves [who] lived there and formed a society of criminals and bandits who raided the Alagoas, where they devastated the cultivated fields."[95] There, the forests provided safe haven for those who live in what would be known as greater and lesser palmares—at the time, about six thousand runaway slaves.[96] While *mu-kambos* (mocambos) had existed for decades, the problem became a particular issue with the arrival of the Dutch in 1630.[97] Fifteen years later, the two mocambos of palmares had grown to ten.[98] In 1644 Maurits ordered a search for palmares, with the intent to destroy the problem. That expedition failed, as did another the following year.[99] Rebellions in São Tomé and preparations for an expedition to Chile thwarted further plans during the time of Dutch rule.

Given the labor shortage, possession of northeastern Brazil and efforts to restart sugar production had by the late 1630s catapulted the Netherlanders into human trafficking. "Without [African] slaves, nothing will get done," complained Maurits to Dutch West India Company officials.[100] On his initiative, the Dutch seized the West African Portuguese-held fort of Elmina in 1638, the year after Eckhout painted his ethnographic portraits. By 1641 the Dutch had seized São Paulo of Luanda in Angola, an important step, for the Dutch, in guaranteeing labor for sugar mills. From 1641 to 1645, the number of Africans trafficked under Dutch flags reached a peak and tripled. It was during this time that the Netherlanders surpassed even the Portuguese as slavers. Seizing Portuguese West African slave trading posts was a victory that "counted higher than any other" as it due to the "great profit it will afford," wrote a certain N. N., "and I doe not doubt but the company shall bee furnished from thence with all sorts of commodities."[101]

Increased slave trade notwithstanding, a shortage of African labor remained a chronic problem due to death by overwork or suicide. In fact, Dutch-commissioned art cataloged the increasingly wretched conditions of African slaves at that time. The following note, for example, was affixed to the back of a bucolic Frans Post rendering of a sugar mill that Maurits had commissioned—and gifted to—Louis XIV in 1679: "Sugar mill powered by water with kilns, where the syrup is extracted from the cane for the making of the sugar. In the mouth of the kiln the fire is so hot that the Negro slaves prefer to die, and for this reason, they poison themselves when they are able, suffering as they do with that heat."[102]

Not all Afro-descended men in Brazil were confined to the cane fields or other backbreaking work reserved for the enslaved. Free Africans were among Portuguese subjects who professed and proved their unswerving loyalty to high-ranking officials—among them an enduring hero of the Pernambucan uprising, Henrique Dias. According to one witness, his help—and enduring loyalty—arrived unexpectedly: In the midst of one wretched campaign, Dias, a free man of African descent, offered his services and that of his men to General Matias de Albuquerque. "It seemed to him [Dias] that we needed his person," wrote a contemporary, "and this the general accepted, with a few men of his color." Dias distinguished himself from the start.

Dias was no hopeful martyr, however, and would be rewarded many times over—to a point. Indeed, when his left hand was shattered in battle, he ordered the surgeon to take it off at the wrist. "I still have my right hand with which to fight the Dutch!" he proclaimed.[103] Dias would rise to the rank of commander. Albuquerque gave him free rein to lead his swelling company of Afro-descended soldiers—they became known as the Henriques—provided that all men were free.[104] In 1638, with no end to the war in sight, the Dutch offered pardons to the leaders of the Portuguese resistance, including Henrique Dias. He scoffed, writing that his own men included Angolans, men from Minas, and creoles. They were "ill-tempered, badly behaved men who neither feared nor obeyed anyone."[105] News of Dias's continued efforts and sacrifice against the Dutch reached the Crown. After the Dutch defeat at the 1638 Battle of Bahia, Dias was given the title of fidalgo and named to the Order of Santiago. "And without doubt," a contemporary chronicler recalled, "this was just [merited] because of the blood he spilled from many wounds" for the Portuguese.[106] The allegiance of Afro-Brazilians was increasingly accepted by the elite as it became clear the Portuguese could not "continue to hold Brazil without the help of the African soldier."[107]

Contrary to Maurits-commissioned depictions of "wild nations" of Brazil, many Afro-descended, Indigenous, and mixed-descent men served the Portuguese cause, even as the Dutch expanded their reach in northeastern Brazil. In 1639 Maurits biographer Caspar van Barlaeus sent to his future patron a description of how a small Dutch fleet of ships routed the mighty Spanish Armada at the Battle of Downs. "I, too, together with our sailors, am befogged and blinded by the smoke and fog," Barlaeus had exulted, "so it is hardly possible for me to recognize and distinguish friend from foe and one ship from another."[108] On the ground, and in the battle for Brazil, the scene might have been more hazy: marginalized people chose the side that best served their interests. The Dutch never fielded an all-Black regiment led by an Afro-descended commander; nor were Indigenous troops commanded by an openly lauded Potiguar, as in the case of Felipe Camarão. The Old Dutch West India Company (OWIC) archive appears to offer silence on non-Dutch men like Calabar who helped their cause decisively.[109] The stories of soldiers like Antônio Felipe Camarão and Henrique Dias offer an initial glance at how and why subaltern soldiers seized the opportunity to serve the Portuguese and gain recognition for their efforts.

Not Always Going Dutch: New Christians and "Divided" Men

By the time Recife was fully in Dutch hands and under the leadership of Johan Maurits, the Jewish community clustered in and about Joodenstraat, or Jew Street, from where they conducted all manner of business.[110] Maurits's painters did not include New Christians as portrait-worthy subjects. It is true that they were less "native" to Brazil than the Tupi or Tapuya portrayed by Eckhout or Post, but their presence there had been established in the sixteenth century.[111] From 1630, however, New Christians and Jews proved essential to the Dutch Grand Design. In Pernambuco they provided translation, tax farming, and slave auction services on and around Joodenstraat, the street where most lived.

In return they were granted the right to practice Judaism if they so desired—and they did. They also served in the local militia on all days but the Sabbath.[112] They received economic benefits—at first. Unlike Afro-descended residents of the Dutch-held territory, they bore arms; but like them, they gained neither social nor cultural acceptance from West India Company officials.

Portugal's first lease of South American land, in 1502, went to New Christian Fernão Noronha, a merchant and explorer, perhaps a partial solution to claim more territory for the Crown. By that time, Portugal's Edict of Expulsion (1496) had gone into effect. However, unlike the Spanish goal to completely drive out its Jewish population, Portugal leaned toward forcible conversions. Noronha's exploratory contributions aside, the edict led to several bans on emigration and an underground resistance in Portugal. But the formal establishment of the captaincy system in Brazil and the Inquisition in Portugal, both of which occurred in the 1530s, prompted the first large wave of New Christian and Jewish Portuguese to Brazil—about the same time as forced arrivals from West Africa. It is estimated that New Christians made up about 14 percent of the white population of Pernambuco. The wide expanse of the Atlantic served as a temporary inquisitional buffer for suspected Judaizers and *conversos*; away from the long arm of the Holy Inquisition, or Santo Ofício, New Christians helped settle and build Brazil. They became *mestres do açucar* (masters of sugar) as they owned and ran engenhos, and served as *lavradores* and artisans, merchants, and more.[113]

In the early years of the Iberian union (1580–1640), the Inquisition did make it to Bahia, casting doubt on newly arrived and well-established New Christians and distinguishing them from the old. For instance, toward the last decade of the sixteenth century, Gregório Nunes, born of a New Christian mother, fled persecution to Brazil. In 1591 he was hauled before the Santo Ofício in Bahia and accused of reciting verses of Bandarra's *Trovas*. As noted earlier, believing in and discussing a possible "return of the king" was a crime during Philippine rule.[114] During the 1624 Dutch invasion of Salvador, New and Old Christians alike fled into the interior; it is possible that during this time Jesuit novice António Vieira came into contact with the mystical-prophetical work.

In Dutch-held Pernambuco, the "divided man"—neither Jew not Christian—not only earned temporary protection from the reach of the Santo Ofício but also engaged, from 1630, in new economic activities.[115] During the time of the Dutch, some served as tax farmers, collecting taxes; others as spies for the Portuguese. Most of the new arrivals in New Holland (Nova Holanda), as the colony was sometimes known, sided with the Dutch and engaged in intermediary activities from the start.[116] As the Old Christians spoke no Dutch and only a handful of WIC officers spoke Portuguese, Jews and New Christians served as translators.[117] They also engaged in not only agriculture but up to 63 percent of the tax farming and eventually all aspects of slave auctions.[118]

The 1635 Spanish-Luso-Brazilian army withdrawal from Pernambuco encouraged the expansion of the Jewish community, either by way of conversion (or reconversion in the case of newly minted New Christians) or transatlantic migration from Europe. By 1636 Zur Israel, the first synagogue in the New World, had opened its doors in Recife. Less than a decade later the next big wave of Jews and New Christians arrived, this time from Amsterdam, and in 1649 Magen Abraham opened its doors in Maurícia (Mauritsstad), a town on the island of Antônio Vaz named for Johan Maurits.[119] For many, Brazil was the "land of opportunity."[120]

As with most residents of Dutch Brazil, Jewish and New Christian loyalty to or betrayal of either the Portuguese or the Dutch proved a matter of context—and perhaps opportunity. For example, in Brazil and Amsterdam, established New Christians like Gaspar Dias Ferreira collaborated with *and* spied on the Dutch. A fair number of Old Christian moradores cooperated with the enemy to keep the peace, but Portuguese like Father Calado suspected Dias Ferreira of more. In the first place, he "lived among them [the Dutch] with his wife, and children inside the fortifications, to get more land with the Dutch."[121] There he served as adviser to Governor-General Johan Maurits and sat on his local council, and despite being under suspicion as a New Christian—for no Jews or New Christians were eligible to serve on the council—he acted as Maurits's secretary and adviser. It was in this capacity that Dias Ferreira journeyed with the governor-general for the second Battle of Bahia, in 1638.[122] According to Father Manoel Calado, who often dined with Maurits—and was invited to live with him—Dias Ferreira conspired with an infamous Dutch commander known as Pè de Pau (Peg Leg) to "grab more land."[123] The Luso-Brazilian commanders, including Henrique Dias and Felipe Camarão, not only survived the forty-day siege Bahia in April 1638 but routed the Dutch. Maurits returned north to Recife. As the war dragged on, Dias Ferreira strongly advised Maurits to pursue a maritime military strategy rather than waste time and men trying to seize Bahia and push into the interior.

Like Father Manuel de Moraes, Dias Ferreira was on the side of the Dutch but then returned to aid the Portuguese. Unlike Moraes, he would be celebrated as a hero for the Portuguese cause during his lifetime. Dias Ferreira, aware of rising resentment against himself and Dutch rule, left his family and traveled with Johan Maurits upon the governor-general's recall to the United Provinces in in 1644. He was soon charged by the Dutch with treason. Even as Dias Ferreira provided information to Barlaeus, who would write Maurits's biography, local Jews tipped off Amsterdam authorities that Dias was acting as spy for Madrid and Lisbon. In fact, his letters to the king of Portugal had been intercepted; in them he warned of the importance of Brazil to the Portuguese Empire and of the necessity of holding onto Angola.[124] He was turned in by local Jews, who passed the letters on to the States General. Dias Ferreira was then jailed but managed to escape to Lisbon within a few days of his sentence. He was hailed there as a hero.[125]

A comparative treatment of disloyal Portuguese yet remains; the story of Calabar is shared as either a curiosity or only a cautionary tale to would-be traitors. But what of those who crossed over to the Dutch and then back? The "dark" priest Manoel de Moraes and Gaspar Dias Ferreira directly aided the Dutch, but both returned to the Portuguese fold. One was jailed, and the other hailed as a hero. Perhaps this was because the former, as a Jesuit priest imbued with traditional Portuguese values, first fought against the Dutch but then led his own men against the Portuguese, a double betrayal of the Catholic Church and the Portuguese crown. Dias Ferreira, as a suspected New Christian and Calvinist convert, advised Maurits in military action but never picked up arms against his former compatriots. Perhaps expectations were not as high for him as for Moraes given the "stain" of his religious ancestry; neither did their respective penances compare. The former priest offered chaplain services and last rites to wounded and dying soldiers—but only after being captured in Maranhão; the New Christian smuggled strategic information from Amsterdam to Lisbon, was imprisoned by the Dutch, and escaped to the metropole. Finally, the degree and nature of betrayal may have accounted for their different treatment upon return to Lisbon.

In April 1640, in the aptly named Church of Our Lady of Good Help, St.

Anthony's namesake, António Vieira, lamented the trials of the Portuguese. The Dutch were set to try yet again to take Bahia of Salvador. Then he harkened back to the origin myth of the Portuguese overseas empire, reminding listeners that the trials—borne of Portuguese exceptionalism as God's chosen people— were only temporary. Why abandon the Portuguese cause now?

> After so much danger, disgrace, and after so many terrible deaths ... what lands have we [your faithful] gained to thus lose! ... To the Dutch you've delivered Brazil, the Indies ... the world is in your hands, as for us, the Portuguese and the Spanish, You have left us, repudiated us, undone us, and finished us off. But I remind You Majesty O Lord, those You cast out, You may one day seek and not find. ... You may look for me tomorrow and not find me.[126]

With or without spiritual aid, marginalized moradores negotiated their own on-the-ground reactions to the Dutch in Brazil. That is, they reshaped their roles as subjects of Portugal and took unexpected action that directed the course of the war. In Dutch-held Brazil, non-elite voices rang distinct from the chorus of European men who staked claim, like Maurits, to the seventeenth-century Atlantic world. Domingo Fernandes Calabar and Manuel de Moraes crossed over to aid the Dutch, the former nearly single-handedly causing the withdrawal of the Spanish-Luso-Brazilian army to Bahia in 1635. Both turned the tide of war in favor of the Netherlanders. Absent clear directives from the newly restored Portuguese crown (1640), hardened Luso-Brazilian, Indigenous, and Afro-descended guerrilla fighters overcame the odds to mount a resistance that cut across ethnicity, class, and gender. Though the Portuguese elite traditionally considered Indigenous men and those of African and mixed descent to have "tainted blood," Felipe Camarão and Henrique Dias received regnal recognition and were nominated for high honors.

Given the aesthetic production and prolific output of the Dutch, it is tempting—and reasonable—to cast the Dutch in Brazil as a remarkable achievement of an upstart colony. Frans Post's painting of Fort Frederick Hendrick (Figure 7) imagines a well-ordered world under Dutch—specifically Maurits's—control.[127] We see three unshod figures—bare feet a sign of slavery for them all—either walking to or from Fort Frederick Hendrick.[128] Far

Figure 7. Frans Post, *Fort Frederick Hendrik*, 1640, oil on canvas, 66 × 88 cm. Collection of the Ricardo Brennand Institute, Recife, PE, Brazil.

from being the passive subjects portrayed under Dutch rule, Luso-Brazilian men—and, as we'll soon see, women—affected the outcome of the war. Felipe Camarão and Henrique Dias are now permanent fixtures in Brazilian history for their heroic, if perhaps embellished, acts against the Dutch.

Against the visual evidence, overlooked Portuguese-language texts reveal that the Dutch occupation of Brazil served as a time of opportunity for marginalized subjects, regardless of which side they chose. The military St. Anthony, *Father* Anthony, and the records of resistance fighters in seventeenth-century Brazil point the way to a study of on-the-ground improvisation during the long struggle against the Dutch. These records afford us a glimpse of the overlooked and game-changing actions of Luso-Brazilians during the "Divine War of Liberation," as the conflict in Brazil was known, to final victory in 1654. Salvation, then, came neither from above nor from the metropole but from the unlikeliest of sources—non-elite Portuguese subjects in Brazil.

CHAPTER FOUR

Mistress, Mother, Soldier, Spy

Luso-Brazilian Women of Dutch-Contested Brazil

ON APRIL 24, 1646, one year into the Pernambucan uprising, several hundred half-starved Dutch West India Company soldiers sailed the short distance from the island of Itamaracá to São Lourenço do Tejucupapo. Alerted to the enemy, local townsmen hastened to blockade the main route to the village. But the Dutch pushed through an unlikely path—a mangrove swamp—where they encountered rebel women in the wait. There, with a crucifix in one hand and a sword in the other, a woman who may or may not have been called Maria Camarão urged the women to battle—or so the story goes.[1] In another account, not one but four Marias led an all-female assault against the Dutch. Three times the enemy charged; three times the defenders stood their ground and pushed back. Side by side the women—wives, mothers, sisters, and daughters armed with sticks, pots of boiling water "with peppers," and pans—held off the enemy, fighting until at last the Dutch withdrew.[2]

This female ferocity, unremarked in the official records and correspondence, was yet noted at the time and the story was burnished through the years.[3] In 1648, writing from the front, Father Manoel Calado took note of the women of Tejucupapo in his account of the war.[4] Teacher-turned-chronicler Diogo Lopes de Santiago described their involvement in even greater detail. Possibly basing his account on Calado's, he praised the female warriors for putting aside their "natural womanly fear" to pick up arms and fight with their men.[5] Santiago's manuscript, written between 1661 and 1675, languished unnoticed until Frei Rafael de Jesus then incorporated whole tracts of the work in his widely

Figure 8. Tereza Costa Rêgo, *Women of Tejucupapo*. Collection of the family, Recife, PE, Brazil.

circulated *O castrioto Lusitano* (1679).[6] And two centuries later, well after Brazil's independence from Portugal, emperor Dom Pedro II visited the town of Tejucupapo "out of curiosity and respect for our tradition." He then publicly acknowledged the women who took up arms and defied the Dutch.[7] National recognition of the women of Tejucupapo continues to be manifested in art, song, and drama (Figure 8).

Soldierly *portuguesa* lore predates the Luso–Dutch conflict to at least the fourteenth century, when a local *padeira*, or baker, confronted seven Spanish soldiers in her shop. They had hidden there after defeat by the Portuguese at the Battle of Aljubarrota. Surviving Spanish then scattered—in this case to the wrong paderia. A "corpulent, manly" baker named Brites de Almeida found seven Castilians hiding in her oven. Armed only with her baker's spade, she beat them to death. Then she cooked them, according to the tale, with her own bread.[8] Legend also has it that after dealing with her would-be attackers, the "baker of Aljubarrota" formed an all-female corps, leading the women into battle against hated Castilians. In this way she helped secure Portuguese independence. More than a century later, in Lisbon, women stood defiant and

armed against the old enemy. Philip II of Spain's ascension to the Portuguese throne in 1580 revived memories of the padeira of Aljubarrota; this time, Lisboeta women wielded pans against the enemy and launched into battle. The results were less than memorable, but what lingered were stories of female resistance.[9]

After the 1640 dissolution of the dual crowns, chronicler Francisco Brandão began writing the history of Portugal. He would include the oft-repeated legend of the warrior-baker of Aljubarrota. To that end, he interviewed the oldest living residents of Alcoçaba, which included the village of Aljubarrota in its parish. His efforts unearthed not only memories but also the famed baker's spade, hidden during the Iberian union and buried in a wall for safekeeping from the Spanish.[10] Now the spade was removed from the wall and displayed for public viewing.

At critical moments, Portuguese women defended their kingdom against invaders; in conflict-ridden Brazil, this manifested in ways unexpected. During the Dutch invasion of northeastern Brazil, necessity pushed the bounds of women's work. As in Portugal, this work sometimes included picking up arms and joining the defense. Women also demonstrated practical and economic strength. In Dutch-contested Brazil, as in Portugal, elite women inherited property or brought it to a marriage, affording themselves a measure of independence. This also meant the ability to wield landed power, even—and especially—during crisis.[11] In the absence of husbands, brothers, and fathers, women ran their own engenhos. They also worked and leased land to active or retired Dutch West India Company officers or leased land *from* them. And they married Dutch.

The legend of the padeira of Aljubarrota is even now common lore, but in the battle against the Dutch, who remembered what Luso-Brazilian women did, why, and to what end? Some Dutch West India Company soldiers remarked on their seductive ways, even blaming them for poor performance in battle. On the other hand, former soldiers and chroniclers included—or imagined—female sacrifice and martial heroics. Duarte de Albuquerque, Diogo Lopes de Santiago, and Francisco Brito Freire, who fought against the Dutch, highlighted how women exhorted their men to battle. Some women took up arms against the Netherlanders; others urged all their sons to the fight. Memorialists not only stressed *patriota* contributions in terms of the number of sons women sent to battle. They also praised women's efforts in critical, desperate times—how, like the padeira of Aljubarrota and the women of Lisbon, they fought side by side with the men.

Such evidence, fragmented across records, correspondence, and surveys, points to women's contributions and constraints. Real or imagined, female physical daring in the face of certain death—recorded, recollected, and circulated in early modern Portugal—is traceable from Portugal's early struggle to throw off Spain. In Brazil, martial women have been memorialized in local and national lore, the built environment, and the lived experience. While their more genteel peers have been at best confined to the archives, soldierly women have been celebrated out in the open. Today, what is remembered of the women of Dutch Brazil seems to remain—as in the Battle of Tejucupapo—almost in living memory.

Landed Ladies, Noblewomen

In seventeenth-century Western Europe, women worked—whether single, married, or widowed. They even migrated for economic opportunity. They lived in groups or alone, by necessity or by choice. They raised children with or without the help of men.¹² Like men, women were expected to work and carry out tasks; indeed, this was the norm for everyone except small children. Gendered notions of productivity became more accepted in late eighteenth-century Europe—when, for example, homebound wives and daughters, a sign of manly status, became more the norm.¹³

Early modern Portuguese women may have toiled for the kingdom, even taking up arms, but Iberian law also offered women a measure of economic opportunity and protection. Portuguese women had the right—though not always enjoyed—of dowry and inheritance.¹⁴ Portuguese wives could and did also claim and manage their deceased father's or husband's assets. A woman's inheritance was not always shared with her husband; legally it was hers alone. Further, men could not dispose of immoveable property—such as an engenho—without the consent of their wives.¹⁵ And according to the law, women were not required to cover their deceased husband's debts. In seventeenth-century Portugal, women over the age of twenty-five engaged in a number of businesses, could also become creditors, and were expected, as was the case with men, to pay their own debts in full.¹⁶

A woman's *dote*, or dowry, could offer even greater security. A women might also, as necessity warranted, obtain an advance on her dowry from her inheritance. On paper at least, sons and daughters inherited equally. But marriages that included a *contrato de dote* permanently secured for the wife any and all such property, including money, goods, or land. Dote had another economic meaning as well: this was the payment a man made for sullying a woman's honor.¹⁷ In this case, the payment would cover convent or other costs associated with living out life unmarried.

Brazil also served, for Crown and church, as a partial solution to the problem of orphan girls—a pressing issue in the case of fidalgos who died while in service overseas, leaving their daughters bereft of a dowry and with it the prospect of marriage. For those who could afford it, convent life was an option in the metropole, but another solution was had abroad: female orphans of men in service of the state could be granted a dowry by the Crown, and some were sent to help populate distant claims.¹⁸ In 1603, however, officials considered Goa to be too distant for such young ladies, whose average age was twelve. That year, the Mesa da Consciência, a royal council created to find moral solutions to social issues, determined that only three girls would be sent to Goa each year, with the rest shipped off to Brazil. Once there they were to marry and help foster settler communities. The demand for Portuguese-born wives may have been weak: a 1606 suggestion offered any man who married an orphan girl a minor position in the newly created high court of Salvador. António Cristovão Vieira Ravasco took up this offer, wedding an orphaned Maria de Azevedo. Parents of the future Jesuit priest António Vieira, they traveled from Madeira to Salvador, together with their son.[19]

Land grants also helped women stake claim in Brazil. "Men control the seas," went the saying in early modern North Portugal, "but women rule the land."[20] In contested northeastern Brazil, this seemed also to have been true. News of Pedro Cabral's westerly landfall in 1500 spread quickly, and within decades French and English swarmed the coast claiming resources. Dona Brites de Albuquerque, wife of Pernambuco's first donatary, ruled the captaincy in his absence and after his death.[21] And from at least the first decade of the seventeenth century, women requested and received land from donataries—a survival strategy for Crown and settler. This practice, deriving from medieval Portuguese custom, encouraged petitioners to demonstrate the ability to hold and cultivate the land for family and for kingdom—one way to stake claim to land during the reconquista and divide it up among Christian settlers.[22] In this way, Portuguese women helped secure colonial claims.

Through the seventeenth century, widowed and otherwise single women could and did request sesmarias by submitting to the donatary of the captaincy a formal petition or request. This included the name, providence, and "qualifications" of the petitioner, as well as the specific land requested. Land-seeking women proved their worth and potential through their stock of cattle and oxen, clear indicators that they could be self-sufficient and, in the case of potential sugar engenhos, grind cane. In most cases, this also meant assurances of livestock that would graze until ready for market or consumption, or for use in sugar cultivation. The second part of the petition included justifications for soliciting the land—through a letter, for example, from the captain-major or governor responsible for the territory. In this way the petitioner demonstrated that any land granted could be put to maximum use. The scribe would then verify that the plot requested had not been granted to another.[23]

This strategy, an attempt to bolster colonialization in Brazil, enabled elite widows and daughters the ability to negotiate the most trying conditions.

Angela de Morais, for example, petitioned for land in Rio Grande do Norte; on February 26, 1605, she received her league of land on the Rio Cunhau. Whether she held onto it for long is unknown.[24] But by the time of the Dutch challenge, Lusophone women had long owned and managed property, reaping economic and social benefits from such work—a matter of practicality and precedence.

The Dutch in Brazil surveyed territory under their control, revealing that women owned, managed, and worked land even in the contested captaincies. Adrian van der Dussen's 1638 overview, describing Dutch-held captaincies and the people of Brazil, indicates the economic clout of northeastern Luso-Brazilian women: with or without husbands, they owned farms and ran sugar mills. They also rented out land to and contracted lavradores—Dutch and Portuguese men—for the purpose, presumably, of getting out the safra and selling sugar on the domestic or world market. The female owners, however, were not equal to men in terms of property ownership; of the five surveyed Pernambucan parishes, women owned about 10 percent of the engenhos.[25]

Most elite women worked within the confines of their homes. This prompted at least one Dutch soldier to note that Portuguese men "are very jealous of their women and ever keep them shut away, recognizing that those from their own nation are inclined to corrupt other women."[26] But the landed ladies of the northeast also tended to see themselves as "moons among the stars" for their access, despite relative isolation, to resources and their ability to wield them.[27] While most remained rooted in engenho life, some also ventured off for religious services. As the war dragged on, necessity prompted flight, of course, and longer-distance ventures into the backlands or farther south.

In print and in paint, routines and rituals of elite women were captured by more than a few other Dutch West India Company men—a very different scene. Portuguese women, observed English soldier Cuthbert Pudsey, "must be carried [even a short distance from their homes] betwixt two slaves, in a hangmatt of great vallewe," and protected from the harsh sun by a richly embroidered canopy.[28] Like Pudsey, soldier-turned-scribe Zacharias Wagner turned to chronicling after his years in service and even described the same scenes as Pudsey (see Figure 9). Unlike Frans Post or Albert Eckhout, artists schooled and handpicked by Maurits to render Dutch rule, the self-taught Wagner portrayed quotidian images of life in Brazil. This included his own sketches of wealthy Portuguese women in his autobiographical work. Well-dressed and socially authoritative, apparently

Figure 9. Zacharias Wagener, *Slaves Carrying a Covered Hammock, Brazil*, 1630. In Ferrão and Soares 1997.

even during Dutch rule, elite women traveled about in palanquins. Wagner noted that: "The wives and children of notable and wealthy Portuguese are transported in this manner, by two strong slaves, to the houses of their friends or to church; they hang the beautiful cloths of velvet or damask over poles so that the sun does not burn them strongly. They also take behind them a variety of beautiful and tasty fruits as a present for those that they wish to visit."[29]

At least one English soldier recalled Luso-Brazilian women as lazy, spoiled, and inclined to sloth. This veteran of the 1624 Dutch assault on Salvador described the Luso-Brazilian woman as a childish seductress, keener on comfort than on practical action. Like Pudsey and Wagner, "I. B." commented on how Portuguese women were carried about in coaches and chairs. Poorer women made do with hammocks: "For daintinesse," he scorned, "[Portuguese women] may not set a foote on the ground." He added, however, that women *could* move faster if they so chose, recalling "[a] time they were glad to make use of their feete to save their lives."[30] He was likely referring to the initial invasion, when the town was under heavy artillery fire. Then the refugees fled for cover in the surrounding matos—and, as they were able, the nearest aldeia.

Such views, if they were more widely shared, did little to dissuade West India Company officers from marrying local women. The opportunity to build family wealth not otherwise available proved more appealing, for some, than signing on for another extended contract. By 1631, observed Pudsey of the Portuguese and Dutch, "more & more they marry together." He noted that the sergeant major of orders was the first to marry a Portuguese woman of no insubstantial means—"a sugar mynes daughter, being she," he wrote, and "heire to her father."[31] Perhaps this was what soon prompted a *predikant*, or Dutch preacher, to complain in a letter to the High Council that "our men run after them very much."[32]

Pudsey and the predikant may well have been thinking about thrice-married Dona Ana Paes. Widowed at age nineteen after the death of her first husband, Captain João Correia da Silva, she went on to marry two West India Company officers, Charles Tourlon and Gijsbert de With. To each marriage, she brought with her a substantial fortune in sugar-producing land. Her Engenho Casa Forte—which would at various times also be known as Engenho Tourlon, Engenho Nassau, and, with her third marriage, Engenho de Withe—was located on a rich expanse along the Capiberibe River. By Pudsey's standards, Ana Paes could qualify as a woman of "high quality" and "good rank." She was not only propertied and resourceful, but her beauty could bring one to tears.[33]

By all accounts, Dona Ana Paes was far from retiring, slothful, and unengaged, contrary to the scenes portrayed by Wagener, I. B., and Pudsey. Educated and fluent in several languages, she was known as a lively woman. She was suspected, by some, of having turned Johan Maurits's head, as the governor-general had her second husband, Captain Charles Tourlon, imprisoned under vague charges of treason and sent off to the Netherlands to be tried. She was not afraid to challenge the governor-general—if even indirectly. In fact, Ana Paes took action on her husband's behalf. She began by penning a protest letter directly to the Council of Zeeland, reminding the men who held her husband captive of his long and illustrious service. Tourlon had distinguished himself in service for the Dutch, she wrote, "knowing justly that he could hope for great prizes." Instead, Dona Ana lamented, "it was his fortune to be punished by being dislodged from his own home."[34] Perhaps her entreaties to the Zeelanders made a difference: Tourlon was never found guilty, and the case against him was tossed. However, he died on his return trip to Brazil.

Ana Paes married yet again, perhaps not without controversy given her own personal wealth and the high standing of her third husband. This union ultimately led to the loss of her personal wealth. Gijsbert de With served as a justice to the High Council in Brazil—and it was with him that she went fully Dutch. In a statement to the High Council explaining why he would marry Ana Paes, de With pointed to the fact that she had previously married Tourlon, had converted to Calvinism, and was prepared to raise all her children in the Calvinist faith. This was all proof positive, he wrote, that she preferred the Dutch "to her own kind."[35] In fact, she bore two more children with him—Kornelius and Elizabeth—raising both in the Calvinist tradition. She sold the Engenho Antônio, another jewel in her dowry, to João Fernandes Vieira—though she could not have predicted that this Dutch ally would turn resistance leader for the Portuguese. With the Pernambucan uprising in 1645, her own engenho, Casa Forte ("Strong House"), served for a short time at least as command center for the WIC. On the losing side by 1648, Dona Ana gave up most of her own land; Portuguese inheritance laws did not provide for women who married the enemy. She departed to the United Provinces with de With and their children upon the West India Company's final surrender in 1654.

Clara Neves, on the other hand, held onto the family engenho, despite the fact that her husband, Gaspar Dias Ferreira, was a known collaborator with the Dutch. The property was not even part of her dowry, acquired instead in the first decade of the battle for Brazil. Ferreira, a suspected New Christian, lived inside Mauritsstad city walls with his family, where he served as confidante and adviser to Governor-General Johan Maurits. The Luso-Brazilian sailed with Maurits to the Netherlands in 1644, but he asked his wife to retain and work the family engenho in his stead. The property had been acquired—perhaps by less-than-scrupulous means—in the early years of the war. In Brazil, Neves and her children were harassed by the previous owners, the family of Antonio de Sá. The wartime acquisition—linked with lingering doubts of loyalty—cost the couple their eldest son. He was killed in suspicious circumstances, likely related to a family feud.[36]

Women had power, if even—according to Dutch and English accounts—of a sordid sort. Not only did even "the meanest" women command their porters, but they were compelling survivors too. Pudsey wrote that the well-adorned, bejeweled, "gentyler kynde of women" proved a challenge for men to resist.[37]

He lambasted siren-like women who "spayred noe treasure for apparel to bewitch their loover's harts," claiming that they seduced men with their "odiferous parfumes."[38] They were also, he proffered, partially responsible for incest that ran rampant among the Portuguese in Brazil, writing that "everyone lay with everyone," including mothers with their own sons.[39] Another chronicler credited Portuguese women with provoking divine anger, which allowed for Dutch conquest, and in general weakening soldierly resolve, as "the Towne of Salvadoe had in it many whores, some of them being left behind."[40] The presence of these same women, he claimed, was the main reason Salvador was won back in 1625 by the Spanish; there the first commander "was not ashamed to go in the middle of the day to a whore-house." However, I. B. also noted that the man was a drunkard, which led to his sudden and unrelated death.[41]

As their husbands fled south from Recife to the stronghold of Bahia to regroup against the Dutch, most wives remained behind to raise families, remarry, and hold onto property as best as they were able. Mistresses—of men and of property—earned little more than offhand remarks from chroniclers, but these offer a glimpse of female social power and economic clout. Clara Neves is not remembered in Portuguese accounts, and Ana Paes earned a passing reference by Father Calado in his *O valeroso Lucideno*—but the stories of these landed ladies indicate their economic power, a legacy and an Atlantic evolution of Portuguese inheritance law. Ana Paes is remembered in Brazil as a woman "ahead of her time." To this day, her property remains a memorial for the bloody Battle of Casa Forte and for the woman who once lived there.

Mothers and Martyrs

Not all Portuguese women attracted Dutch suitors. "Very few . . . are good-looking," wrote a Dutch West India Company officer stationed in Recife. "They are dry of face and dark of skin. While still girls, the women lose their teeth, and because they are used to always sitting, they are not as agile as the Dutch women, and walk about in *chapins* as if they had chairs on their legs."[42]

Duarte de Albuquerque, donatary of Pernambuco and brother of the captaincy's governor-general, who was also commander of resistance forces until 1635, might have argued that the less physically appealing women were worn down by motherly sacrifice. Albuquerque highlighted their contributions in producing sons for battle—and losing them. And so "it is only just," he stressed, "to make note of their brave feats."[43] Albuquerque recorded, for example, that on April 30, 1635, Maria de Sousa received word that her third son had died in the war. His elder brothers had already predeceased him in battle. Her response, he wrote, was an "example of Portuguese female valor." Upon receiving the terrible news, she turned directly to her twelve- and fourteen-year-old sons. Rather than drawing them close, she put a sword in each of their hands and urged them to battle: "In this moment, my sons, your father and I have received the news of the death of your brother Estevão, which is the third . . . I've lost, in addition to a son-in-law. But instead of diverting you from the same dangers, I'm putting you right in their path. So here and here take the sword and give your life with the same honor as your brothers, for God, for king, and for pátria."[44] The boys then signed up for duty, joining their deceased brothers' regiment. Albuquerque noted that they distinguished themselves with valor and highlighted their mother's efforts. They "proved they were sons of that mother," he wrote, "who demonstrated, how patriotic she was: matron, without doubt, deserving to be remembered for her elegant suffering."[45] Rather than divert her children from danger, Maria de Sousa put them in harm's way—the most heroic act, he noted, a mother could make for kingdom and for God.

Luso-Brazilian mothers negotiated against the Dutch off the battlefield too—until they were accused by the Dutch of subversive acts. In early March 1641, Dona Jerônima de Almeida of Porto Calvo, a noblewoman and mother of nine daughters and three sons, was turned in to West India Company officials for treason.[46] She had whipped an enslaved person, who then disclosed to the Dutch damning evidence against her: packets of letters from Bahia, where her husband was active in the resistance.[47]

Dutch authorities hauled Dona Jerônima from her twelve children, her engenho, and her home in Porto Calvo to be tried in Recife. The wife of a "principal morador," Rodrigo Barros Pimentel, she would, under normal circumstances, travel in comfort and style.[48] But she was not likely transported in a sedan or even a hammock, as befitting her status and means. After a thorough investigation, Dona Jerônima was charged with aiding and abetting suspected West India Company traitor Gerrit Craeijesteijn.

In his account, the sheriff stated that Craeijesteijn sent her a letter in which he asked her to act as an intermediary for Portuguese resistance captain Paulo da Cunha. Dona Jerônima handled this request through a certain Pedro d' Andrade Barbosa, who had heard that the captain had come to the engenho Moro. Barbosa indicated that Craeijesteijn should come immediately, and he did. Arriving there, Craeijesteijn spoke with the Portuguese captain as well as other officers on the "enemy" side.[49] The letter, written in Portuguese, was one of the bundle intercepted by the Dutch. It proved damning indeed, with Craeijesteijn indicating that Dona Jerônima needed to keep her guard up. "Not on [her] life" was she to reveal anything about such a rendezvous.[50] If pressed, she was to say that she was unaware of Paulo da Cunha.[51]

In her deposition to Dutch West India Company officials, Dona Jerônima confirmed the meeting but claimed ignorance of any conspiracy. She could neither "read nor write," she explained, did not know of such things, and was busy making dinner the night she supposedly engaged in treason.[52] Evidence notwithstanding (including her own letter to Craeijesteijn), she pled that could not have been involved in strategic moves against the Dutch. Her plea came to no avail. She was sentenced to death by hanging.

Dona Jerônima's female peers then took action. They went en masse to Governor-General Johan Maurits to intervene on her behalf. Likely among them and serving as spokeswoman was Dona Ana Paes, well-known for her outspoken ways. Padre Manoel Calado had described Ana Paes as a "free" woman, suggesting that she was given—or affected—more liberties than was the norm for an elite Luso-Brazilian woman.[53] As a group they negotiated Dona Jerônima's release. They declined Johan Maurits's offer to dine with him that evening, demurring that as married women it would be improper, but instead sent him several chests of sugar. Thanks in part to her countrywomen, Dona Jerônima was pardoned.[54]

The actions of the landed ladies highlight an agency that has often been obscured by Dutch- and English-language records. These were no sequestered wives who were helpless, passive, frivolous, and hidden from sight. And for elite women like Dona Jerônima, womanly chores and duties—making dinner, for instance—may have served as more than evidence of ignorance. Instead, as in the case of the wife of resistance leader and landowner Rodrigo Pimentel, these duties served as cover for possible insurrection. Portuguese women may have appeared isolated from society in their homes or on their engenhos. But as grantees of sesmarias and engenho owners, they proved productive, even engaging in resistance against the Dutch.

"Noble feats" of Martial Women

On March 12, 1625, Dutch West India commander Piet Heyn escaped the Iberian reconquest of Salvador but then joined in on an attack on the little fishing town of Nossa Senhora da Vitória in the captaincy of Espírito Santo. In an act of desperation—or, according to legend, heroism—sixteen-year-old Maria Ortiz repelled Dutch troops almost single-handedly. According to one story, her father was away and had warned his wife and daughter to take care. When the Dutch troops swarmed into town, Maria—then sixteen or twenty-one, depending on the source—tossed boiling water on the head of the Dutch captain, forcing their defeat. She then exhorted other women to do the same, forcing an enemy retreat.[55]

As the war in Brazil heated up and Portugal wrenched free from Spain, a very different story on women made the rounds in Portugal. The century prior, the Madeira-born "people's poet" Baltasar Dias had warned men off marriage in his book-length poem *Malícia das Mulheres* (Malice of Women).[56] Written in letter form, this catalog of women's vices and litany of husbands' woes made clear the dangers of such union. The narrator described married men as imprisoned. "I don't want to marry/because I have no desire to do so," Dias wrote, concluding that nuptials would only lead to a life of misery.[57] Dias likely wrote the piece in 1540, around the time inquisitorial efforts in Portugal picked up pace. *Malícia* circulated widely and informally, prompting the blind poet to seek his fortune in Lisbon. But the work's slam on the sacrament of marriage was enough to keep it from the official press for nearly a century. In 1640, during a time of crisis, upheaval, and change, and with a readership craving old certainties and traditions, *Malícia* proved more than popular it had in its first printing.[58]

Multiple reprintings in the century that followed indicate that *Malícia*'s readers in Portugal may not have known—or cared—how local chroniclers wove women into the battle for Brazil. But after the Divine War of Liberation from the Dutch in 1654, Lisbon's printers ran hot with tales of the Luso-Brazilian resistance. These included the feats of female patriotas. Donatary Duarte de Albuquerque, lord proprietor of beleaguered Pernambuco, praised the sacrifice of mothers as they exhorted their sons to battle; twenty years after the printing of Albuquerque's *Memórias diárias*, Brito Freire repeated the same stories in a hardly disguised act of plagiarism. By that time, Queen Mariana of Spain had recognized Portugal's sovereignty and with it the legitimacy of the Portuguese crown.[59]

Including women in circulating stories of fierce on-the-ground American resistance may well have served as a reminder—even if indirect—that resistance included heroics from all classes and "types" in Portugal and Brazil, including and especially women. For a short while at least, literary demand for Portuguese women portrayed as allies and defenders, rather than malicious upstarts, indicated a readership that idealized women as prepared to resist outsider rule, whatever form it might take. Mother-martyrs would defend their families and kingdom to the death.

After the final surrender of the Dutch in Brazil, chroniclers reserved their most effusive praise for women who did physical battle. Rather than flee Dutch invaders when they charged her home, wrote Francisco Brito Freire, Jeronyma Mendez, wife of a barber, "did not desert the room like others." She lay in wait behind a door and stabbed to death the first enemy soldier through. Writing from Lisbon forty-two years after this event and after continental recognition of Portugal's status as an independent kingdom, Freire praised the actions of the woman he identified as hailing from Fáro in the kingdom of the Algarve.[60] As governor and captain-general of Pernambuco from 1661 to 1665, Freire had spent a portion of his time in battle against the Dutch, though at the time of the alleged stabbing he was in the service of the Crown elsewhere. Indeed, large portions of his hagiographic *Nova Lusitania: historica da guerra Brasílica* are lifted from contemporary chronicler accounts. But for the lifelong soldier, the martial role of women anchored—or at least amplified—the new history of Portugal.

Writers also praised Indigenous women for serving in battle. Clara "the Warrior" Camarão fought side by side with her husband, Felipe António Camarão, a Potiguar soldier for the Portuguese. After the betrayal of Jesuit Manoel de Moraes, the "Commander of All Indians," Felipe Camarão had assumed leadership of the regiment.[61] In one losing battle against the Dutch, Clara purportedly picked up and wielded arms against the enemy. Ignoring the shrieks of the "ladies of Porto Calvo," she marched to the front.[62] The record is scanty, but at least one eighteenth-century writer marked her ferocity in battle, comparing her to, among others, a third-century queen who conquered Egypt and challenged Rome. He describes her courage as a highlight of the war against the Dutch as she rode into battle with sword and shield, "seen by the admiring Dutch and to our own applause in one of the most dangerous conflicts at her husband's side." He explains that "such noble feats obscure the memory of Zenobia of Palupia; of Camilla, Queen of Vulcans; Semiramis, Queen of Babylon."[63] The eighteenth-century author and Benedictine monk Domingos Loreto Couto described her feats and that of other women, noting their "manly" actions as they fought against the Dutch.[64] His work, sourced mostly orally, remained unpublished until the twentieth century.

References to Clara Camarão have been derived mainly from the work of chronicler Diogo Lopes de Santiago—as have other remarkable stories of female resistance.[65] Teacher and friar, Santiago had set aside his instructional duties to chronicle and fight in the battle against the Dutch; for him, the contributions of women deserved mention. In April 1646, scouts for the Portuguese spotted Dutch boats cruising the coast of Recife.[66] They suspected a traitor in their midst. Shortly before the sighting, Captains Paulo da Cunha and Francisco Lopes had herded three hundred cows from Rio Grande into town, now held by the Portuguese; this information may have been relayed to the other side.[67] Starving Dutch soldiers trapped on the island of Itamaracá could only receive food from Recife. They well knew that the fields of São Lourenço were rich and abundant in crops, including mandioca, beans, and "spiny fruits." Desperate, they planned to invade São Lourenço da Tejucupapo by cover of night. The enemy navigated the dark waters "now by sail, now by oar."[68] They encountered two Portuguese hastening across the path to safety: "Don't run as we are all friends," called out the enemy sergeant major, who also threatened them if they did.[69] The Battle of Tejucupapo soon began.

More than four hundred company soldiers and two hundred Indigenous allies engaged in pitched battle with one hundred Portuguese men, who first assisted and then joined the women of town. One woman, wrote Santiago, held a cross in hand and exhorted the men to battle; others helped ready water and prepared gunpowder. Still others set about praying with fervor, calling upon God and all the saints to free them from the furious Dutch. When the invaders hurled themselves to battle for the third time, the women of Tejucupapo picked up arms too. The Dutch fled, launching themselves into their boats so quickly that their weapons were left strewn about, as were tools with which to dig up manioc.[70] For Santiago, as he made clear to his readers, the female valor that turned the tide of battle was nothing short of historic—and divine—intervention.

Henrique Dias and His Daughters: Inheritance, Legacy, and Memory

Women helped secure family fortune and estates through and beyond the Luso–Dutch battle for Brazil. This proved critical, especially in the case of Black men like Henrique Dias. The renowned commander had been offered—and then denied—select merits afforded to men of "pure blood." Leveraging inheritance though his daughters helped him partially skirt the issue of his own "tainted" blood.

Indeed, by the time Henrique Dias sailed from Bahia to Lisbon in June 1656, he could prove more than two decades of dedicated service to the Portuguese. In his twenty-three years of fighting the Dutch, he had earned serious injuries—the worst of which were documented by local chroniclers. After the Battle of Porto Calvo, for instance (1637), his left hand shattered and infected, Dias was said to have ordered the surgeon to amputate it at the wrist. He would use his right hand, he swore, for revenge.[71] Seven years later, he was shot clean through the leg. He kept on fighting and then seared and sealed the wound with a piece of sheep's wool fried in fish oil. "And in this way," wrote the observer, "he was healed in a few days without having to see the surgeon."[72] For his valor, the Black commander was promised—but never awarded—significant honors, not once but twice, by the Crown. So with the Dutch surrender and departure from Brazil (1654), Dias, now commander of a Black and mixed-descent regiment of four hundred men, began waging a different sort of war—across the Atlantic and in the metropole.

Overseas service in Brazil, since the sixteenth century, had offered an opportunity—however limited—for marginalized men to advance their status. Twenty years elapsed between nomination and award for the Black soldier Manuel Gonçalves Doria, who ultimately earned entrance, in 1647, to the Order of Santiago.[73] At that time, the war had started to tip toward the Portuguese. But with the final ouster of the Dutch, Dias's heritage now proved problematic. With his case to claim honors now stalled, he turned to leveraging inheritance law—so that his four daughters could indirectly claim his awards.

Not long after the first Portuguese encounter with the Americas, non-elite men, through their expansionary efforts in the northeast and the interior, began to gain access to the Portuguese fidalgueira. And with the English, French, and eventually more persistent Dutch challenge for Brazil, men on the margins gained recognition for their soldierly efforts to defend the colony. This included Henrique Dias. In 1633, when the tide turned toward the Dutch, he had offered his services—and that of his companions—to ground commander Matias de Albuquerque. These Albuquerque accepted—though not without reserve, unable as he was to distinguish between free and once-enslaved Black men.

Dias and his men acquitted themselves well in that battle and beyond. He received a formal "promotion," a September 4, 1639, letter of patent delivered to him in Bahia by the new viceroy of Brazil, Fernando Mascarenhas. Philip IV, highlighting the sacrifice of Dias's left hand at the Battle of Porto Calvo, named the soldier "Governor of Creoles, Negros and Mulattos of Brazil."[74] There was more: the king nominated Dias to a military order of his choice and gave handsome compensation from the royal treasury, effective immediately.[75]

Despite regnal recognition of Henrique Dias's past and continuing heroics, from Lisbon, the Mesa da Consciência e Ordens (Board of Conscience and Orders) held up Dias's entrance into a military order of his choice. Formed in 1532, this board was meant to resolve matters that addressed royal "obligations of conscience," but it foundered under centuries-old regulations. With the expansion of the Portuguese maritime empire, its work came to include administration and gatekeeping of the military orders of Avis, Santiago, and Christ. Here, the Mesa da Consciência ensured "purity of blood"—that is, applicants to the orders could not be of Moorish or Jewish descent; they could not be engaged in manual labor or descended from manual laborers. The procedure? Upon receiving an application, the board appointed two men—a member of the order and a cleric—to investigate the appointee's background, including his heritage traced to grandparents. When the origins of the person were in a remote town, a local member of the order—a military man—would undertake the investigation.

In the war-torn Brazilian northeast, contemporary chroniclers seemed more impressed with Dias than with the Mesa da Consciência e Ordens, and they inked in his status with a vengeance. Padre Manuel Calado, for example, addressed and then dismissed Dias's heritage. Writing from the front lines, Calado insisted that though Dias was "black in color [he was] white in effort and achievement," and that through his valor, Dias "repaired any defects in his nature." That is—his military exploits for Portugal made him noble.[76]

One year after Philip IV had nominated Dias to a military order of his choice, the now impatient king informed the Mesa da Consciência e Ordens that he had appointed an ambassador to Rome to expedite this award; he would bypass the board. But the 1640 December restoration of Portugal, and with it the dissolution of the Iberian crowns, arrested the whole process.

In the years that followed, and as the conflict dragged on, the restored Portuguese king, Dom João IV, also acknowledged Henrique Dias for his effort, awarding him entrance to a military order. He amassed a loyal following; by the time of Dutch surrender, Dias's highly engaged *terço*, or regiment, made up about 10–12 percent of the fighting force. In fact, the Henriques, as they came to be known, would not be disbanded for another century. Yet the Black commander never received his proper due.

So in 1656, two years after the Dutch surrender, Dias arrived in Lisbon to personally claim his award. The death of Dom João IV disrupted this process. Dias then reached out to regent queen Luisa de Gusmão—and a new solution was offered to the council. By now, Dias had been awarded homes and property abandoned in Brazil by the Dutch, but his entrance to the fidalgueira—and with it that of his descendants—was still blocked.

Iberian law guaranteed bequests, generally in the form of immutable land, to women. Awards and titles, also considered property, could be transferable to future generations. Henrique Dias, unable to formally advance further, petitioned to secure his titles through his daughters. He asked if their future husbands could claim the military titles and with these familial wealth, honor, and social legitimacy. In this way, Dias sidestepped an investigation into his own heritage.

He succeeded. Henrique Dias secured special dispensations and an unusual dowry for his daughters. Their "inheritance"—his awards from Dom Felipe and Dom João IV for his past service—would go instead to his current and future sons-in-law. In 1657, still in Lisbon, Dias asked that his benefits go to his son-in-law Pedro de Valdoveço, a "very noble person." The board then launched an investigation into his background, which determined that "his grandparents came from Africa; but it is not known if they were slaves." As he was known to be a "noble man," the matter was dropped and Valdoveço assumed the honors. Dias then secured in writing the promise that future husbands of his other daughters would receive merits as well.

The Luso–Dutch conflict may have offered space, however slim, for Luso-Brazilian women of African descent to help negotiate wealth and status. Henrique Dias's solution—leveraging inheritance law—sidestepped the issue of his "defects," allowing at least part of his family to formally claim honor. But by the first decade of the eighteenth century, it seemed that even this "solution" was untenable. Whereas his mixed-descent son-in-law of "noble blood" received the titles in 1657, his youngest daughter's husband would not. In 1711 Amaro Cardigo, husband of Benta Henriques, petitioned multiple times to inherit his deceased father-in-law's titles. Fair enough—after thirty years of soldierly service, he had met all the conditions required. But the Mesa da Consciência found that one of his grandparents was of African descent and a former slave. Between the "tainted blood" and "deficit" wrought by manual labor, his petition was denied.[77]

In Living Memory

Nearly four hundred years after the Dutch invasion, the "women of Tejucupapo," cast in ever heroic terms, have become part of the lived experience of the now-impoverished place. A rural town, Tejucupapo is deplete of the resources and work that attract capital and industry. One of the main sources of revenue remains fishing. "Life in Tejucupapo is very hard," says Luzia Maria da Silva, founder and president of the Women's Association of Tejucupapo, "especially for women." More than forty years ago, as she lay ill at the Hospital of Santo Amaro and near death, she recalled the stories her grandmother had told her of the valor of the fighting women of Tejucupapo. "So I promised God that should I live, I would dedicate my life to sharing their story."[78]

Thanks to Luzia Maria's vision and persistence, every April since 1995, the women of Tejucupapo have reenacted the Battle of Tejecupapo.[79] "Take your position," she calls over a megaphone, and then begins to recount the whole story. When she orders participants to charge, costumed men and women mime battle. Outdoors and across a broad field, they engage in exuberant theater, and heartfelt they reenact the unlikely moment when the women beat off the Dutch.[80] Luzia Maria, by day a nurse in a local school, feels strongly that the whole experience is far more than one battle; it gives the women of Tejucupapo hope and shows them who they can be. Men participate as the Dutch, ready to assault the town and "die" on the field. "This is what we live for," she says. "The men around here don't do much at all."[81]

Unlike the *donas do engenho* Ana Paes, Jerônima, and Clara Neves, neither Maria Ortiz, Clara Camarão, nor the women of Tejucupapo made it into the Dutch or Portuguese contemporary official record. But they are woven into regional and national memory. An *escadaria* (set of hillside steps), built in the 1920s where Ortiz was presumed to have lived, remains dedicated to her and was recently renovated.[82] Today the fighting women are enshrined in Brazilian national memory.[83]

A good story bears retelling, and with each iteration of the Dutch expulsion from Brazil, tales of martial women became more firmly entrenched in the Luso-Brazilian imagination—a tradition, and a warning to would-be invaders perhaps, that took root in Portugal with early renditions of the padeira d'Aljubarrota. At home and abroad, Portuguese women could—and did—pick up arms and resist; they calculated how best to maintain family and property. Crown chronicler Francisco Brandão intentionally interviewed the oldest living residents of Alcoçaba, who "recalled" Brites de Alameida's role in defeating the Spanish. Writing in 1732, José Soares da Silva noted how the those "residents [had] feared Philip II would extinguish this memory" and were glad of the chance to tell this violent, marvelous story. He and chroniclers who followed took pains to substantiate the story, adding luster to the legend of the baker.[84]

On and off the battlefield, Luso-Brazilian women engaged with the enemy. During the time of the Dutch, resistance and Crown chroniclers depicted real or imagined women's economic, social, and military actions, crafting a narrative of heroic resistance and a Luso-Brazilian identity distinct from the metropole. In contested Brazil, and again across the Atlantic, former military men and priests recorded the deeds of Luso-Brazilian women. They were mistresses—of men and of their own property; they bore and sacrificed sons who went into battle. Women also served as soldiers, and some may have even been spies. These accounts reveal women's freedoms, constraints, and contributions as they coped with contested Brazil. For some, this included marriage to the Dutch; for others it meant taking up arms and confronting battle. In Brazil and during the Luso–Dutch war, women negotiated a new status—one traceable from the earliest days of Portugal, defined even then against an enemy invader.

CHAPTER FIVE

"Hunger, the Biggest Battle"

Finding an Army, Fueling Resistance

ON JUNE 1, 1635, Antônio Carvalho, a recruit from Madeira, was caught stealing from an orange grove outside Recife. The Dutch West India Company soldier who had found him there taunted Carvalho, asking if he wanted to return to the besieged Forte Real do Bom Jesus. The stronghold, which had been built between the Dutch-held towns of Olinda and Recife in the first few months of the invasion, had long hampered Netherlandish expansion beyond this narrow slice of Pernambuco. Two years prior, the Dutch had managed to set up positions around the fort; now they began what would become three months of near-continuous shelling. The Dutch soldier knew well that the besieged men and women were starving and that some risked death to forage, as Carvalho was doing now. Did he want to return to the misery of his camp? "I do," replied Carvalho, "I have *dôces* (sweets) there, which I can eat to temper the sourness of this here orange." The enemy, commented the local chronicler, was "on this occasion a gentleman," as he allowed Carvalho to return unharmed and having tasted of at least one orange.[1]

This "orange grove incident," an interlude in the ongoing Luso–Dutch war in Brazil, points to a common enemy: hunger. By 1635 the Dutch and Portuguese had, for nearly four decades, been battling for resources the world over, and arguably no region was more critical to them than the Brazilian northeast. Both sides had committed atrocities in the decades-long war for Brazil, but between burning fields and poaching livestock, the greatest challenge, for Dutch and Portuguese alike, was to fend off starvation. Both endured the task of not only feeding troops on the move but also meeting the needs of their respective settler populations.[2] They engaged in a food war, not only pushing the enemy to starvation but also pirating each other's shipments of provisions, which they diverted to their own men.

Despite the initial Dutch success in seizing Olinda, the seat of Pernambuco and main port of Recife, the guerrilla resistance, on home territory, had the greater margin of advantage in the first two years of the war (1630–1632). During that time, Matias de Albuquerque, governor of Pernambuco, and his Portuguese troops confined the invaders to the two towns, a strategy that had worked in Salvador five years prior. This tactic worked temporarily. Though they had ransacked the storehouses of the São Bento monastery and elsewhere, the WIC troops, culled by hunger and disease, were almost entirely dependent on transatlantic shipments of provisions. So they could hardly break from their siege-like positions.[3]

As the Dutch West India ships became more adept at blockading Brazil's coast, the 1625 success of the Iberian armada was not repeated. The much-hailed rescue fleets commanded by António de Oquendo (1631), Luis de Rojas y Borja (1635), and Fernando de Mascarenhas (1639) failed to liberate the northeast and stem the tide of Dutch advance. The Spanish, building on past strength, continued to privilege maritime rescue efforts, but getting help to ground troops proved a challenge—and feeding them even more so.[4] The Iberian crown authorized shipments of troops, provisions, and munitions to Brazil, but soldiers generally had rations enough only for the crossing. These supplies were halved (or worse) as the situation warranted. Once on the ground, Luso-Spanish-Neapolitan troops often had to fend for themselves.[5]

Who would join the Portuguese cause—and why—when the backlands provided easy escape from soldiering? The 1638 Siege of Bahia, a turning point in the broader battle for Brazil, indicates that for both soldiers and provisioners, the conflict offered opportunity for those of "tainted" blood, including entrance to coveted military orders and the fidalgueira, and with these hereditary titles and annual pensions. Petitions, correspondence, and post-conflict relations not only reveal *how* soldiers were recruited and kept fed but also *why* men would agree to this service in the first place. Luso-Brazilian men sought to distinguish themselves in the war against the Dutch, their strategies extending beyond military service to include feeding soldiers.[6] After 1640, provisioners turned to

Lisbon, rather than Madrid, to persuade João IV that their auxiliary efforts in the war merited distinction. Their petitions often requested entrance to the coveted Portuguese military orders of Christ, Avis, and Santiago—and of course the titles and pensions that accompanied such distinction.

The Dutch–Portuguese war over Brazil also increased the demand for manioc, a root crop long prized by Indigenous peoples. Luso-Brazilians soon transformed this highly nutritious and hardy plant from Indigenous food to a weapon of war. Feeding troops with manioc and its derived *farinha da guerra*, or war flour, helped augment food provisions—a fact well recognized by the Dutch. Not only did the Dutch attempt to promote manioc production, but they also intercepted supply lines, burning Portuguese ships laden with this flour.[7] But for the Portuguese resistance, this locally grown and procured crop helped hold hunger at bay, leading to a seemingly improbable victory against the Dutch.

Military logistics and soldierly persuasion point to the logic, in the face of Spanish and Dutch imperial might, of the Luso-Brazilian guerrilla-won war. Providing for soldiers mattered. War-prompted changes in culinary habits also make clear that who ate what—and how—made a difference in the outcome. The challenge of feeding thousands of troops and colonists on the move influenced how Spain, then Portugal, administered Brazil; from at least 1638, with no aid from Europe in sight, Brazil-based Portuguese took matters into their own hands by creating and making firm connections from coastal towns to the backlands. From 1640, the Portuguese increasingly drew Angola and the Atlantic islands of Madeira, Cabo Verde, and the Azores into circuits of support. With the dissolution of the dual crowns and recall of Spanish and Italian troops, local soldiers and provisioners more fully assumed the burdens of recruitment and provisioning. In so doing, they gained not just on the Dutch in Brazil but in the Portuguese Atlantic world—and with it, a social, political, and economic prominence that resonated across the Atlantic.

Recruitment and Provisioning: From Early Philippine Rule to the 1638 Siege of Bahia

The Portuguese marked the early years of the Iberian union through public displays of fealty to the Spanish, and in his entrance to Lisbon, Philip II of

Spain appeared to reciprocate the attention. En route to the city from Tomar, the king "praised the spectacle" celebrating his acclamation in 1580. He then swore to uphold Portuguese autonomy even after the kingdom was absorbed into the Spanish Empire.[8]

And so the first Spanish monarch of the dual crown sailed into Lisbon on the royal galleon, part of a spectacular fleet as still more boats joined the royal process down the Tagus River, vying for recognition as most beautiful and "gallant" ship. The loveliest among them were painted many colors, brightly decked out for the occasion.[9] From the youths who followed his royal carriage to Lisbon to the nobility joining his swelling entourage and the "vulgar people," wrote Afonso Guerreiro, it seemed that the whole country had turned out to welcome the Spanish king.[10] Smarting from the terrible loss of Portugal's autonomy, he was not among the celebrants. Philipe de Aguilar, one of the city *vereadores* (councilors), lined up to greet the new king, kissed his hand, and offered Philip II of Spain—now also Philip I of Portugal—the key to the city. This would, he claimed, "open all its doors and those of the loyal hearts of its citizens."[11] With the dual crown, a once-divided Catholic world now appeared united.

Though the new king managed affairs from Lisbon for three years, his rule of Portugal proved less direct than anticipated. This was partly for the sake of political expediency; he had promised that the Spanish and Portuguese overseas empires would be administered separately. So the affairs of the newly formed Council of Portugal were conducted in Portuguese. Only Portuguese—and not Spanish—received appointments in Portugal, and the Portuguese could serve in other Spanish kingdoms as well.[12] Philip's administration had installed the Conselho da India in Portugal by 1604 to provide for and supply cargo and overseas grants of land or title; however, jurisdictional strife between this administrative organ and Portugal's Mesa da Consciência e Ordens, which managed religious affairs even in the colonies, led to its extinction.[13] These actions indicated a measure of respect for Portugal's sovereignty, but with it came expectation of support for the larger Spanish Empire as needed.

The Dutch threat and conquest of Portugal's—now Spain's—overseas colonies, however, prompted direct intervention by the Iberian crown. From the first, most decorated, and only successful "journey of the [Luso-Spanish] vassals" through 1640, the Spanish steered men, munitions, and provisions across the South Atlantic to dislodge the Dutch in Brazil.[14] Over the next four decades, for instance, the Philippine-installed Conselho da Fazenda (Council of Treasury) meant generally to maintain and oversee Portugal's possessions to the east, evolved in administrative structure, as did its reach; its authority now extended to Mina, Guinea, and Brazil as well as São Tomé and Cape Verde.[15] As a result, individuals sent petitions directly to Spain, with the bulk of requests and permissions regarding the war against the Dutch flowing through official channels.

Like his grandfather, Philip IV (r. 1621–1640) proved a tireless administrator, though his handling of Portugal hastened the rupture of a once-solid union. He dispensed with ceremonial pleasantries and, with his valido Count-Duke Olivares, pushed for greater Luso–Spanish coordination—specifically with regard to military recruitment—in the wider European conflict. In the case of Dutch-threatened Brazil, a strong Iberian union manifested, from 1624, in the Spanish-led joint armadas. The rescue attempts, including the 1625 "journey of the vassals," now served to project Iberian power in the peripheral space of the South Atlantic colony. But this lasted little more than a decade.[16]

Despite the loss of Salvador, Dutch West India Company investors never lost sight of their goal to "take the land of Brazil."[17] One lesson from their short-lived hold was that Portuguese in Brazil would not rise up en masse and join them in their fight against Spain. In widely read "motives" to take Brazil, Jan Andries Moerbeeck had highlighted the injustice of the king of Spain, who "illegally took possession of the lands and cities" belonging to Portugal. Luso-Brazilians might have agreed, and also with Moerbeeck's view that there were "reasons to hope for the assistance of Divine Justice, in the work of the Company in Brazil, which belongs to the Portuguese Crown."[18] Of course his prediction—or pitch—that Portuguese in Brazil would welcome Dutch rule proved quite wrong.[19]

Portuguese subjects with direct connection to Brazil needed no prompting to defend their homeland against the second, enduring attack of the Dutch in Brazil. In 1629, at first word that the Dutch were heading to take northeastern Brazil, Matias de Albuquerque, brother of Pernambuco's donatary Duarte de Albuquerque Coelho, departed from Lisbon to the family captaincy with his own detachment of twenty-seven men. Of course, this was no match for 13,500 soldiers preparing to disembark just north of Recife; he aimed instead to repair fortifications, round up local troops, and hold the Dutch at bay while he waited for reinforcements from Lisbon and Madrid.[20] Albuquerque drew from and depended on local militias, but the 650 ground troops he mustered at the onset of the second Dutch attack in 1630 lacked weapons and training.[21] He and his men retreated to the backlands as first Olinda and then Recife fell to the Dutch.

The shortage—or relative absence—of local troops was in large part due to Spanish preference for skilled, loyal soldiers for the war in Brazil.[22] This was part of a long-standing strategy to send outsiders to the front. "There is no surer strength than that of foreign soldiers," noted one contemporary tactician.[23] This included men from the Spanish army in Flanders who received more formal training relative to soldiers in the guerrilla resistance. More importantly, however, they posed less of a threat to the existing (Spanish) power structure. A professional army, loyal to Spain, was expected to get the job done in Brazil—and leave.[24]

Bagnuolo also appeared skeptical of the Luso-Brazilians' ability to perform in the heat of battle. The 1631 Luso-Spanish-Neapolitan rescue armada disembarked seven hundred men, including the future ground commander, who marched overland to the royal fort Bom Jesus. The experience left a deep impression on him. Upon the death of Luis de Rojas y Borja, Bagnuolo assumed leadership of Matias de Albuquerque's regiment, to which Indigenous and Black troops had reported. But despite an ongoing shortage of soldiers, Bagnuolo made no real effort to recruit more troops, at least not in the first five years of hostilities. The Neapolitan's scorn for these *soldados da terra* was rooted in his opinion that they had signed on only for steady pay, had little experience and even less loyalty, and had the habit of disappearing into dense thicket at the first sight of action.[25]

Well before the invasion of 1630, local authorities in Portugal regularly up rounded recruits to fight in the enduring Spanish–Dutch war, using unemployed men as "voluntary contributions" to Philip IV's joint army and protecting Iberian interests.[26] The Unión de Armas (Union of Arms) created a sixteen-thousand-strong reserve force of Portuguese. Yet this did not solve recruitment issues for the Luso–Dutch war in Brazil—one indication of Spanish priorities.[27] The war at home presented immediate concerns; the troubled colony across the Atlantic, ever a drain on the Spanish treasury, prompted—or encouraged—the colonists step up.

From a distance of two hundred years, an English historian observed that "warfare in Brazil was not to be learnt in regular camps and cultivated countries," though the recruitment efforts—a measure against unemployment and unrest—were cast wide.[28] Improvisation helped ramp up soldierly supply, as engaged officers made direct requests to take on soldiers drawn beyond the bounds of the Habsburg Empire. For instance, Manuel Pires Bezerra, captain of the ship *Nossa Senhora*, petitioned Philip IV for permission to take on two English artillerymen, as the forty men he had under his command were neither sufficient nor experienced. He complained of the dearth of Portuguese men with such skill, noting they were needed on large ships sailing with recruits from northern Portugal to Bahia. The captain requested that the foreigners help man weapons en route to Brazil, asking license to bring aboard these "friends" who would aid the Luso cause and were "confederates of your majesty."[29]

But by 1635, Portuguese prospects against the Dutch in Brazil had dimmed, and Crown and local officials fielded new alternatives regarding recruitment. This included more open enlistment of Afro-descended men, some of whom may have been on the run from enslavement. That year, the loss of the Forte Real do Bom Jesus and subsequent retreat south of Spanish-Luso-Brazilian troops meant that many soldiers returned to the metropole. Even more died of exhaustion or illness. The number of foreign troops continued to decline—from 1,950 to 1,000 in the following year—with only a handful of Spanish and seventy Neapolitans remaining in Brazil for the war effort by the end of 1636.[30] At the same time, however, the number of soldiers in the Terço da Gente Preta, Henrique Dias's all-Black regiment, climbed from "forty Angolan blacks" to eighty men in 1636 to more than four hundred by 1652.[31] These allegedly were not men who worked on the engenhos; not only would refuge in the army damage planter–military relations, but the sale of sugar, so dependent on African labor, helped finance the war against the Dutch.[32] Still, not a few runaways made their way to and were mixed in with and accepted into the Dias regiment—a far better alternative than risking having *crioulos* (Brazilian-born people of African descent) fight for the Dutch.

The Black troops were so reliable, however, that Dom Jorge de Mascarenhas, the newly appointed viceroy of Brazil, proposed actively recruiting them from the mocambos. Salvador's municipal council rejected this proposition on the grounds "that it is in no way appropriate to make concessions nor give space to the slaves or compromise," although they might be enticed to battle by the prospect of royal favors. The council, concerned with the long-term implications of this idea, eventually dismissed the suggestion that Henrique Dias himself visit the mocambos with a "priest fluent in the language of the blacks, to bring them to us and enlist them in his regiment."[33]

As the Luso–Dutch war in the Atlantic expanded to include West Africa, so too did the demand there for soldiers, clergy, and basic provisions. Petitions included specific, often modest numbers of men for such service, suggesting an awareness of the challenges of recruitment during this extended conflict. Portuguese-held West African strongholds braced for conflict after the Dutch seizure of Elmina in 1637; Captain Jusé (or José) Martins sent a request to the regional governor at Mina, Manuel da Cunha, for twelve extra men at São Tomé. The specificity did not extend to provisions. For example, his request for the Castle of Axim (or Axém), cataloged as one long sentence, included a cleric, ten soldiers, and biscuits, wheat, olives, and wine for the soldiers, as well as *aguardente* for the Black captains.[34] A liquor made from distilled sugar cane that is flavored with anise, arguardente, wrote Martins, was a cheap substitute for wine."[35] In his personal notes, Manuel da Cunha reviewed and supported the request of José Martins. He agreed that spiritual help was warranted, writing that at Axim, one cleric of "infallible strength" was needed to give assistance to the Christians—"whites and black"—in the castle and the nearby aldeia.[36] Thus the ongoing effort to recruit soldiers included ancillary physical and spiritual sustenance so they could perform their duties.

As the Dutch seemed to realize their Grand Design, securing first the Brazilian northeast and then strongholds along the Portuguese African Atlantic coast, fresh suggestions to pull men from Portugal and the Atlantic islands—anywhere but Brazil—came pouring in to the Crown through the 1630s. For instance, Captain João Rodrigues de Sousa, writing from Brazil, suggested that Philip IV should round up unemployed men in the town of Lamego in northern Portugal to help with the war effort.[37] Captain Manoel Coelho de Figueiroa sent out a request to the Conselho da Fazenda to enlist new soldiers, "for lack of men," from the Azores.[38] Conscious, perhaps, of loyalties a married man might have for family over a kingdom, including and especially that which was across the Atlantic, Figueiroa specifically requested single men. He offered no explanation beyond this request. Two years later, in April of 1638, the Conselho da Fazenda approved another request to recruit one thousand men, also from the Azores. Marital status did not appear to be an issue.[39]

Food insecurity may well have checked prospective soldiers for the Portuguese from dashing across the Atlantic. Natural hardships of soldierly life aside, the prospect of a monthslong voyage without adequate provisioning may have been less than persuasive, even for the unemployed. In the United Provinces, enterprising recruiters promised of decent rations, even as they rounded up stragglers and locked them in Texel boarding houses before they shipped out. But the Iberians made no such offer to their own men. The Dutch seemed to make good on their promise—in the early weeks of service at least. For instance, Stephen Behaim of the Dutch West India Company wrote to his brothers of his rich weekly allotment of provisions; this included wine, cheese, and salted fish. (Within a year he was found wandering, half-mad, and ill-nourished.)[40] By contrast, Iberian fare was simpler. Provisions for Portuguese soldiers, wrote Luis Mendes de Vasconcelos in his *Military Arts* (1612), should consist of "grain, wheat and biscuits," as these were "most necessary for sustenance," a policy pursued in the ongoing conflict against the Dutch.[41] As an important part of ship preparations, the procurement and distribution of sustenance for the transatlantic voyage—but not beyond—meant sourcing dried beef, wine, and biscuits. Beyond that, Portuguese soldiers generally provided for themselves on the ground.

Chronic food shortages in Portugal may well have been one reason for the push for Portuguese soldierly self-sufficiency. From at least the fifteenth century, Portugal suffered from cyclical drought. One solution was that merchants exchanged salt from Setúbal for scarce wheat procured elsewhere on the continent. The broader goal for the kingdom was to secure a stable enough source of grain, in particular for Lisbon, the most densely populated Portuguese city at the time.

Procuring wheat for a transatlantic crossing to Brazil proved an additional strain to the royal and municipal treasuries. By June 1630, with the Dutch firmly entrenched in Pernambuco, Philip II (IV of Spain) wrote to the Lisbon municipal council that he would send a rescue armada—but reinforcements had to follow, as well as other aid, lest they lose the South Atlantic stronghold.[42] This was followed up by another urgent letter procuring a quantity vast enough for the armada.[43] The Lisbon council agreed to offer a substantial portion to start organizing provisioning of the armada, but an ongoing wheat crisis required the mobilization of networks beyond state borders.⁴⁴ In a June 1, 1630, letter, the king requested that city officials reach out to local merchants who had networks and connections with Sicily, Germany, and France, so they might send from there the largest quantity of wheat possible to handle the shortage in Lisbon.⁴⁵ Another royal letter followed, this time in starker terms: the Spanish king of Portugal demanded support from Lisbon to prevent the Dutch from taking Pernambuco and, by extension, to save Brazil. This, he stated, should be the first order of business.⁴⁶ The shortage of domestic grain, then, meant that merchants did double duty in securing wheat for the kingdom *and* for the armada—no small feat. Stretching thin procured supplies guaranteed that the recruits for the war in Brazil would have just enough sustenance to survive the crossing.

The challenge in provisioning reveals regnal disconnect and resident frustration over the king's uneven approach to his vassals in Portugal. Lisboetas expressed concern that they bore an undue burden, relative to other towns, of procuring supplies for the kingdom *and* for overseas expeditions. This led to a breakdown in negotiations between city council and Crown; Lisboetas, dealing with their own crises, seemed far less concerned with the situation in Brazil. For instance, to meet the king's demands, the council had asked permission to ship in grain from Andalusia and Sicily and had sent an emissary to solicit sacks of the product for the city.⁴⁷ The council then discovered that, in fact, the southern Portuguese region of Algarve was plentiful in wheat but it was too expensive for Lisbon to purchase. This was due to a tax that Lisbon, and not the Algarve, had to pay on the wheat. When challenged, the Crown resolved that the Lisbon city council should proceed to obtain the wheat however it could and get to making biscuits for the armada heading to Brazil.⁴⁸ Two days later, on September 2, 1630, Philip IV acknowledged Lisbon's efforts in "attending the very necessity of helping the state of Brazil and expelling from the captaincy of Pernambuco the Dutch who have occupied it."⁴⁹ But did the Dutch threat to Brazil matter to Lisboetas?

As this epistolary exchange dragged on, conditions for Dutch and Iberian soldiers worsened in Brazil. Dutch West India Company soldiers long depended on imported foodstuffs and were at particular risk of starvation while out on campaign. But because of the war-torn countryside outside of Recife, "there is not a single cultivated acre, field, or meadow, only dense brush and untillable forest everywhere. It is also utterly without bread, wine, and barley—almost everything needed to sustain life," wrote WIC soldier Stephan Behaim to his brothers Lucas and Frederich in 1635. Starvation threatened both belligerents, and Behaim also noted that for the WIC troops, the items "must be imported from Holland and Zeeland at great cost and peril."[50] He noted, however, that "soldiers here are provisioned according to need. I still receive each week enough bread, meat, bacon, plums, beans, berries, barley, vinegar, olive oil, and sometimes wine to get along rather well." That would change as the war dragged on. The collapse of sugar prices in Amsterdam through the 1630s meant that such exports from both Dutch and Portuguese Brazil bought less.[51]

Amid this crisis, independent merchants and shipowners found their merchandise and ships tied up in port for the war effort. They included Margarida Vareira, a shipowner and merchant from the northern Portuguese port city of Viana do Castelo.[52] In her *requerimiento*, or request, to Philip III of Portugal (IV of Spain), Vareira sought the return of her ship the *Bom Jesus*, which had been embargoed for the war in Pernambuco. She asked for the return of her ship and its cargo of wine, claiming it had been destined for Rio de Janeiro to sustain the spirits of the soldiers in the ongoing war against the Dutch. It was eventually deemed too small to be of use. Her petition was granted and her ship returned.[53]

The struggle to supply and provision troops affected life for people on both sides of the Atlantic. It also directly affected the outcome of key battles. Brazil's Forte Real do Bom Jesus, constructed under the direction of Matias de Albuquerque in the first month of the 1630 Dutch invasion, had for nearly five years held men, munitions, and provisions to fuel attacks on Dutch troops in either Olinda or Recife.[54] But the fort also blocked Dutch access to the engenhos along the Capiberibe River.[55] With the help of turncoat Domingo Fernandes Calabar, the Dutch West India Company broke free of those two towns and after three months of continuous shelling destroyed this strategically located stronghold. In the end, "Neither the valor not the consistency of the defenders [could] prevent its loss; because in the end [they] lacked sustenance; they ate horses, leather, dogs, cats, rats." They also lacked ammunition. After three months and three days, the survivors filed out of the fort.[56]

During the long siege, a few men begged for and were granted permission to slip out and obtain provisions.[57] This was not without danger; Madeirense

António Carvalho had been caught foraging in an orange grove, though he was finally released to return to the fort by a Dutch West India Company soldier. On June 6, the besieged soldiers and residents surrendered to the Dutch, who razed the fort by the end of the next day. By that time, the resistance had retreated to Fort Nazaré, where the situation was worse: "Those at [the nearby] Fort Nazaré," wrote a local chronicler, "had already run out of food [and had] not even filthy animals, and with the enemy so close to the trenches they were forced to surrender under the same conditions [as those of Forte do Bom Jesus]."[58] The lessons of this defeat, hastened by the lack of food, no doubt came in handy during the Siege of Bahia just a few years later.

The 1638 Siege of Bahia: Portuguese Victory, "and Spain did not even come to the rescue"

"Experience has taught us that the conquest of Brazil is permanently threatened by Bahia of all Saints," wrote West India Company officer Adrian van der Dussen, "and while the Spanish are masters of Bahia they will have many opportunities to molest us, by land and by seas."[59] The Dutch had secured the two main towns of Pernambuco by 1630, but without Bahia, the West India Company gains were at best temporary.[60] Even as West India Company control expanded from 1635 through 1641, ongoing resistance originating from Bahia set company efforts back on a regular basis, resulting in a significant loss of life and property. As van der Dussen stressed in his survey on northeastern Brazilian captaincies, the stealth of resistance fighters made it "impossible to track [them], and our soldiers are not as familiar with the *matos*." The threat to the cane fields was almost continuous. Despite the Dutch blockade of the northeast coast, the "Spanish have the best port" in Bahia, so he bemoaned, "We are in a perpetual state of war."[61]

It would take a formidable challenge by the Dutch to conquer Bahia. Dutch accounts said the Portuguese tolerated hardship better than the non-acclimated Dutch WIC soldiers, acknowledging that the enemy could make do without olives, butter, wine, and an abundance of meat: "They know better than ours to subject themselves to extremes, like the lack of sustenance, etc. [while] company soldiers were loaded down with their rations and highly dependent on what food would be shipped to them."[62] Despite the European inclination to scorn American-born recruits, one contemporary argued that because of sheer hardiness, "one natural born soldier of Brazil was worth two from the Kingdom [of Portugal], given life-long acclimation to the tropical conditions."[63]

For the Portuguese, bolstering Bahia meant holding the line south of the São Francisco River to protect the resistance stronghold. It was from Salvador that the Luso-Brazilians could and did push back against the Dutch—to devastating effect. West India Company soldiers garrisoned the easterly portion of the São Francisco River, but that did not stop the guerrillas from stealing across the riverain border and torching Dutch-controlled cane fields. Farther north in Recife, removed from such direct threats, governor-general of Dutch-held Brazil Johan Maurits van Nassau-Siegen (1636–1644) confirmed to West India Company directors that a Bahia in Portuguese hands meant perpetual harassment of Dutch Brazil. Nassau shared that a local spy explained how the resistance fighters planned yet another trip across the river to do damage. The informant detailed how up to 150 men—fifty whites and the rest under Henrique Dias, "captain and governor of the negros"—had orders to burn the cane fields of Pernambuco between Sirinhaém and the *várzea*. This would destroy the Dutch economy to the north. They would return back across the San Francisco River, explained the man known as Diabinho (Little Devil), unless they received word from a long-expected rescue Spanish armada.[64] This was a very real fear for the Dutch, evocative of the failure of 1625: pitched resistance from the backlands and a full-frontal maritime assault by sea. Diabinho was right—but too late, as the resistance was able to carry out its plan and set fire to a large swathe of cane fields; the fire was only put out toward dawn. Still, for his effort, Nassau gave him his own small patrol and made "captain of the mato" (woods). His task was to scour thicket for "men of all races" who would fight for the Portuguese.[65]

In 1638 Nassau's men seized Portugal's West African fort at Mina, making good on phase two of the Dutch Grand Design, but the problem of rebel activity from Bahia persisted. This threatened to undo all progress in Dutch Brazil. Vexed by the constant attacks, in early 1638 Nassau ordered another assault on the Portuguese captaincy. His fleet would set sail from the Dutch stronghold of Recife. The governor-general's concern was prompted not only by unpredictable attacks on the cane fields; his men had also intercepted letters that pointed toward increasingly organized resistance from Bahia. He had also received several bold (but unverifiable) claims from the United Provinces. Chief among these was that the enemy was floundering due to lack of provisions. Other dubious claims included that the Portuguese would soon cross over to the Dutch side and that the governor of Bahia was at odds and fighting with the Count of Bagnuolo. Despite his doubts about the trustworthiness of these reports, Nassau still felt it important to attack Bahia before the arrival of another Luso-Spanish armada.[66] In light of yet another anticipated armada from Madrid, Nassau set in motion the plan to sail south and take Bahia, choosing to act sooner rather than later.

On March 20, resistance captain Sebastião Souto intercepted a letter from Recife indicating that Nassau's fleet was headed to the Bay of All Saints. While the West India Company had caused damage there over the prior decade, it would now assault Salvador with full intent to conquer, a feat not accomplished since 1624. The Portuguese forwarded the letter—along with two Dutch prisoners they had captured, for good measure—to Count of Bagnuolo, commander of the land troops, who was stationed fourteen leagues north of Bahia.[67] Upon receiving the news, the Count ordered a thorough inventory of the storehouses. The accounting made clear the dearth of supplies. The storehouses contained "some flour, but lacked salted meat, fish, salt, and everything needed to sustain a defense."[68] Given the situation, he authorized the purchase of cattle, wine, olives, and other such provisions for the soldiers.[69]

When word of the impending Dutch attack arrived in Madrid, Philip IV ordered preparations for the grandest Luso–Spanish rescue armada yet, but Luso-Brazilian soldiers went on the offensive almost immediately. Captain Sebastião Souto received an alert from a local morador of two Dutch ships laden with brazilwood that had sunk just off the coast and ten leagues north of Bahia, and with his men, he set off to investigate. They found twenty-five of the crew holed up in a nearby coastal church. They killed nineteen and imprisoned two; the remaining six escaped. In one captive's pocket, Souto found a letter confirming the Dutch governor-general's plans to besiege Bahia yet again. This, along with the two prisoners, he sent on to Count of Bagnuolo, who sent on word to the governor of Bahia.[70] By now, Dutch West India Company troops and ships were massing on the São Francisco River in preparation to head south to take the capital city of Portuguese America. Spies reported that the Dutch had meat, grain, and other "refreshments" in stock.[71] Away from Dutch-held Brazil, West India Company supplies could only be replenished by sea, an uncertain option at best given Portuguese control of the Bay of All Saints; the vast quantities of provisions indicated readiness for a drawn-out battle. The governor then relayed this news to Count of Bagnuolo, commander of the Luso-Spanish-Brazilian troops.

Salvador's residents had proved unwilling to brace for yet another possible attack—at least not until the arrival in Bahia of Souto's two Dutch prisoners and the intercepted letter, After all, the Dutch had been expelled a decade earlier and Salvador they had survived sporadic shelling since. Duarte de Albuquerque Coelho, donatary of Pernambuco and brother of commander Matias de Albuquerque, was not impressed by what he perceived as local complacency, noting that residents had done little in the past decade to fortify the town.[72] But the arrival of the prisoners and written proof of an impending invasion changed that. The town's residents were now "convinced that the enemy was upon her."[73]

The first sightings of the Dutch caused confusion; the resistance army did little to reassure the townspeople of Salvador. At arrival of enemy ships in the Bay of All Saints, Count of Bagnuolo and Duarte de Albuquerque Coelho set out to occupy the engenho of New Christian Diogo Muniz Teles before the Dutch could do the same.[74] This move proved critical, as the property occupied a favorable position above the city. From this vantage point, they spied the full Dutch fleet in the bay, which vastly outnumbered the resistance troops on the ground. The panoramic view contributed to the Count's decision to avoid a direct engagement with the enemy; he would wait for reinforcements. The townspeople threatened that if indeed the army wouldn't engage the enemy, then they themselves would decide who would govern them.[75] Partly to quell such protests and also to "do something," the Count, nineteen of own his men, and two terços from Bahia set out for the site where the West India troops had been seen. Not finding them, the men returned to the city. There they prepared for the siege with Henrique Dias, Felipe Camarão, and their men, who took up the rearguard.[76]

As the troops made camp around the city, military–morador tensions continued to run high, in no small part due to the pressure to provide for thousands of troops. Local resistance to the Count's command, however, was a more serious concern. On April 20, when Bahian officials made clear their disregard for the portly Neapolitan commander, Governor Pedro da Silva stepped in to mediate. This was for the sake of a united front—or, as it seemed to others, an act of self-preservation: "This generous act astonished all who knew what it was to be responsible for a stronghold; it seemed to some that he did so to have a companion in the loss [of Bahia], which seemed inevitable," wrote an onlooker, "because if the governor had high hopes, no one would believe that he would part from the glory of victory."[77]

Beyond battle strategy and loyalty, contemporary accounts make clear that good camp conditions and a steady supply of food roused Luso-Brazilian morale. Early on, Henrique Dias, the Indigenous commander Felipe Camarão, and eight hundred men left Salvador to procure food, but the army's provisioner-general soon established reliable local supply lines.[78] A few weeks after the appearance of the Dutch fleet in the Bay of All Saints, "it didn't even seem like we were under siege," an eyewitness observed, "as we had fresh meat, and walked freely about the camp."[79] Between May 5 and May 7, two ships laden with more than two thousand bushels of flour sailed in to make delivery to the Portuguese. During this time, the head of provisioning also took in nearly three hundred cows and one hundred sheep, locally purchased and delivered overland.[80] These "served as great help to the wounded and infirm."[81]

The nearly monthlong siege revealed the strength of local Luso-Brazilian troop networks, as well as the determination of Dutch forces in their quest to gain all of Brazil. An anonymous Portuguese eyewitness to the battle wrote that the Dutch force had landed on Bahia and inflicted enough damage that Bahia was in a "miserable state," with the ground troop commander, Italian Count of Bagnuolo, entrenched outside the city.[82] The following Thursday, however, the count, spurred on by the "great insolence of the enemy," engaged the Dutch in a furious nine-hour battle, aided by Indigenous troops led by Felipe Camarão.[83] The Dutch Siege of Bahia began in earnest, but as one observer wrote, "Every day hope grew that we could resist." Help came from around the country."[84] Men from as far away as São Paulo came streaming in to help the defense.[85]

Maurits's report to the Heeren XIX, the "Nineteen Gentlemen" of the Dutch West India Company council, made clear that he was caught off-guard by the resistance of the combined Portuguese forces: "the garrison of the governor with 2000 soldiers, as many Portuguese and Spanish, and the forces of Bagnuolo numbering 1400 soldiers and eight hundred '*brasilienses*' [Tupinambá Indians]" and "the inhabitants of the city with three thousand men, the priests and students having taken up arms and two companies of cavalry and field men (gente do campo) the mulatos and negros are also armed." The governor-general of Dutch Brazil took counsel and decided to withdraw "for the safety of the State" and "before God could punish us."[86] By nine in the morning on May 19, Maurits of Nassau had petitioned for and was granted a ceasefire to collect and bury the dead.[87]

With only a supply line from Pernambuco, Maurits's men continued to fare poorly when hostilities recommenced. One week after Maurits had asked for and was granted a reprieve to collect his dead, the next and last battle resulted in more than two thousand Dutch West India casualties and the abrupt departure of the would-be invaders.[88] But before departing, Maurits kissed the hand of the Count of Bagnuolo—a detail not included in his report home.[89] He seemed ashamed, wrote an onlooker. Unbelievably, the Luso-Brazilian land forces had protected the capital city, and, wrote the same chronicler, "Spain did not even come to the rescue."[90] On May 26, the Dutch started picking up their equipment and making ready to depart. Two days later, Nassau's armada lifted anchor at night and slipped back north. Portuguese spies reported that Nassau's fleet arrived back in Recife on June 5.[91] Nassau wrote to the High Council that at the end of the siege, "we retired in good order and that night." Contrary to Portuguese reports, Maurits added, "The enemy perceived nothing of our retreat."[92]

Under the command of the Neapolitan General Bagnuolo, the guerrilla resistance army, supported by local officials and sustained by locally purchased supplies, had routed the invaders within forty days. Nearby moradores also brought provisions to wounded and infirm soldiers; medic Manoel Fernandes de Figueiredo noted that it was with "much charity" that the local farmers brought to the hospital eggs, bread, wine, sweets, and chickens.[93] The damage done to Bagnuolo's troops was severe enough, but the men received aid from the bishop of Bahia and clergy, who comforted the wounded, granted them their last rites, and helped tend to those recovering. Indeed, the hospital was well stocked thanks to the church; the bishop had sent eggs, wine, water, sweets, and chickens.[94]

The acquisition and inventory of provisions make it clear that sustenance was a critical factor in the outcome of the Siege of Bahia—and the battle for Brazil.

Timed properly, the destruction of food supplies could have tipped the scales the other way, a fact not lost on Maurits, whose naval forces burned a Portuguese ship full of flour in the Bay of Camamu.[95] After Maurits lifted sail for a return trip to Pernambuco, what was left behind, particularly provisions, was set upon and duly recorded. Dutch-discarded items included seventy-five flasks of wine, goats, much grain, and legumes, as well as bread.[96] Stew-filled cauldrons and "still-baking bread" served, for the Luso-Brazilians, as proof positive of the enemy's hasty and ignominious defeat.[97] One contemporary writer included livestock in his count of the dead. This served both as reference and indicator of success; though 449 bullets were found lodged in the doors and even inner walls of the homes of moradores, "no one [inside the city walls] was killed or wounded except for one horse and one ox."[98]

The long Dutch siege of Bahia and the success of the guerrilla resistance indicate the strength of local and inter-captaincy coordination. The West India officers planned for a sweeping invasion, but Luso-Brazilians had routed invaders and sent them packing. Initial morador resistance gave way to gratitude for the defense; hostility toward Philip IV's commander in chief gave way to grudging acceptance of his leadership. But with restoration of Portugal in 1640, and a break from Spanish-appointed posts, Luso-Brazilians came to coordinate military movements in ever increasing numbers.

Changing the Guard, Emptying the Pantry? Portugal's Restoration, 1640

Events during the 1630s had led Portuguese resentment of Spanish rule to increase throughout the decade. With Iberian treasuries running low, Count-Duke Olivares, Philip IV's councilor, had introduced a host of fiscal measures in Portugal through the 1630s, including sweeping taxes designed to extract funds from municipal councils, the nobility, and even the Portuguese clergy. A few years later, the *real d'agua*, urban taxes on the retailing of wine and meat (in addition to those on salt), contributed to swelling discontent. With continued crop failures, Portuguese peasants strained under increasing fiscal demands and the inability to pay for simple foodstuffs. Tax and grain revolts broke out in Évora and quickly spread through southern Portugal; unlike the riots of 1637–1638, these were not readily put down.[99] In the summer of 1640, the

Catalan revolt against Spain prompted the demand for additional Portuguese recruits to confront this new threat.

By this time, the Portuguese nobility had split neatly on the issue of loyalty to Spain: they either sided with Philip IV, rounding up troops to suppress the Catalan revolt, or, like Dom João, the Duke of Braganza, they kept a low profile in the Portuguese countryside.[100] On December 1, 1640, in a near bloodless coup in Lisbon, the Forty Conspirators (*conjurados*) ousted the Spanish and installed Dom João of Braganza as the first Portuguese king in sixty years. The conspirators killed Miguel de Vasconcelos, Spain's last secretary of state for Portugal, and escorted Margaret of Savoy (Duquesa da Mantua), who had been ruling in Philip IV's name, to the Spanish border. The uprising went so smoothly, and was so successful, that it strained the credulity of even the most seasoned observers. Clearly, the will of heaven manifested in the swift overthrow of Spanish rule.[101] This was a surprise even to most Portuguese nobility, many of whom had either been summoned to or resided at the court in Madrid, and still others who were generally disengaged from politics.[102]

For Portuguese subjects in Brazil, these events meant that requests regarding the Luso–Dutch war were no longer routed to Philip IV of Spain but directly to Lisbon and to the new administrative structures that evolved with the new government. Even prior to his formal acclamation in 1641, Dom João and his cabinet partially reorganized the structure of the government for defensive purposes, as Portugal was now threatened by Spanish troops massing at the border and the Dutch continued sacking Portuguese possessions abroad. They created the Council of War (Conselho da Guerra) in preparation for hostilities against Spain and by 1642 the Overseas Council (Conselho Ultramarino).[103] The Council of War, designed to manage military concerns at home and abroad, originally oversaw the provisioning of men and supplies. Because of administrative conflicts between the two councils, the Conselho Ultramarino came to have control over matters in Brazil.[104]

In Brazil, the December 1640 restoration of Portugal meant more than a changing of the guard: now the Portuguese would be directly responsible for their own fate. This meant, first, disarming Neapolitans and Spanish soldiers in Bahia in early 1641. As their services were no longer required by the Spanish, most returned to Europe. Still, about seventy Neapolitans and Spanish swore loyalty to the Portuguese and opted to stay on and fight for the Portuguese against the Dutch. They were then sent to Pernambuco to support a direct attack on Dutch Brazil.[105]

Increasingly, local recruitment proved to a solid solution to the continuing need for soldiers, as did the formation of local militias. Prior to restoration, the Spanish command had concerns about the loyalty and ability of Luso-Brazilians. This changed as the war dragged on in the 1640s and need trumped politics—and concerns about social propriety. Now Indigenous, Afro-descended, and men of mixed descent recruited from Pernambuco comprised the Infantaria Natural. Up to one-fifth of the Infantaria's troops were registered as Black or *pardo* and not as members of the Henriques.[106] These men were recruited from the margins of subsistence living, surviving through hard labor in the cane fields or through brazilwood extraction.[107] The post-restoration exodus of troops meant that the moradores and resistance fighters were largely on their own.[108]

Local recruits, however, were too few in number to complete the task of driving out the Dutch, and the Overseas Council (Conselho Ultramarino) stepped up this drive; from the 1640s, increasing numbers of men were drawn from the Azores. In 1645 two hundred soldiers, in what appears to have been the largest deployment from the Azores to date, departed on two caravels set for Rio and Bahia to fight against the Dutch. The Overseas Council, prompted by requests from Rio de Janeiro, gave orders to recruit still more.[109] In the following year, the Overseas Council passed on to Dom João IV a report about four captains who had been to the Azores to recruit men—an indication of the urgent efforts under way.[110] The captains had hoped to round up two thousand prospective soldiers—or at least the "largest number possible." They came away shy of that number, however, and were disappointed in the quality of the men, who jumped at the opportunity for off-island adventure.[111]

The enticement for Atlantic island men to join up was real. Under Portuguese inheritance law, generous grants and hereditary titles could even be passed on to daughters. For example, given his service in the first and second battles for Bahia (1624 and 1638), Azorean Francisco Duarte had earned entrance to the Order of Christ and a generous pension. Upon his death, Dom João IV decreed that the pension and title would pass to Duarte's wife and only child, Marianna de Costa—and to Marianna's future husband at the time of their marriage.[112] And all around the Lusophone Atlantic, more than a few loyal Portuguese gained reward during and beyond the battle for Brazil.[113]

Food Scarcity, Improvisation, and Honor

Like recruitment, provisioning also provides a window on a changing Portuguese Atlantic world. In Lisbon, ships loaded up with attention to rations; procurers sought enough salt, flour, dried meat, and wine for the journey.[114] Certain groups, however, merited select provisions. For instance, the municipal council from Rio de Janeiro requested "white biscuits for the captains."[115] This was a standard, an imperative for armada vessels.[116] Captain Manuel da Cunha, in his request for help at Axim, requested twelve to fifteen barrels of wine, writing that three barrels would go to the *povo preto* (Black people) since it rendered them "more agreeable and content."[117] Along with biscuits, legumes, grain, olive oil, and wine, another captain requested brandy for the "capitães negros," though he offered it as a cheap substitution for wine. He also asked for a clergyman.[118]

As the guerrilla resistance in Brazil began to rely less on transatlantic help from either the Spanish or, from 1640, the Portuguese monarchy, it improvised new strategies not only to obtain men but also to find the provisions with which to feed them. Manioc, a regional staple in northeastern Brazil, took on a new role in the colony's gastronomy. It was cheap food with which to provision the marginalized soldiers, men who played a crucial role in turning the tide against the Dutch after the period of Spanish rule had come to an end.[119]

It was during this war that grain and wheat were more readily replaced by manioc, a once disdained food (by Europeans) of the Tupinambá peoples. Soldiers were provided with salted meat and dried and salted fish.[120] However, manioc had the extra benefit, given its high fiber content, of being filling. Provisions from the Portuguese metropole helped support a monoculture littoral long devoted to growing sugar cane, but with the interruption of supply ships, the demand for this basic food increased.[121]

Who would feed the soldiers, why, and how—and to what end? For the non-elite, fighting off the Dutch offered unexpected opportunity—the possibility of joining high status military orders—as did feeding soldiers for the Portuguese. Petitions to Philip IV and, after 1640, Dom João IV indicate the importance of provisioning. Petitioners for such mercês demonstrated their loyalty through personal sacrifice—in providing for the soldiers, they gave up profit and pay. For instance, Antônio Barbosa, who had once fought under Matias de Albuquerque, gave up sugar cane production to plant crops for the infantry.[122] Others claimed they had sold provisions at low cost or willingly supplied the soldiers with manioc and meat at little or no profit, and for this they wanted acknowledgement, payment, or both. Manuel Álvares Deusdará's petition was accompanied by letters of support from none other than Matias de Albuquerque and Bagnuolo, who wrote that "without him it would not have been possible to sustain the war for so long." Luis Barbalho sold some of his slaves so he would have the resources to send to Paraíba.[123] Thomas Pottes, an Englishman married to a Portuguese woman, had served as medic during the war, but he also highlighted in his petition the fact that he supplied cattle to moradores; in his case he sought merely to recoup losses sustained during the conflict.[124]

Manioc: Flour of Land, Flour of War

Between a long rainy season and the ongoing war, the agricultural enterprise in the Brazilian northeast was a gamble, and with the exception of manioc, the harvest was met with bated breath. "It is just like an act of copulation," one seventeenth-century planter from the northeast complained, "in which the participant does not know whether he has achieved something, or whether the result will be a boy or a girl, sound or deformed, until the birth is achieved."[125] But manioc, the principal food of the Tupinambá, had the extra advantage of being hardy and easy to grow—as the Dutch well appreciated.[126] Albert Eckhout's rendition of manioc, a simple plant with hard, sticklike roots, highlights its importance (Figure 10). Early adventurers and moradores had obtained the crop easily from the Tupinambá, who were willing to part with their surplus in exchange for token gifts. But more permanent settlements, including aldeias, warranted planned cultivation. In the late sixteenth century, Jesuits had introduced systematic planting. By the early seventeenth century, the flour from manioc was considered basic sustenance for all residents of Brazil, but it was not yet used in military provisioning.

Until the Dutch conquest of Pernambuco, manioc flour was considered a

Figure 10. Albert Eckhout, *Manioc*, seventeenth century, oil on canvas, 93 × 93 cm. Courtesy of the National Museum of Denmark.

low-status Luso-Brazilian staple, a likely reflection of its production for domestic rather than global consumption. The Portuguese called manioc flour *farinha de pau* ("stick flour"), while the moradores termed the product *farinha da terra* ("flour of the land"). After the arrival of the Dutch, it came to be known by a third term, *farinha da guerra*.[127] Manioc, like the Luso-Brazilian soldier, was hardy and resilient. Indigenous warriors had long taken this flour of war, ground to an extra-dry paste, out on journeys or into skirmishes. As one contemporary author wrote, "They [the Tupinambá] would wrap this flour in leaves and in this way, if it falls in the river or rains from above, it won't get wet."[128]

Once considered "pagan food" of the Indigenous, manioc became integrated into the resistance army's military rations during the Luso–Dutch war. Of all the edible food that sustained moradores, planters, Indigenous people, and enslaved people, manioc was considered the best.[129] Mixed with water, manioc flour and especially the extra-dry flour of war produced a feeling of satiety—a boon to provisioners trying to stretch supplies enough to feed armies of men. Ground manioc could be mixed with beans or absorbed in a broth or sauce, where it acted like a thickener. It was also mixed up as a porridge.[130] Finally, manioc served as payment for soldiers in time of cash scarcity. Given the shortage of food as the war dragged on, this came to be seen as a regular form of wages.[131]

Post-siege demand for local defense proved consequential to manioc planters. They had long asked for extra military protection, but an expanding garrison strained local food production. As soldiers poured into newly fortified Salvador, a local grain cartel pressured planters to produce more manioc.[132] This group included the sugarocracy—the sugar-producing elite—who colluded with municipal officials, the military, and the Crown to ensure the production of farinha da terra and its distribution from the captaincy of Ilhéus to Salvador, center of sugar production.[133] Some planters resisted. Antônio de Couros Carneiro, the wealthiest planter and captain-major of the Ilheús, had been forced to centralize production of farinha and its distribution to Bahia. It was shipped from the 1640s at his expense. He had been initially supportive of extra military protection, but this came at a cost. The garrison would also ensure the regular and timely delivery of farinha from Ilheús to Bahia, for which Carneiro received delayed or no compensation.[134]

As the Luso–Dutch war for Brazil dragged on through its second decade, the biggest battle, wrote Duarte de Albuquerque Coelho, "was against hunger," noting that it "was felt by all." He was referencing the 1635 fall of the Bom Jesus, but he might as well have predicted the next nearly twenty years too.[135] Soldiers not only engaged in food warfare—emptying enemy storehouses, blockading besieged towns, burning fields and ships of food—but with starvation a near daily threat, they switched to the other side as warranted. Inconsistent Spanish and Portuguese support prior to and just after the restoration of Portugal led to unexpected opportunities to wage war against the Dutch and the incentives to do so. Enterprising merchants, engenho owners, and former soldiers stepped up to sustain the troops. They would petition, as they were able, for their own material sustenance: compensated funds or at the very least some sort of acknowledgement.

The 1635 loss of the Forte Real do Bom Jesus and the long march south to Bahia led, within a decade, to a reckoning in recruitment and provisioning. Transatlantic supply lines, never a sure bet given the Dutch blockade of the northeast coast, waned in the context of the 1640 restoration. Now Portugal waged a two-front war at home and abroad—with Spanish troops at the border and the Dutch in the South Atlantic. Since then, the recruitment of soldiers from the Atlantic islands, as well as the formation of local militias, indicates strategic decision-making that went beyond hunkering down in royal forts and eating down supplies. The strain led to coalescing and increasingly independent on-the-ground efforts, and an emergent Luso-Brazilian identity centered on food. For this reason, manioc flour now has a privileged place at the Pernambucan table and is known as a food of resistance, inseparable from the Luso–Dutch conflict and indispensable in victory.[136]

CHAPTER SIX

"All Men Have Death in Common"

Restoration, Coordination, and Conflict

WHEN THE FORTY CONSPIRATORS stormed Lisbon's Ribeira Palace, ending six decades of Spanish rule, they were likely unaware of the transatlantic ripples they set in motion. But the December 1, 1640, actions of *os conjurados*, as they came to be known, were met immediately with popular approval: a mob outside the palace relished the defenestration of Miguel de Vasconcelos, pouncing on Philip IV's secretary of state when he was tossed their way. The Portuguese *povo*, long resentful of funding and fighting Spain's multi-front wars, then got in their punches. And so the insurrectionists rode a wild wave of unrest to action. With Dom João IV, the eighth Duke of Braganza, now set to claim the throne, an end to the Luso–Dutch Atlantic war seemed at hand—and with it a reshaping of Iberian–American ventures.

By land and by sea, Luso–Spanish exchange within the Americas had spurred, since the century prior, the trade of silver for slaves. This attracted attention from the Dutch, who sought access to Peruvian silver, Brazilian "white gold," (sugar) and African labor to produce both. Joris van Spilbergen's 1614 route around South America hints at Dutch American ambition: he stopped over in São Vicente, sailed through the Straits of Magellan, and then lurked briefly in Arica—an entrepôt for Potosí silver. As he and his men "found no ships or galleons for shipping silver," they then set back out for sea.[1] Sixteen years later, the Dutch West India Company's Grand Design (Groot Desseyn) set into motion war extending from northeastern Brazil to Angola. By 1641 Dutch soldiers had marched into and seized the northern captaincy of

Maranhão, as well as Portuguese-held Luanda, Benguela, and São Tomé. For access to silver and slave markets, the Dutch and the Portuguese also considered seizing Spanish claims—most notably Buenos Aires.[2]

An independent Portugal offered tepid support to its South Atlantic colonies. Waning enthusiasm for the colony aside, the beleaguered kingdom now faced a Spanish challenge on the border. The new king would launch no rescue armadas to Brazil, aiming instead to defend Portugal from invasion and collapse. At any rate, only the first rescue attempt against the Dutch—the 1625 Luso-Spanish "voyage of the vassals" for Bahia—had succeeded. Like his ousted Spanish predecessor, restored king Dom João IV raised taxes to fund the war effort. This was met without protest; with war at his doorstep, Dom João diverted resources closer to home.

The regime change stoked Iberian tensions abroad. Across the Atlantic, Portuguese *capa e espada*—military aristocrats—negotiated new terrain, wending through divided interests and loyalties. When his wife and sons fled across the Portuguese border to Madrid, the viceroy of Brazil, Dom Jorge de Mascarenhas, was recalled from his new post in Bahia and replaced by one of the conjurados. Accused of treason, he was shipped to Lisbon in chains. But Salvador de Sá, son of a Spaniard and married to a Spanish woman, managed to evade this fate. A *peruleiro*, or merchant engaged in Peru-based commerce, Sá amassed riches in Potosí; grandson of the third governor-general of Brazil and son of the governor-general of Rio de Janeiro, he had also earned praise for participating in the 1625 reconquest of Bahia. With the restoration of Portugal, a once "unified," now divided South America meant for Sá an orientation that would eventually turn east—away from Spanish silver. His Iberian American connections mostly severed, his focus now shifted as he pursued the reconquest of Angola. His success there helped turn his fortunes solidly to Brazil.

Through the 1640s, a mostly untethered Luso-Brazilian resistance coordinated a different sort of restoration: Portuguese rule to the Brazilian northeast and in West Africa. For Portugal, independence meant the very real threat of Spanish invasion and, with it, diminished aid to Dutch-challenged Brazil. Across the Atlantic, the restoration of Portugal prompted Castilians and Portuguese to take sides and at least partially unwind mutual interests. In Brazil, Luso-Brazilian peruleiros and planters, driven by a mutual demand for forced labor, collided and colluded to reconquer Angola and oust the Dutch. The restoration of Portugal would prompt a new Luso-Brazilian reaction to the Dutch, as backlands resistance became transatlantic battle.

The Restoration of Portugal

In October 1640, at the far end of the Almada palace gardens, anti-Madrid conspirators plotted the overthrow of Spanish rule. Lesser nobility who bore the brunt of Philippine demands, they protested, among other abuses, Spanish indifference to the Dutch conquests in Brazil—except as an excuse to further raise taxes. By late fall, the men determined to install Dom Joaõ, the eighth Duke of Braganza, as rightful king of Portugal. The duke was, after all, directly descended from Catharine of Braganza, heir to the throne after the untimely death of Dom Sebastião; by dint of gender, she had been forced to cede power to Philip II of Spain.[3] Sixty years later, aware of a threat against Spanish rule, Phillip IV's valido Count-Duke Olivares summoned Dom João to Madrid.[4] The latter demurred and remained in his rural estate. Meanwhile, in Lisbon, fellow conjurados gathered through the fall to determine how best to execute their plan.

The conspirators appreciated public sentiment against the Spanish but also understood that Portuguese elite remained largely loyal to Philip IV. From the inception of Philippine rule in 1580, the first Spanish king of Portugal offered incentives to guarantee Luso loyalty. This process began with the acclamation of Philip I of Portugal (II of Spain) at Tomar, where he guaranteed privileges for the elite class, access to Spanish markets, and continued Portuguese control of their overseas colonies.[5] For this reason, the conspirators kept their numbers small and meetings secret; they understood the enemy from within—like the Portuguese secretary of state to Spain, Miguel de Vasconcelos. But the middle nobility, including the conspirators, chafed at increasing pressure to round up recruits for Spain's wars. Ongoing conflicts also weighed on the working class of Portugal, responsible for the heaviest burden of taxes to finance the continental and overseas war against the Dutch.

So at nine in the morning on December 1, 1640, with Philip IV's troops away confronting rebellion in Catalonia, the conspirators scaled the fence from the

Almada Gardens to the Ribeira Palace. Some might have even found their way in through an underground tunnel. They first tracked down Miguel de Vasconcelos, who was hiding in a closet. He was shot on-site, his body then tossed out the window to the mob below. By now a large crowd had gathered at the Paço da Terreiro, Lisbon's largest plaza.[6] By the end of the day, the conjurados had imprisoned Margaret of Savoy, cousin to Philip IV and vicereine of Portugal. The Rio Tejo continued to flow, as it ever had, past the Paço da Terreiro into the Atlantic, but the landscape had changed. Now crowds packed the plaza, cheering the ouster of the Spanish and the conspirators, one of whom hoisted high the flag of Lisbon.[7]

The unexpected news of a Portuguese king spread quickly—at least through Lisbon. The Duke of Braganza, ensconced in Villa Viçosa, did not make it to the city that fateful day; indeed, he would "change nothing of the Duke of Braganza by being the King of Portugal," ever preferring hunting and music to regnal concerns.[8] Still, Dom João IV consolidated his position over the next few weeks. He left for Lisbon on the third of December, first taking up residence in Ribeira Palace as citywide Masses and celebrations took place. Within two weeks, the eighth Duke of Braganza was crowned king; it took another seven days for the word of his acclamation to reach Braga, Portugal's northernmost town.

Recovering Brazil from the Dutch was no immediate priority for the kingdom. Now Portugal girded for war against an old enemy, Spain. At the end of January, after securing the succession of his children to the crown, João IV turned to domestic matters, which ranged from the shortage of bread to the threat of Spanish reconquest.[9] In a departure from his Spanish predecessor Philip IV, the Portuguese king did not bid the municipal council of Lisbon for aid to liberate Brazil. Neither did he indicate much concern to the council regarding Dutch conquest or the Netherlanders overrunning and seizing both Maranhão and Angola later that year. He offered no explanatory defense when raising taxes, which he did within half a year. The Casa de Vinte e Quatro approved his hike of an extra five *reis* on meat and wine; this passed to the people without much drama, given the guilds' consent.[10] The three estates also agreed to substantial funding—1.8 million cruzados over three years—for an army of twenty thousand soldiers, four hundred horses, and further recruitment of men for the conflicts ahead.[11]

By 1642 the court of Dom João IV had created the Conselho Ultramarino (Overseas Council), streamlining administration over colonial claims. This included Dutch-contested Brazil. Nearly half a century prior, the Spanish-created Conselho da India (Council of Indies), tending to Portuguese colonial claims, had for a short time at least wielded enormous power—even as it collided with three long-running Portuguese institutions. From 1604 to 1614 it coexisted with and ultimately caved to the High Court (Desembargo do Paço); the Board of Conscience and Orders (Mesa da Consciência e Ordens); and the Council of Treasury (Conselho da Fazenda).[12] Though the council's functions were later absorbed by those three competitor bodies, the Spanish approach—greater oversight over the Americas and Portuguese overseas claims—lay the foundation for future such efforts after restoration. Dom João and his cabinet first created the Council of War (Conselho da Guerra) in preparation for hostilities against Spain, and, by 1642, the Overseas Council (Conselho Ultramarino).[13] Though the Council of War, designed to manage military concerns at home and abroad, originally oversaw the provisioning of men and supplies, administrative turf wars meant the Conselho Ultramarino would oversee matters in Brazil.[14] The royal resolutions also affirmed that anyone who could raise a company of men and head to Brazil was under the jurisdiction of the Overseas Council but that those who went with the armada would be controlled by the War Council.

For the Portuguese, centuries-old habits and networks of exchange bound social networks connecting the military elite. The newly formed Overseas Council, comprised of a one-to-two ratio of *letrados* and former military men, included more than a few, such as Salvador de Sá and Jorge Mascarenhas, who had fought against the Dutch.[15] The latter, after pleading his case and being released from prison, joined the Overseas Council. For his experience abroad, he would also serve as council president, adding special weight to descriptions of game-changing battles.[16] Yet ever under suspicion thanks to his Madrid-based family, Mascarenhas would be imprisoned at least three times.[17] None of that mattered in 1643 when the newly formed council met to discuss Brazil. From Lisbon, the council members considered support for the colony, a potential attack on Buenos Aires, and a reconquest of Angola. But in the end, recruitment and funding for the Brazil-based ventures would come from Luso-Brazilian planters and peruleiros.

Divided America: Closing the Iberian Border

The Portuguese rebellion of December 1, 1640, so upset Madrid that all public talk of it there was prohibited on pain of death. This was the first, and for a few weeks only, decisive Spanish action on the matter. The disaster at Downs (1639) and the Catalan revolt (June 1640) paled by comparison; a sleepless Count of Olivares did little more at first than sift through the worst news of his tenure.[18] The empire now stood to lose its Portuguese colonies abroad—and anywhere with a strong Lusophone presence. For a short time at least, inaction was the order of the day.

The Portuguese high elite had profited from the union of the Iberian crowns—and were ready to swear fealty once again. They included the sons of Brazil's viceroy, Dom Jorge Mascarenhas, who had sailed to Spain under cover of night.[19] In the metropole, Olivares tasked them with keeping the faith. They were so effective that across the border, and for the next twenty years, Portuguese loyalists would quell anti-Braganza conspiracies.[20]

Oceans away, the news soon filtered to Spanish America, where—given the ubiquitous Portuguese presence—the consequences for Philip IV ran especially deep. From Potosí to Guanajuato, 80 percent of the world's silver flowed around the globe. It was this trade, since 1550, that had laid the fiscal foundation of the Spanish Empire.[21] Despite restrictions on "gypsies and Portuguese," the incentive for transcontinental exchange was strong.[22] The exchange of silver for enslaved persons benefited those who split liege loyalty for profit. In the late sixteenth century, merchants, muleteers, and other Portuguese men contributed to the burgeoning trade and cross-boundary exchange; even the bishop of Tucumán, Dom Francisco de Vitória, sent silver to Brazil in exchange for slaves.

The Iberian union had encouraged trans-imperial exchange in the Americas, a process not easily undone.[23] In the 1630s, English merchants sailing from Cadiz noted that Spanish America needed an inflow of twenty-two thousand enslaved Angolans to survive and that this fell to the Portuguese, who held the bulk of *asientos*, or permissions for this trade.[24] Through the early seventeenth century, peruleiro interest—including that of the Sá family—intensified around the exchange of Angolans for silver. Salvador de Sá's father, Martim de Sá, had set out to search for mines in Rio Grande as early as 1619.[25]

Padre Almeida, Sá's confessor, had urged him on to Spanish America years later—the same year the Dutch invaded Recife. In 1630, with the priest's blessing, Sá journeyed from Rio de Janeiro to Rio de la Plata to Peru. As northeastern Brazil fell to the Dutch, Sá fought battles in Spanish America and made his own conquests there too. Within years, he became one of the richest men in Tucumán, making a fortune through marriage and mining.[26] In 1635, when the Luso-Spanish-Brazilian army, defeated by the Dutch, withdrew from Pernambuco and streamed south to Bahia, Sá reversed course and returned to Rio de Janeiro. He received the governorship of the captaincy but did not relinquish his peruleiro plans. Silver—obtained by the sale of African captives—financed the war efforts, as he would later point out to the Portuguese king.

On January 10, 1641, Madrid ordered sealed the borders between Portugal and its colonies; intra-imperial Iberian commerce was to come to a halt.[27] By the late 1630s, reassignments of minor Portuguese officials from Spanish port cities to the interior had actually anticipated Portugal's break, but the news of Portugal's revolt, when it reached Cartagena, caught Iberian officials, soldiers, and merchants off-guard.[28] After the Count of Torres's armada had failed in January 1640 to oust the Dutch from Brazil, Spanish and Portuguese commanders Juan Vega Bazán and Francisco Dias Pimentel sailed to Cartagena with fifteen hundred men. Within a year, Spanish concern about the mostly Portuguese men quartering in one of their most important American ports proved well founded. The Portuguese slave trafficker João Paes de Carvalho, held for questioning, was found bearing instructions from Lisbon for one of the captains: Rodrigo Lobo was to sail to the Azores with most of the fleet.[29]

Dias Pimentel and other Portuguese elite who expressed fealty to Spain received regnal approbation, but unexpected incomers were met with suspicion. In August 1641, the second Count of Castelo Melhor, João Rodrigues de Vasconcelos, was detained soon after arriving from Brazil. Officials accused him of planning to instigate revolt and to abscond with a Spanish silver ship. Once again, Rodrigo Lobo appeared as a person of interest in the apprehended papers. The count denied the charge but was imprisoned. He was freed, ironically, by Dutch corsairs who whisked him to Portugal. It was then, in 1642, that the rest of the Portuguese armada and its crew, which had been sequestered in Cartagena, were sent to Cadiz—under the command of Dias Pimentel, who remained resolutely loyal to Madrid.[30]

In Brazil, Madrid-appointed Portuguese officials also faced suspicion. "All men have death in common," mused Dom Fernando Mascarenhas, the Count of Torre, "distinguished only by those whose memory live forever."[31] Torres had anticipated, perhaps, that his own fortune was sunk. Until 1640 the Count of Torre had led a long and distinguished overseas career. Named governor-general of Brazil in 1637, he would command the largest armada ever to cross the Atlantic, the last Luso–Spanish rescue attempt to oust the Dutch from the Brazilian northeast. Torres's five-day naval battle against the Dutch—a draw off the coast of Recife—proved remarkable only for the twelve hundred reinforcements disembarked—too far south of his target to make a difference. Within half a year, Torres would be replaced by his uncle Dom Jorge de Mascarenhas, the Marquis de Montalvão. Torres was then imprisoned, sent on to Lisbon, and remembered mostly—or only—as an example of dilatory folly. Soon after Portugal's independence from Spain, his uncle too would be sent back in chains.[32]

The post-restoration willingness of Portuguese governors in Angola to gain goods for moradores (settlers) kept strong the Spanish silver-for-slaves trade. Direct commerce between Spain and Portugal may have been prohibited, but colonial "governors closed their eyes": Cartagena, Buenos Aires, and Vera Cruz continued to receive and exchange captives for silver.[33] From the early 1640s, peruleiro and governor of Rio de Janeiro Salvador de Sá sent his own ships to Angola and back for the purpose of trafficking Africans through the Rio de la Plata route to Peru—though with little success. He was also accused of misappropriating treasury funds for his personal use and gain in Rio de la Plata.[34] One commissioned such venture resulted in the Spanish capture of two ships; the governor of Buenos Aires imprisoned the captain, priest, and crew and then sent them all on to Chile. When the captain of the other ship dared asked that his eighty captives on board be released to him, he was put to death.[35]

From 1641 on, with or without asientos, Spanish merchants purchased captives from all European-controlled American ports—including those commanded by the Portuguese.[36] The demand for labor remained high. In New Spain, the enslaved worked not only in the silver mines but also in agriculture, given strong export demand for cacao.[37] During the union of the crowns, up to 60 percent of enslaved persons in the Americas were in fact sent to Spanish America—many transported from the Rio de la Plata region through riverine routes and overland—via Portuguese, Dutch, English, and French who obtained asiento. Indigenous resistance, as well as the end of the *encomienda* and requerimento systems, prompted increased human trafficking from Africa. Most of the captives disembarked at Rio de Janeiro and (before the Dutch era) Pernambuco, Bahia, and Buenos Aires.[38]

A June 1641 earthquake nearly leveled Caracas, but with the restoration of Portugal, another threat emerged: a severe labor shortage.[39] The town had evolved from a small community of mostly *encomenderos* to a thriving urban center built on the trade of cacao for African captives. As the Portuguese had held the bulk of asientos, the end of the Iberian union threatened not only unrest but also the end of a steady supply of forced labor—whether in mines or in agricultural work. In Madrid, enterprising merchants sprung to action. That December, for instance, Simão Peres Soares sought royal dispensation to send a ship to Angola. This would shore up loyalty for Spain, he proposed, and he could pick up and ship much-needed captives to the colonies.[40] The Council of Indies delayed on the decision, eventually assenting to Soares's suggestion. It was too late: by mid-April 1641, Luso-leaning subjects in Luanda had declared for Dom João IV and Portugal.[41]

Dutch and Portuguese belligerents viewed Brazil and Angola as one field of battle—and taken together, a sure route to riches.[42] Claiming Angola meant guaranteeing labor for Brazilian sugar mills and Spanish silver mines. Brazil had also served Spain as a buffer from its silver-minded competitors, including and especially the Dutch. In 1637, on the initiative of Governor-General Johan Maurits, the Company captured the West African Portuguese-held fort of Elmina; by 1641 his troops had gained São Paulo of Luanda in Angola too. By 1643 he had sent an expedition to establish an outpost in Chile; this proved unsuccessful. Still, laying claim to Portuguese-controlled slaving posts, noted a Dutch-favoring Englishman, would rake in much-needed profit for the WIC, "and I doe not doubt but the company shall bee furnished from thence with all sorts of commodities."[43]

After conquest in Angola, Johan Maurits offered the Dutch West India Company directors an apologia of sorts for his undirected action. Noting the confusion—and opportunity—wrought by the "revolt of Portugal against Spain," he had decided it was vital to attack the city of Sao Paulo of Luanda: "The moment we gain control of the commerce of blacks not only would our [labor] difficulties cease . . . and the loss of traffic in Negros would hurt . . . the Spanish as much, as they cannot employ the Indians to such work [as done by

Africans] in the exploration of mines and silver in Peru, and this could cause a severe loss in wealth in New Spain." At any rate, he argued, well aware that the independence of Portugal from Spain meant a Luso–Dutch truce, he "didn't know if Angola was for Spain or Portugal."[44]

Overland trans-American trade, grooved in during and after the Iberian union, helped stem the Dutch advance and fund Luso-Brazilian efforts for Brazil. By 1643, the peruleiro Salvador de Sá, now governor-general of Rio de Janeiro, proposed to the War Council a takeover of Buenos Aires; in this way the Portuguese could secure the silver-for-enslaved Africans exchange.[45] Five years later, Jesuit padre António Vieira ventured a similar scheme, suggesting the conquest of the Rio de la Plata region to ensure a steady supply of bullion; he noted that the route from Rio de la Plata to Potosí, while precarious, was nonetheless faster. Weather depending, this route was also more reliable than maritime voyages from Rio or Bahia to Cartagena or Callao, as currents and climate routinely steered ships off their mark.[46]

Divided Loyalties, Common Interests: Soldiers, *Peruleiros* and Planters

When the Dutch attacked Recife in 1630, commander Pernambuco Matias de Albuquerque mused on Netherlandish motivation, noting that without Brazil, Spain was on its heels. The Dutch revolt against its old enemy—manifesting in the Grand Design on Brazil and the South Atlantic—would now play out in the second-richest sugar-producing captaincy in the colony. Absent a Portuguese buffer, the Spanish Empire could lose control of the West Indies and "most of its [maritime] navigational ability" toward the viceroyalty of Peru—cutting off access to its silver mines and ships.[47] So the news of restoration, when it reached Brazil at the end of January 1641, stunned Iberian officials into confusion.[48] With Portugal no longer bound to Spain, was the war against the Dutch now over?

Word of the restored Braganza king filtered out, at first, to an uncertain reception. After his ship dropped anchor in in the Bay of All Saints, the Jesuit priest Francisco e Vilhena came ashore to deliver the report directly to Dom Jorge de Mascarenhas, the Marquis de Montalvão. As viceroy of Brazil and longtime administrator for Philip IV of Spain, Mascarenhas had served the

Spanish crown since his youth; his distinguished domestic and overseas career began when he became comptroller of the Portuguese royal household in 1602 and peaked in his 1639 appointment as viceroy of Brazil, a position newly created just for him.[49] Unsure of the next move, he counseled caution, as "the king of Spain was the king of Portugal and had much power to make extraordinary punishments on those who were traitors."[50] But Mascarenhas then acknowledged Dom João IV and shared the news with the heads of four religious orders and municipal officials. He next debriefed the military, ordering Neapolitans and Spanish soldiers disarmed. Most were sent back to Europe, but about seventy Neapolitans and Spanish swore loyalty to the Portuguese. Opting to stay on and fight for the Portuguese against the Dutch, they were sent to Pernambuco for a direct attack on Dutch Brazil.[51]

In war-torn Brazil, the restoration of the Portuguese monarchy prompted jubilation. Upon hearing the news in Bahia, the field master raised his sword and cried, "We have our king of Portugal and this is Dom João, duke of Braganza, to whom the legitimate right of the kingdom belongs!" Others joined in, shouting "Viva king Dom João of Portugal"—including Viceroy Mascarenhas, anxious to demonstrate his fealty to the Crown. The refrain of "Viva Dom João!" rang out through Salvador. After a celebratory Mass at the nearby Church of Sé, the moradores thanked God for having given the Portuguese, at long last, their king, "and what a king!" The viceroy ordered celebratory blasts from the city's forts and from ships anchored in the bay. At nightfall, residents put lights in their windows and doors. They celebrated all through the next day.[52]

The governor of Bahia sent letters to Recife, capital of Dutch-held Brazil. These Governor-General Johan Maurits received "with great friendship," celebrating in his customary expansive style; even the horses were decked out for the occasion.[53] With a truce on the horizon, festivities continued in Dutch Brazil through the month of April, and Maurits set up a number of jousting and other games; he hosted the performance of a French comedy, delivered "with much ostentation." Together, both Portuguese and Dutch West India Company troops indulged in a monthlong celebration.[54]

Those who had openly and loyally served the Spanish—like Viceroy Mascarenhas—had less reason to celebrate. Salvador de Sá, now governor of Rio de Janeiro, was in church when he received word. Like Mascarenhas, he expressed hesitation.⁵⁵ The son of a Spaniard and part of a third generation of leaders in Rio de Janeiro, he had enjoyed—as had his father and grandfather before him—great prestige in Madrid. He stood more to lose than his influence, however, as he was now cut off from his vast interests in Potosí.⁵⁶ Yet Sá carried on his duties, next sending word to the unpredictable, conflict-ridden captaincy of São Vicente.⁵⁷ There the king was acclaimed quickly, though the interior capital—also São Vicente—proved less receptive to Dom João IV. This town, largely populated by Castilians since 1583, had maintained strong commercial ties with Paraguay and connections to Potosí. It refused to accept a Portuguese king, instead electing Amador Bueno, son of Sevillian-born colonialist and member of the local elite, to lead them. (Bueno declined, declaring loyalty to Braganza rule.) The Indigenous-hunting Paulistas had crossed Philip IV in 1640; now the captaincy's recent division between São Vicente and Itanhaém—and with it the expulsion of Portugal's Countess of Vimeira as donatary—proved problematic.⁵⁸ Intra-captaincy dissent was evident even in 1639, when unknown Sebastianists disseminated writings that claimed King Sebastian would return as the rightful king of Portugal. They also declared that the pope would excommunicate anyone who took up arms against them. Two Jesuits were accused of the deed and expelled from the captaincy. This stoked conflict between two great families of São Vicente, the Pires (Portuguese) and the Camargos (Castilians), which threatened to tear the captaincy apart. In the end, Dom João IV was acclaimed in São Vicente by April 13, 1641—but by far fewer elite than those who had voted to expel the Jesuits.⁵⁹

At last, with São Vicente rounding out captaincy congratulations, the Marquis of Montalvão, Dom Jorge de Mascarenhas, sent his son Fernandes to Lisbon to assure the king of Brazil's support. Montalvão was on shaky ground. His wife and other children, residing in Lisbon during the coup, had fled to Madrid; once in Portugal, Fernandes was nearly lynched by an irate mob. But on the same ship as Montalvão's son, Fathers António Vieira and Simão Vasconcellos rounded out the celebratory convoy sailing east for the acclamation of Dom João IV.⁶⁰ In the millenarian milieu of the seventeenth century, the Jesuits claimed that the Braganza monarch was the *real* returned king, on the throne to restore Portugal to greatness. Vieira took seriously his own role as God's representative. He claimed to serve the Portuguese monarch (and by extension, Portugal), as God's sovereign on earth.⁶¹ Thus the Jesuits went beyond congratulations, helping lay down textual and oral validation of King João IV. Vieira gained the new king's confidence, eventually serving in the capacity of personal adviser and diplomat.

Delivering news of restoration to Portuguese claims proved a fraught undertaking elsewhere, given the potential for conflict between Castilian and Luso troops and with it the prospect of further loss for the Portuguese.[62] In mid-December, the treasury suggested that Dom João send word to the Atlantic islands so vital to the kingdom; Madeira, Cabo Verde, the Azores, and São Tomé routinely provisioned vessels for the Atlantic crossing and also served, for the Portuguese, as a proven source of recruitment.[63]

Atlantic island reception of the king proved uncertain at best. The Pernambucan governor of Cabo Verde welcomed the report, but he had more to celebrate than his Castilian peer based in the Azores. When Captain-Major Francisco de Ornelas Câmara sailed to his native Azores on December 21, he delivered the news of restoration first to the largest island, Terceira. There he offered to the Spanish commander, Don Ávarão de Viveiros, great honors should he submit fully to the Braganza king. In response, Viveiros sequestered himself in the main fort, waiting for a rescue armada from Spain. The armada never materialized. The Portuguese cause had more traction on the island of São Miguel, populated as it was with far fewer Castilians. Madeira residents proved receptive to the news; they had already been alerted to the acclamation by an English ship out of Sevilla. A royal letter addressed to Madeirenses arrived on January 9, 1641; the residents hailed João as their king just two days later.[64] For the most part, non-Portuguese soldiers were disarmed and sent packing to the Canary Islands.

Resounding support in Angola for Dom João IV did little to fend off a Dutch attack. In August 1641, smarting from yet another failed attempt to take Bahia, Johan Maurits sent an expedition to claim Luanda. "Without [African] slaves, nothing will get done," he complained to Dutch West India Company officials.[65] By August 26, 1641, the Dutch had seized Luanda, next capturing Benguela, Axim, and São Tomé.

Losing Luanda to the Dutch caused severe consternation among Portuguese priests, planters, and peruleiros. Without a dependable supply of forced labor, Brazil—and by extension Portugal—would not be able to finance and sustain the war against the Dutch. More broadly, the whole Portuguese

American colonial enterprise was now at risk. "Brazil cried out at this sorrow," wrote Father Simão de Vasconcellos, out of "brotherhood" with Angola. The resulting damage caused by the Dutch, he wrote, "to human eyes seemed irreparable." Now the commerce in captives was lost. "And while these two states cried, our Portugal could hardly laugh, as on one, and the other, depended so much."[66]

From Bahia, the governor-general of Brazil, António Teles da Silva, warned Dom João IV in 1643 that "without [Angola] Your Majesty does not have Brazil, because settlers will lose heart without slaves or the sugar mills, [and] will dismantle them." He then drove home his point: "And Your Majesty's Customs will lose the rights on their sugars."[67] The urgency to restore Angola was real. As early as February 1641, slavers had petitioned for and received authorization to carry on trade for silver with the Castilian Indies. With this access now restricted, funds brought in by the sugar trade took on greater importance, but both planters and peruleiros needed slave labor out of Africa to get the job done. Above all else, the reconquest of Angola was needed to defeat the Dutch in Brazil; and in Lisbon, the direct link between sustaining a colony in Brazil and Angolan captives was made clear.[68]

It would take more than prayers and handwringing to restore the Portuguese in West Africa and, with this, control of the slave trade to the Americas. Bahia, in its continued—and successful—resistance to the Dutch, remained the central coordination point in the enduring war. Inter-captaincy conflict soon surfaced.[69] António Teles da Silva, one of the Forty Conspirators who had placed the Duke of Braganza on the throne, had replaced the Marquis de Montalvão as governor-general of Brazil. There was no love lost between him and another former Madrid loyalist—Salvador de Sá. Teles da Silva supported the planters and strategized against the Dutch, while Sá pitched his own plans to Dom João IV and had his sights set farther east.[70]

The War and Overseas Councils finally considered the problem of Angola in 1643.[71] That same year, Sá made his case to the king in person, shaping an approach based on his peruleiro experience. Without slaves, he reasoned, it was "largely difficult to relaunch the Rio de Janeiro–Buenos Aires exchange" for silver. In this way, he highlighted the importance of the Peruvian trade, the need to control the region, and, with it, access to the mines of Potosí. The Overseas Council decided that the South Atlantic solution rested on the reconquest of Angola, demurring from Sá's other suggestion: an outright attack on the Rio de la Plata region.[72]

Crown and council agreed to reconquer Angola but punted on provisioning and recruitment—to severe consequences for the mission. In 1644, as the Spanish–Portuguese border Battle of Montijito drew resources and men, Lisbon had more immediate concerns. In the reconquest of Angola, men and materiel would have to be supplied out of Brazil, which needed slaves to survive, reasoned Crown attorney and the Royal Treasury's Fernão de Matos de Carvalhoso—skirting the fact that Portugal's fortunes were tied to this enterprise as well. He suggested that Rio de Janeiro serve as central command for provisioning and recruitment, with nearby captaincies lending help as needed. However, Sá planned to put the burden on Bahia, São Vicente, and their Indigenous troops. In 1644 ships sailed from both Bahia and Rio de Janeiro for this first, most unsuccessful reconquest. From the Bahian fleet, one column of 107 soldiers was nearly wiped out by the Jaga; only four men survived. From Rio, Sá's appointed commander, Francisco Souto Maior, was not successful either, though his forces managed to load two thousand captives on five slave-trading ships and head back to Rio de Janeiro.[73]

As the war in Brazil carried on, a disastrous battle at Tamandaré lay bare inter-captaincy—and interpersonal—concerns. In mid-1645, governor-general António Teles da Silva sent two Portuguese regiments to Dutch-held Recife as an offer of assistance against Luso insurgents threatening the colony. To recapture Pernambuco, he had strategized a one-two punch in Recife: the planters and guerrilla fighters would rise up in the backlands, and commander Jerônimo Serrão de Paiva would lead the naval attack on the Dutch-held captaincy. António Teles da Silva now ordered Sá to distract the Dutch and lend naval support in Recife. This he protested; his ships were no match for the Dutch West India Company fleet. Sá weighed anchor for a few days and then decided against confronting the Dutch navy. He proceeded to Lisbon, leaving Serrão de Paiva to fend for himself.[74] Paiva's men landed south of Recife, in Tamandaré, but without Sá's support, the August 1645 uprising meant that the "Divine War of Liberty" proved less than inspired. The sixteen caravels under Paiva's command may have successfully disembarked Portuguese troops, but the entire fleet was destroyed.

With land victories at Mount Tabocas and Casa Forte (1645), Lusophone

Atlantic coordination against the Netherlanders yet seemed possible. Sá, now in Lisbon and serving on the Overseas Council, applied but was rejected for the vacant governorship in Macao. Dom João IV turned him down—perhaps due to his Spanish background and abiding interest in the silver trade.[75] His actions at Tamandaré notwithstanding, Sá instead received his letters patent as governor-general of Angola and began preparations for reconquest.[76] Yet despite agreement on the importance of the mission and evidence that the 1644 mission to Angola had failed for want of support, Sá was unable to muster much help. So early in 1648 he sailed from Lisbon to Rio de Janeiro and made ready for reconquest. From there he provided the resources and rallied support to the point that he was formally recognized as nearly single-handedly having organized the successful mission to retake Angola. Sá was granted in one swoop governorships of both Rio de Janeiro and Angola, as "your help," remarked the court, "was the most important that could have been sent."[77]

Restoring Angola, Shoring Up Brazil

Despite his long campaign to reclaim Angola, neither local support nor his own long experience helped Sá determine exactly when to embark on this next, critical phase of the war against the Dutch. He had waged a successful campaign to build and command a reconquest armada, but now the governor-general of Rio de Janeiro wavered as the hour of departure approached. The formidable West India Company fleet had made ready, months earlier, to cross the Atlantic and crush the Luso-Brazilian resistance and was now heading toward the Bay of All Saints. Defending the colonial capital seemed the most prudent and loyal course of action, but Sá's locally mustered men, some of whom had defended Bahia during the 1638 siege, were ready to head east. He was torn: retake Luanda or stay put and fight, just as the Dutch were cruising toward them? The success of both plans was needed to save Brazil.

The deciding factor to retake Angola, it seems, came from above—and through—Sá's personal confessor, Padre João d'Almeida. Any lingering doubts appeared erased by Almeida's encouragement—or rather explicit instructions— to set easterly course for Africa. In October 1647, six years after the Dutch had seized Angola, divine favor had indeed seemed to bless the voyage. The commander should depart on the feast day of St. Michael the Archangel, the priest urged, and further, Sá should take St. Michael as patron saint for the voyage.[78] Sà followed the priest's instructions and set sail. He made good on his promise to Almeida: after a token skirmish with Dutch West India Company troops manning the Luandan forts, Sá proved victorious. With the colony now in Portuguese hands, he erected a new Catholic church at St. Paul of Luanda.

Perhaps no region was more vital to Portuguese and Spanish America than Angola, but Sá's own plan to recapture the African west coast clashed with resistance leaders in Brazil, who directed attacks against the Dutch. Commander and planter João Fernandes Vieira fretted that Sá's attack on Angola would draw Spanish attention back to Brazil. But Sá pushed back, mustering troops in Rio, Bahia, and Angola. They were mostly Brazilian-born or -raised men, hardened by combat against the Dutch and driven by prospects wrought only by war. The reconquest of the colony would salvage not only Brazil—and by extension Portugal—but also the careers of Luso-Brazilians like Sá, caught between Lisbon and Madrid. His mission to reclaim Luanda and Portuguese Angola from the Dutch was not the first,[79] but the timing and nature of Sá's conquest of Angola for Brazil points to far-flung Luso-Brazilian social-commercial connections, including Jesuits who would spur him on.[80]

On August 16, 1648, seven years after the Netherlanders captured Luanda, the Portuguese proved victorious. In July 1648, less than a month after arriving off the coast of Angola, the Dutch surrendered. Benguela fell to them shortly thereafter, as did São Tomé. Dutch West India troops marched out and were sent packing, save for a handful of French Catholic soldiers and others who decided they would sign on with the Portuguese.[81] Within months, Sá's "first New World colonists' task force," sailing from Rio de Janeiro, had all but retaken their West African claims with fortuitous timing and relative ease.[82] With much of Angola controlled now by the Portuguese, the "Divine War of Liberty" in Pernambuco seemed more than violent prayer in action; now Portuguese reach re-extended across the South Atlantic (Map 2).

Notwithstanding a ban on intra-Iberian exchange, Dom João IV granted to select Spanish merchants the opportunity to enslave Congolese each year—in exchange for silver of course.[83] The bullion helped finance Portugal's conflicts until the Brazilian gold rush a few decades on. In 1654, the year of the Dutch surrender in Brazil, Dom João I approved the Overseas Council's suggestion

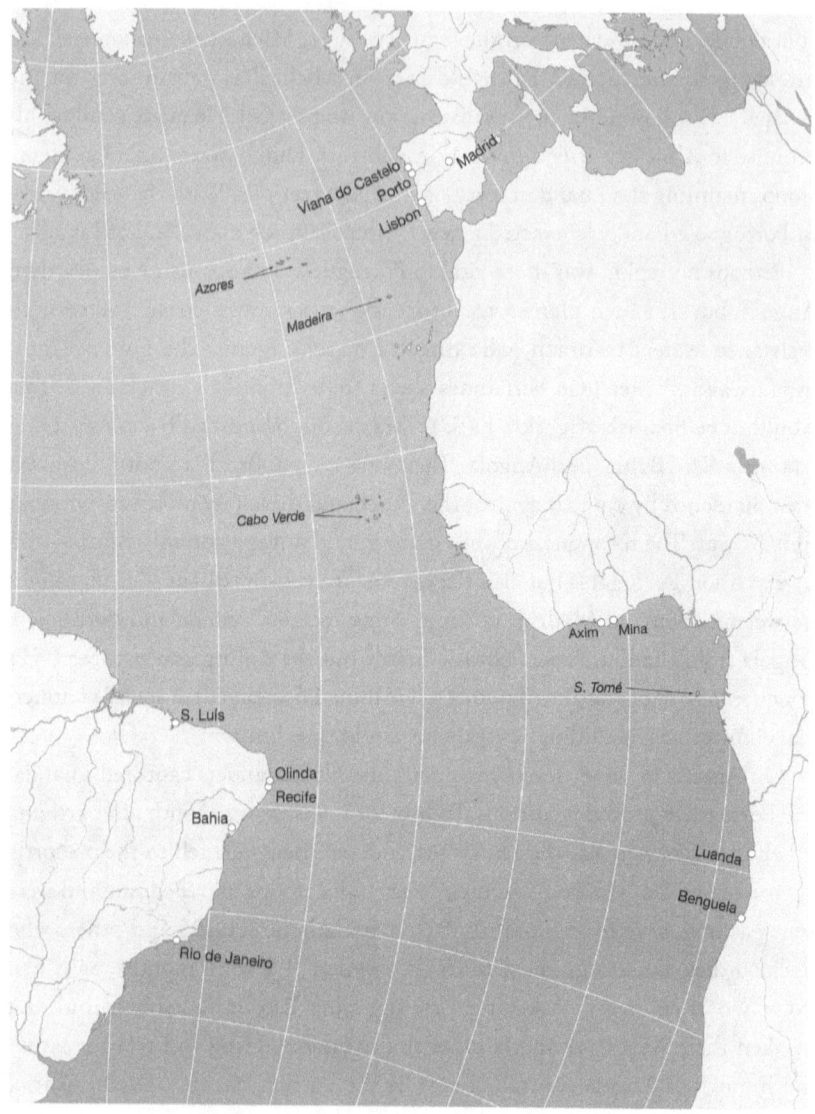

Map 2. The Portuguese Atlantic world, 1649. By Martin von Wyss, @mvw maps, © Suzanne Litrel, 2019.

that no more than two ships from Spain could be admitted in Angola at the same time; he still noted that without Spanish ships bringing jugs of wine, "there would be no commerce."[84] During his tenure in Angola, Governor Bartolomé de Vasconcelos de Cunha had received at least one ship from Puerto Rico and another from Havana. He hoped this would help open up Buenos Aires; in exchange for enslaved captives, the governor expected to have his own ships return from Rio de la Plata laden with silver.[85]

From Brazil, planters protested such Spanish involvement in Portuguese trade. João Fernandes Vieira, leader of the Pernambucan revolt and Recife's wealthiest planter, argued that African captives should not be sent to Spanish America—they should be shipped to Brazil. There they would work on engenhos, "which would result in the conservation of life, sustenance, and commerce of her moradores, and the importance to the exports and imports of this Reign."[86]

Luso-Brazilians may have had an edge in the market, however, engaging as they did in trade for captives with *zimbo*. "Fished" off the coast of Benguela, the cowrie shell was the "most tractable money" in circulation.[87] Beyond West Africa, traders from Brazil had best access to this shell, harvested as it was from select Bahian beaches. Dutch West India Company slavers were unable to trade in zimbo as Bahia—whose beaches yielded a rich harvest—remained outside the scope of their control. This practice began at the turn of the century and continued past restoration. Cowrie harvesting and distribution, by nature a challenge to assess, escaped taxation, frustrating Crown officials. By the end of the eighteenth century, Brazilian shells made up 94 percent of all zimbo imported to and circulating in Luanda.[88]

Reconquest and a Resistance "Personality"

Portugal's independence from Spain spurred Luso-Brazilians to mine resources at home, encouraging a new dynamic in crown–colony relations. The battle for Brazil would promote sugar production far south of Pernambuco—beyond Bahia to Rio de Janeiro, seat of the oligarchic Sá family. A decade after the dissolution of the dual crowns, Luso-Brazilian peruleiro interests shifted from silver to sugar. Salvador de Sá returned from his governorship in Angola

(1648–1652) with several hundred enslaved Africans. He then developed five sugar mills and forty cattle ranches. As governor of Rio de Janeiro in 1660–1661, he turned from mining to planting and expanded the captaincy's commercial agricultural prospects.[89]

Absent Crown support, from 1641, Luso-Brazilian planters, peruleiros, and transatlantic traders forced outcomes against the Dutch in Brazil and the South Atlantic. Sá's successful reconquest of Luanda and Benguela tipped the war solidly for the Portuguese. Rio de la Plata colonists still exchanged silver for Angolans—for whom Luso-Brazilians traded, in Luanda, for zimbo. This exchange helped fund the war effort. The last Dutch West India Company troops left Brazil in 1654, less than a decade after the Luso-Brazilian reconquest of Angola. There, as elsewhere in the South Atlantic, Luso-Brazilians started to "form their own personality" while shoring up an independent Portugal.[90] Their transatlantic actions, rooted in local and personal interests, hint at more than crown–colony concerns: they also point to regional rifts, fissures that would widen in the years to come.

CHAPTER SEVEN

Discourse, Diplomacy, and the Commercialization of War

IN THE SPRING OF 1643, Francisco de Sousa Coutinho, newly arrived Portuguese ambassador to the United Provinces, faced his erstwhile enemies in the Ridderzaal, or Knight's Hall, at The Hague (Figure 11). There—alone and in front of representatives from Amsterdam and Zeeland, majority holders of the Dutch East and West India Companies—the emissary braced for his reception. In theory, the States General ruled over the so-called Generality Lands, which now included northeastern Brazil, Angola, and Maranhão. But Sousa Coutinho had been deployed to end the Luso–Dutch war—however this could be achieved. A ratified truce to regain territory and cease hostilities had already failed, as Netherlanders continued to seize Portuguese global claims. A career diplomat, Sousa Coutinho was familiar with the emissarial approach of combining "noble lies with underlying truth." It was this discursive weapon he now deployed.[1]

"The judgement of men can be wrong," he began. "Forgive us if we have erred."[2] Francisco de Sousa Coutinho regretted that the Portuguese had ever tolerated the dual crown. The deep freeze of Dutch winter had eased to a tolerable cold, and he hoped for an interstate thaw too. Bridging a decades-long enmity, he stated that the Portuguese and the Dutch had suffered long enough at the hands of the Spanish.[3] For any shareholder who had given Andries Moerbeeck's *Motives to Take Brazil* a glance two decades prior, this was no small irony: at last, the Portuguese were embracing the Dutch over their old cousins, the Spanish. The ambassador now cast the Portuguese and the Dutch as brothers in arms, invoking a mutual hatred of Spain.[4] The decades-long conflict had

Figure 11. Bartholomeus van Bassen, *The Great Assembly of the States-General*, circa 1651, oil on panel and copper, 52 × 66 cm. Courtesy of the Rijksmuseum, The Hague.

disrupted trade, sent thousands to their deaths, and otherwise cost them all dear.

At home and abroad, early challenges to Braganza rule had prompted the creation of the War and Overseas Councils—and a network of emissaries, based in Paris, that unfurled across western Europe. The results were uneven. Over the next few years, as Sousa Coutinho parried Dutch diplomatic feints, representatives of restored Portugal sought political, economic, military, and cultural connections—and with these, allies against Spain wherever they could be found. In Portugal and across western Europe, this forced the strategic change. But Portuguese bibliophiles, religious leaders, and merchants—many in exile—negotiated liminal spaces. They mustered prestige and capital to help the Crown's cause in commerce and war. From 1641, Portugal's governing, diplomatic, and commercial agents worked to assure Brazil's restoration. Discursive attempts to end the Luso–Dutch Atlantic war fell short.

What on-the-ground action—on the continent and in Brazil—yielded results? In the colony, entrenched fighting carried on. By 1645 resistance against Dutch rule had erupted into open war. This forced metropole response. With the clear success of Luso-Brazilian action from 1648, the king authorized the charter of the Brazil General Company. Sousa Coutinho would withdraw from The Hague; from Portugal's ambassadorial headquarters in Paris, the Marquis de Niza packed up too. But behind-the-scenes efforts manifested, in 1649, in the Brazil General Company—an armed escort for the sugar fleet and an idea whose time had come. In Brazil and in Europe, unusual negotiations fostered renewed hope for Portugal and the near restoration, by 1654, of the kingdom and its Atlantic reach.

All the (Restored) King's Councils, All the King's Men

The December 1640 restoration of Braganza rule may have sparked festivities in Portuguese- and Dutch-held Brazil, but the king's first order of business, despite good overseas cheer, was to save his kingdom—all of it. Johan Maurits, governor-general of Dutch Brazil, would mark the restoration of Portugal with an extravagant, days-long celebration with future resistance leaders, including João Fernandes Vieira.[5]

The Portuguese had more immediate concerns. Besides quelling internal threats to Braganza rule, this involved protecting and reclaiming territory abroad.[6] In the metropole, the conspiracy of 1641, manifested by the church and recalcitrant nobles—stealth supporters of Madrid—unsettled even the most fervent Braganza devotees. Abroad, Dutch West India Company soldiers campaigned in Portuguese-held Angola, expanding WIC-held territory. Now the old belligerents appeared ready to parley, as Spain offered to unload Brazil to the Dutch. Such "peace talks," however, did little more than stir Portuguese ire.[7]

Within a week of acclamation, João "The Restorer" set to work, creating new councils and appointing to these his most trusted allies. The king now formed the Council of War to coordinate local, regional, and continental logistics. This group addressed military and related appointments for the war against the Spanish, a reach that would extend to the Portuguese Atlantic islands.

Appointees to this council and other plum assignments naturally included the Forty Conspirators—acknowledgements of deep loyalty and the king's continued favor. Weighty roles led to special opportunities. One such loyalist, António Teles da Silva, sat on this new council. In a continuing indication of regnal favor, he would also serve, by 1643, as governor-general of Brazil.[8]

Troop recalcitrance—an enduring problem—proved a challenge for the War Council, but the continuing conflict also meant opportunity for officers hardened in Dutch-challenged Brazil.[9] The tepid rewards of serving on the Spanish front mustered weak recruitment, best remedied by known war heroes like Pernambucan commander Matias de Albuquerque. Disgraced in 1635, Albuquerque had been imprisoned by the Spanish for his failure to contain the Dutch. He was now released for duty from the Castelo de São Jorge. Albuquerque's experience served him well—as did the faith placed in him by the Crown. He received not only a seat on the War Council but also a patent to lead the continental war against Spain. He succeeded, quickly mustering about six thousand troops; on May 26, 1644, he and his men took the border town of Montijo without a fight and carried on.[10] The king now awarded the once-jailed lieutenant governor of Pernambuco the title of Count of Alegrete, and he became known to the Portuguese as the "hero of two continents."

Dom João IV also authorized, in 1642, the creation of the Overseas Council to "recover what was lost in the past"—a vague mandate yet distinct from the War Council's mission of protecting the kingdom's borders.[11] At first the Overseas Council proved hardly distinguishable in structure from its short-lived predecessor, Madrid's own Indies Council (1604–1614). This institution, hampered by the entrenched Mesa da Consciência (Board of Conscience), the Desembargo do Paço (which oversaw the justice system), and the Conselho da Fazenda (Treasury Council), had lasted hardly more than a decade.[12] But while the Indies Council focused on the Carreira da Índia, or the India trade, the Atlantic-centric mission of the Braganza regime's Overseas Council focused on Portugal's most accessible and profitable colony: Brazil—and with it Angola.

Between the Council of War and the Overseas Council, overlapping spheres of influence and similar missions—preparing for war and recovering previously held ground—led to conflicts of power, authority, and scope. The resulting delays had consequences for Brazil. In 1643, for example, the Overseas Council insisted on the right to prepare men for a rescue armada to Brazil. The War

Council objected, insisting that its own mandate was to recruit and send men to the front—regardless of where that might be.[13]

While the War Council featured fixed numbers of letrados, who served with and balanced out those of "cape and sword"—the aristocrats, or capa e espada[14]—the Overseas Council featured two military men and one letrado. This arrangement worked quite well. The aristocrats, wrote one seventeenth century source, were rash *idiotas* who were apt to act fast without thinking. The letrados, on the other hand, tended to overanalyze and not act all.[15] Military aristocrats had greater authority than letrados in part because they represented and projected the prestige of the Crown abroad.[16] They could also be relied upon for their experience in the field. This was important, as the decentralization of colony–crown communication enabled petitioners to contact the king directly, circumventing hierarchy in Brazil and in Lisbon.[17] The Overseas Council soon swelled with appointees—an indication of its growing importance.

Both councils included lettered and martial men—but military expertise, provenance, and social networks mattered. During the Luso–Dutch wars, Portugal-born men dominated council membership, occupied the presidency, and directed action.[18] The Overseas Council privileged members with experience against the Dutch in Brazil, though Dom Jorge de Mascarenhas (the Marquis de Montalvão), former viceroy of Brazil, fell under suspicion due to his Spanish-favoring family. In 1641 he was sent back to Lisbon and imprisoned, but given his experience and long service, he was rehabilitated. He then served as the first president of the Overseas Council. He would be jailed two more times but retained his council membership up until his death in the prison of the Castle of São Jorge. Salvador de Sá, commander and governor of Rio de Janeiro, evaded such issues despite his own deep connections to Spain. As scion of a powerful family, he seemed a good fit for and was named to the Overseas Council. But Brazilian-raised men such as Sá could only go so far. He confronted resistance, for example, when he laid out his own plans to thwart the Dutch in the Rio de la Plata and retake Angola. After his strategies were met with years-long delays and polite denial, he mustered troops mostly out of Bahia and Rio, took action, and reclaimed Angola for the Portuguese in 1648. Sá kept his seat on the council until he died in 1688 but never served as president.

The Diplomatic Front: Legitimizing Portugal

Far from the battlefield and away from the metropole, Dom João IV deployed men to the diplomatic front—a somewhat ill-prepared effort. From 1580, Portugal's only missions operated in Madrid, Paris, and Rome. Alienated and without direct access to continental concerns, the diplomats operated in Spain's shadow. No foreign emissary took up residence in Lisbon. After the restoration, however, the king improvised by recruiting emissaries from high nobility, the judiciary, and the House of Braganza.[19]

For a few years at least, the Portuguese held out hope that negotiations on Dutch Brazil could be settled. But by 1643, Francisco de Sousa Coutinho had replaced the irascible Tristão de Mendonça Furtado, who headed for Münster to in hopes of gaining French favor during the negotiations. The treaty he had negotiated in June 1641 had been ratified but largely ignored.[20] Furtado's suggestion to attack the Spanish West Indies together fell flat, as did offering Portugal's share of those spoils in exchange for Dutch-held Brazil.[21] Now, prompted by the king's "secret instructions," Sousa Coutinho was to aim for the restitution of all territory seized by the Dutch before and after the 1640 restoration. His next move would be to offer the Dutch two million cruzados for Brazil.[22] The Netherlanders continued their advance on Portuguese possessions overseas. Melaka had already fallen to the Hollanders a few months before Sousa Coutinho's arrival, and this treasure port would not be returned.[23]

Unlike the aristocrat diplomats who scattered across the continent, Francisco de Sousa Coutinho had served the House of Braganza since 1623. His first post was Madrid, where he had arranged the marriage between Dom João IV and Luisa de Guzman. The polyglot Azorean native put to good use his social skills and scholarly inclinations.[24] A genial, quick-witted man, he had also secured recognition of Portugal from Cristina of Sweden during his stay in 1641–1643. For this and his enduring service to the Braganzas, he had been personally chosen by Dom João IV to handle the tricky business of a truce with the Netherlanders. Yet his reputation of tireless servant to Portugal, borne out over the years, did not prevent repeated frustration during his stint at The Hague. Salary delays prompted him to pay his own expenses, but still he kept his counsel.

Upon arrival at Amsterdam, Sousa Coutinho shared with members of the States General that his own great-grandfather had hailed from Dort. But warm conversation aside, his first address aimed to put the Dutch on notice. Knowing well that his elite audience would appreciate the reference to the waning days of the Roman republic, he referred to Book I of Roman poet Lucan's *Pharsalia*, or *Civil Wars*, reminding his audience that "great things collapse under their own weight," from a well-known translation circulating in Leiden since 1640.[25] Sousa Coutinho appeared to be referencing bloated Spain at the end of its days—but he may well have also been describing the overreaching Dutch. Couched between flowery language and expressions of enduring affection, this may also have been a call to roll back Dutch ambitions.

Backed by advanced weaponry, deep capital, and Grotian legal imagination, the States General refused to budge. Most representatives hailed from Amsterdam and Zeeland, states that fielded primary shareholders of the West India Company. They would not be swayed to support peace talks—an enduring issue in the Dutch republic. In 1641–1642, the Dutch West India Company attacked and seized Luanda, São Tomé, and the northern Brazilian territory of Maranhão. Indeed, relations with Portugal appeared, for most members, to be of little relevance. Two years into his assignment, Sousa Coutinho overheard one Dutch official sneer that "all of Portugal isn't worth half of Brazil."[26]

From Paris, ambassador Marquis de Niza, intent on gaining French support against Spain and legitimizing the Portugal, now engaged in epistolary exchanges with scholars within and beyond France. The marquis—a direct descendant of Vasco da Gama—reached out to French scholars intent on supporting Portugal. As part of that task, he and his secretary then responded to detailed inquiries about the restored kingdom. The questions ranged from the history of the kingdom to the lineage of the current king, Dom João IV, to the state of the Portuguese overseas claims. This was the content the scholars needed promote Portugal as a kingdom in its own right.[27]

Besides working directly with French supporters, the marquis also aimed to lay down a Lusitanian print legacy, recirculate origin stories to bolster Portugal's reputation, and purchase stock to bring back home. This "bibliopolitical" strategy, manifested as a library, would serve as physical proof of Portugal's enduring greatness.[28] To that end, the marquis sponsored the first complete printing of sixteenth-century shoemaker Bandarra's *Trovas*, so foundational to what it meant to be Portuguese. The ambassador, a Sebastianist, wrote the preface to the work. Here he drew a direct line to Portugal's proud past and restored hopes, aiming to connect the *Trovas* to Dom João IV—as the newly returned monarch and true heir of the Portuguese throne.

In his quest to legitimize the kingdom, the marquis largely pursued this bibliopolical strategy through intermediaries due to the inquisitorial ban on select works, included anything that smacked of heresy, like the *Trovas*. Exiled cleric Vicente Nogueira was one such man. Deeply learned, he worked in scholarly circles not only for keep—translating, commenting, and writing—but in this case also to pave his way back to Portugal.[29] From Rome, Nogueira had reached out and piqued the marquis's interest in Rabbi Menasseh Ben Israel's millenarian writings. He also offered commentary and contextualization of the rabbi's work.[30] Through him, the marquis, deeply interested in the Old Testament foundation of the *Trovas*, began an indirect correspondence with the rabbi. This space afforded the marquis shelter from charges of heresy; he could not risk reaching out to Jewish members.

Due in part to his own spiritual convictions regarding Christian–Jewish dialogue, Menasseh Ben Israel had long maintained contact with Christians through his published work. Prompted by a belief on the spiritual significance of communication between Jews and Christians, especially on such matters, he responded. In his letters to the marquis—via Nogueira—he also lamented Portuguese persecution of Jews and New Christians. This, to him, was a profound drain on Portugal in terms of lost capital and expertise.[31] Further, he wrote, the continued confiscation of Jewish and New Christian property would hinder the true restoration of Portugal.

Despite best efforts by the Portuguese diplomats—whether through traditional discourse or more nuanced negotiation—the Dutch West India Company's greatest year of expansion occurred after the ratified peace treaty. This should have meant a cessation of hostilities.[32] But from Brazil, Dom João's loyal *conjurado* and governor of Bahia António Teles da Silva could hardly contain himself as the West India Company attacks on Portuguese property continued. This was no "just" war—not even by the barest Groatian standards. The Netherlanders had "taken [our ships]," he wrote to Dutch Brazil's governor-general, Johan Maurits, after one such episode, "and robbed [them] like pirates."[33] Maurits went further, sending troops to Maranhão and Angola. Now the Luso-Brazilian resistance began coordinating in earnest with Teles da Silva. They began plotting not just a reprisal but the end, finally, of the Dutch in Brazil.

Providence, Treason, and the Divine War of Liberation

Tensions between Dutch and Portuguese Brazil finally flared, by 1645, into open conflict. By mid-June, João Fernandes Vieira, former collaborator with and largest creditor to the Dutch, called for an uprising and the start of a "divine war."³⁴ A mixed-descent Madeirense who made his way to Pernambuco at about the age of ten, the young Vieira had soldiered for Matias de Albuquerque against the Dutch. A few years after the Dutch conquests of 1630, however, he began working with a West India Company officer. He would eventually own several engenhos and more than one thousand slaves, marry into an old Pernambucan family, and become the largest creditor to the Dutch West India Company.

For a few months at least, Vieira orchestrated pre-attack planning. On the pretext of visiting his various engenhos, he stored weapons in and around Recife. By May 30, 1645, word reached the Dutch government in Recife that the rebels were planning an attack: proof positive was in an anonymous letter given to the High Council in Recife, signed *A verdade plus ultra* ("The truth plus ultra").³⁵ Not only were dissenters on the move from Paraíba, where they had been gathering, but they soon would confront the Dutch. "How admirable that the [men of the council] feel so secure," wrote the informant, "given that the thicket in Paraíba is rife with many negros, mulatos, and Portuguese and led by [Indigenous commander Felipe] Camarão." The anonymous informant also noted that João Fernandes Vieira, leader of the resistance, was not sleeping at home, was in a state of readiness, and should be imprisoned, along with Francisco Berengeur, his father-in-law.³⁶ This effort was in vain, however, and Vieira remained free. Neither were the WIC soldiers able to imprison other heads of resistance.³⁷

The Dutch government of Recife then dispatched queries to António Teles da Silva regarding whether he had purposefully ordered soldiers across the São Francisco River to provoke conflict. Where Teles da Silva once railed against the Dutch "pirate" attacks, the governor of Bahia now received his own cease-and-desist letter from the Grand Council in Recife. Feigning ignorance, he replied that the upstart Luso-Brazilians acted "in flagrant disrespect of international law" and that he had orders from the king to disperse their rebel troops.³⁸ In fact, da Silva stated, his purpose in sending troops was to sack the runaway slave community of Palmares. He was not interested in conflict with Dutch

Brazil. His response, of course, was an attempt to provide cover for both the guerrilla troops and for the Crown, which was still negotiating other options for Pernambuco.[39]

The Pernambucan uprising against the Dutch seemed, at first, providential. In early August, the Luso-Brazilian resistance dealt a one-two punch to West India Company troops.[40] Short of trained soldiers, Vieira sent his own enslaved men into battle at Tabocas, having promised them freedom in the event of victory. A fortnight later the resistance converged on Casa Forte, Dona Ana Paes's engenho and Dutch stronghold along the Capiberibe River. Wives, mothers, and daughters of resistance leaders had been taken captive and held at the house. They approached the main house to find that the women had been placed at the windows as human shields, but this only spurred on the rebels.

The multiethnic rebel forces proved especially intimidating to the Dutch. As one soldier wrote, the troops "are also formidable from their natural ferocity, constituting as they do of Brazilians, Tapuyas, Negros, Mamelucos ... all natives of this country ... also Portuguese and Italians, whose constitutions enables them to adapt themselves very readily to the terrain, so they can range across the woods, cross the swamps and climb or descend the hills ... with remarkable speed and agility."[41]

The Luso-Brazilian resistance pushed forward, racking up victories unexpected across the Atlantic. Under siege in Recife, the Dutch troops began destroying Maurits's palace on the island of Antônio Vaz—for defensive purposes.[42] Two years later, in the first Battle of Guararapes, Henrique Dias, Felipe Camarão, João Fernandes Vieira, and others converged on the outsized Dutch force. Between April 18–19, 1648, the Dutch were decimated by the resistance. Felipe Camarão, commander of Indigenous forces, would die from his injuries the following month. But resistance continued to surge. Less than a year later, at the second Battle of Guararapes, the forces took revenge. That battle was over in a day. Vieira, however, is still remembered across the Atlantic in his natal home of Madeira (Figure 12).[43]

News of Luso-Brazilian triumph, when it came, derailed diplomacy at The Hague. Behind closed doors and out on the streets, Francisco de Sousa Coutinho faced the direct fury of the Dutch.[44] The *levantamento*, or uprising, had complicated matters greatly, and he appeared to be negotiating in bad faith.[45] Worse, he had received no information or correspondence of any kind

Figure 12. Bust of João Fernandes Vieira, Funchal, Madeira. Author's photo.

from the king for several months. The Dutch demanded swift punishment for the rebels, and the States General threatened to break off talks altogether should they discover that the Portuguese crown supported the uprising in any way.[46]

Facing hostility in chambers and fearing for his physical safety, Sousa Coutinho worried about the "thousand chimera" besieging Dom João IV. According to news now circulating in Amsterdam, Luso-Brazilian guerrillas had advanced and secured the São Francisco River, Porto Calvo, Cabo St. Agostino, Nazareth, and all Dutch-held forts that had fallen to the Portuguese. Recife and the captaincy of Paraíba, however, were still under Dutch control.[47] But "it is just as well that the rebels gained control of the strongholds [in Brazil]," wrote the embattled ambassador to Dom João IV, as more than two years' worth of talks had gone nowhere.[48] He received no response.

As the ground war in Brazil heated up, once-reliable intermediaries for Portugal made only partial headway in diplomatic talks. One concern was the above-mentioned "betrayal," according to reports, of António Teles da Silva, who had pretended to end hostilities while in fact he sent Henrique Dias and his soldiers to attack Recife.[49] A French ambassador now mediating for the Portuguese reported to Sousa Coutinho that in chambers, men "threatened war and more war" and the Zeelanders asked permission to sack the coast of Portugal.[50] In addition, the Zeeland chamber of the Dutch West India Company demanded restitution from Portugal.[51] French negotiators for the Portuguese reported a tense situation in Münster, where the treaty between Spain and the United Provinces was to be ratified. But when it came to Portugal, the Spanish were likewise not interested in general peace.

Francisco de Sousa Coutinho had also tried to finesse tension regarding at least one other "traitor" to the Dutch, and this too impeded his progress. Suspected New Christian and former ally of Johan Maurits, Gaspar Dias Ferreira switch allegiances to Portugal once more. With the Dutch invasion of Pernambuco, Dias Ferreira had lent his translation skills to WIC officers, eventually befriending the Dutch governor-general. He had accepted Maurits's invitation to accompany him upon withdrawal to the United Provinces, journeying to the Netherlands with the governor-general in 1644. But he was soon turned in as a spy for the Portuguese. In fact, he was so valuable to the king that upon his secret instruction, Sousa Coutinho was ordered to offer a large sum, which would be sent for this purpose, "in haste" for his release.[52]

The ransom offer did little to lessen Dutch rage at what they deemed continued acts of treason. Indeed, it was from prison that Gaspar Dias Ferreira carried on secret correspondence with Francisco de Sousa Coutinho, who valued his opinion regarding his experience in Brazil.[53] He also proved his worth by escaping from prison, negating the need for a ransom, though this put the diplomat in an even more difficult position: letters brought by the Dutch ship *Trou van Vlessingen* to West India Company officials in Brazil indicated the depth of Dias Ferreira's betrayal and concern over an increasingly precarious situation in the colony: "It has pained us not a little to know that these perfidious [acts] were discovered and that the bird [has flown the coop]. We hope that all who betrayed us are similarly persecuted, because we have been shamefully betrayed. Nothing happens that the Portuguese don't find out soon; but at [final] reckoning, these traitors will get their prize."[54]

Back in Lisbon, once-traitor and New Christian Dias Ferreira was greeted with a hero's welcome. Dom João IV also nominated him to the Order of Christ.[55] The news, when it came, was welcomed by many in the exiled Jewish community. Some remembered—either directly or through the stories of their elders—how the Portuguese Inquisition took a turn for the worse with the union of the Iberian crowns in 1580. Here was a chance that the exiles might become more than shadow agents outside of Portugal.

By early spring of 1646, Sousa Coutinho, worn down by three years of little progress and Dutch outrage at the uprising in Pernambuco, looked forward to the arrival of and support from Father António Vieira. The Jesuit was "so well-known," he wrote to his good friend, the jurist and longtime secretary António Moniz de Carvalho, "respected and also good company and conversation."[56] He sincerely hoped the Jesuit would spark a resolution to the Luso–Dutch conflict. But the millenarian preacher and Sebastianist would also stall in discursive efforts—until these too were translated into solid aid and clear action for the resistance.

Of Prophecy and Profit: Founding and Funding the Brazil General Company

"Imagine . . . if you would, a transformed world," Vieira wrote to his besieged king from Amsterdam, "of previously impossible hope."[57] But ahead of the first Luso-Brazilian victory at Monte Tabocas he did not foresee the success, from 1645, of the resistance. Preacher, diplomat, and king's adviser, best known for his talent in preaching and writing, António Vieira would serve, by the end of the war, in yet one more role: that of broker. He had already proposed escorting the sugar ships with an armed convoy—a sure way to bring the kingdom badly needed funds.[58] In his quest to spark the material and spiritual restoration of Portugal, had also reached across the confessional divide. This meant forging relationships with the Jewish community.

Faith and finance bolstered support for the Crown and for the resistance in Brazil. From Europe, the cross-continental Portuguese Jewish and New Christian network provided financial aid not only for military but also diplomatic efforts for the kingdom. Baltazar Rodrigues de Matos, for instance, subsidized emissaries from 1644 to 1648. His brother in Rome was key in providing contacts in Rome; their father operated out of Rouen. Matos, working from Lisbon, engaged in the sugar import business and exportation to Italy or Rouen by way of Porto. Matos engaged as well in ventures with Old Christians—as one of the founders of the Brazil General Company.[59]

One Old Christian—António Vieira—was keen on interfaith coordination to solve immediate problems of the Dutch in Brazil and the future of Portugal.[60] Given protection from the Inquisition, he had argued to Dom João IV, financial help might even be obtained from the Jewish or New Christian community in Portugal.[61] In 1646, en route from Paris to his first diplomatic posting at The Hague, Vieira sought capital for the king of Portugal from Jews in Rouen. Short on funds, Dom João IV had wanted to end the war in Brazil and possibly buy Pernambuco back from the Dutch, but he needed capital. Vieira left with this and more: a growing hope for Portugal.[62]

Francisco de Sousa Coutinho had looked forward to Vieira's first posting in 1646, but Vieira, steeped in messianism, also looked to connect to the Jewish community in the Netherlands while on post. His interest in Jewish and New Christian communities likely began in Bahia, where he was first exposed to the Old Testament themes in Bandarra's *Trovas*. His Sebastianist inclinations, evident in his earlier sermons, had not since dimmed. Indeed, at the behest of Jerônimo Nunes da Costa, the diplomatic mission's most influential and helpful adviser, Vieira attended synagogue services in Amsterdam—though at least once he was dragged out by his host for interrupting the rabbi.[63]

Vieira had missed a messianic event that swept the Jewish community in Amsterdam in 1644. The Portuguese Jewish trader Aaron Lévy (António de Montesinos), arriving from the Americas, had made an astounding claim: he had found the lost tribe of Israel. Levy had, he said, witnessed with his own eyes Indigenous Jews reciting prayers on the Colombian highlands. The story convinced the influential Rabbi Menasseh Ben Israel, who had invited Levy to share his account with the synagogue elders, that the end times were near.[64] The thought of Jews lost in the Americas may have been, for him, especially relatable. Born in Madeira, educated in Lisbon, and exiled to Amsterdam, he was, in the expression of his brother, "an exiled Portuguese Jew" since youth. Israel never relinquished his Portuguese name—Manuel Dias Soeiro—and wrote it out beside his Jewish name throughout his life. In recounting the story of Aaron Levy/António Montesinos, Israel described the man as "Portuguese by nation, Jewish by religion." This is how he thought of himself.[65]

Inspired by Levy's account, the revered rabbi would write *The Hope of Israel*

(1652)—but not before an interfaith discussion with Padre Vieira. Menasseh Ben Israel believed that redemption would come to Jews only with their dispersal to the corners of the earth. That they were "found" in the Americas was proof positive that the prophecy was about to be realized.[66] Both the rabbi and the Jesuit believed that communication between Jews and Christians would hasten if not the end times then the preparation for a better future.[67] Like the rabbi, Vieira also believed the New World was not an extension of the Old but rather a space for—and uncovering of—prophecies destined only for the Portuguese.[68] This of course had been articulated in Bandarra's *Trovas*: a mysterious king would one day unite the whole world in a political-spiritual-religious new world order. So for Vieira, the news of the "discovery" of the lost Tribe of Reuben, practicing faith in the Americas, was also a clear sign of transformational times. But while Menasseh Ben Israel believed the Tribe of Reuben had been located, Vieira considered them found but still hidden.[69] The priest was more concerned, however, about dialogue with the Jewish community. In this way he hoped to usher them into the Christian fold.[70]

Financing from exiled Jews proved only a short-term fix, however. Vieira returned to The Hague in 1648 but headed for Lisbon as he and Sousa Coutinho received word of Spanish–Dutch negotiations for peace.[71] In 1648 Vieira wrote his "Opinion in Favor of Giving Pernambuco to the Dutch," more commonly known as his Papel Forte. It was clear to him that the Portuguese had to pull out of the costly, protracted war across the Atlantic.[72] "Let us reserve what we want to do now to the Dutch for a more opportune time," he argued, "when we will not just take what they are returning to us but all of our conquests that they have unjustly possessed."[73] He spelled out eight "inconveniences" of holding onto Pernambuco—not the least was that it would continue to pull scarce resources from Asia. That part of the world and not Brazil, he pointed out, was home to most of the Christians under Portuguese jurisdiction.[74]

Francisco Sousa Coutinho and António Vieira pitched giving up Dutch-held territory in northeastern Brazil, but by 1648 the increasingly victorious Luso-Brazilian resistance offered new options for the Crown. The second Portuguese victory at Guararapes forced Vieira to change tack. With popular Portuguese sentiment now on the side of the insurgents, António Vieira would reconsider the creation of an armed escort fleet to carry provisions from Lisbon to Brazil and return loaded with chests of sugar.[75] Salvador de Sá's persistence in reclaiming Angola (1648) proved critical to the whole enterprise. Absent securing enslaved labor from West Africa, as was well-known, there would be "no Brazil." A steady supply of forced labor would increase sugar production and, with it, badly needed funds for the Portuguese royal treasury.[76]

Prophecy, Capital, and the Brazil General Company

Between the loss of sugar receipts and the cost of fighting a multifront war, Dom João IV's financial woes prompted an Englishman to write that "the king here is a man of no estate." Scattered as it was, his overseas kingdom consisted of possessions in Africa, Goa, Brazil, and Madeira. Though these were "alone bigger than all of Europe put together, poor things God wot, that with good husbanding might only yield about 9 or 10 million every year."[77] In the early years after restoration, when Portugal's treasury seemed beyond replenishing, the king was pressed to hold onto his restored kingdom.

From Brazil, the resistance pushed forward to galvanizing transatlantic results. By 1649, with the second Battle of Guararapes marking another clear victory for the Portuguese, the formation of the Brazil General Company was finally realized. These "war" ships guaranteed revenue for investors in "white gold," among them Dom João IV. António Vieira had first floated the idea to the king in 1643, even then gaining royal support for the plan.[78] Though Vieira would later argue against saving Pernambuco, the plan never disappeared; instead treasury councilor Pedro Fernandes Monteiro persisted with the prospect. Pernambuco, he argued—and by extension all of Brazil—could only be restored from the Dutch with the recovery of Portuguese shipping.[79] The Papel Forte notwithstanding, Vieira reverted to his original position with a zeal, whipping financial support in exchange for a lifting of Inquisitorial restrictions against Jews and New Christians.[80] He also encouraged Dom João IV to participate in the creation of the company as a common shareholder, thus floating the notion of the privatization of defense.[81] The king then granted a charter for the creation of the sugar convoy escort company, which would also have monopoly rights over cod, oil, wine, and flour.

New Christians and Jewish merchants had long formed a below-the-radar alliance with the pro-Braganza Portuguese, no less useful to both groups now.[82]

Even in exile, Duarte Nunes da Costa, for one, welcomed a chance to revive business that had declined with the Dutch attacks on Brazil. His son Jerônimo Nunes da Costa also proved his worth as a well-connected businessman and negotiator based in Amsterdam, gaining an appointment in 1645 as agent for the crown of Portugal. He smoothed diplomatic correspondence between the Dutch and the Portuguese. In May 1649, for instance, when Sousa Coutinho received news of the Dutch loss of Angola to the Portuguese, the States General refused to acknowledge surrender. The diplomat then sent the news to Jerônimo Nunes da Costa, who arranged for copies to be printed up and circulated in Amsterdam. This was proof positive that the Dutch were losing ground.[83] Nunes da Costa was invaluable to the Portuguese king, who named him a knight.[84]

The Nunes da Costa family was among the merchants—Old Christian, New Christian, within and beyond Portugal—who vied for access to the convoy, recognizing the merits of a crown-backed provisioning for the resistance.[85] By shipping supplies to the resistance in Brazil, the venture was to provide a public good—for a fair exchange to investors of course. These and other free agents engaged with the Brazil General Company through their shareholding, subcontracting, and lobbying. The charter gave the highly heterogeneous group of shareholders a monopoly on wine, oil, flour, and cod.[86] By dint of connections and wealth, they gained access to near-guaranteed profits and, of course, Dom João IV.[87] This group included Italians and Englishmen in Lisbon who sought status as New Christians rather than Protestants in order to invest.[88]

Investing merchants—including New Christians—were to gain a reprieve from potential sequestration of goods, barring the most dramatic circumstances, such as enemy invasion of key ports.[89] The sale from Portugal to Brazil of essentials such as flour, oil, cod, and wine would all be under the control of company shareholders. On the return voyages, with chests of taxable sugar protected by the armed convoy, the Portuguese crown would be able to replenish its long-drained treasury.

The royal charter of March 10, 1649, made official the creation of the Brazil General Company—one route to provisioning and funding the besieged colony and kingdom. As a contemporary noted, "[One] can't deny the benefits the convoy of the Company have brought to the city [of Lisbon] . . . with more than 100,000 chests of sugar and other fruits of that state [Brazil]."[90] In this way the company fleet replenished the treasury of Dom João IV and helped pay for the war against the Dutch.[91] The armada of well-stocked ships not only supplied provisions essential to the moradores but also returned to Lisbon laden with "white gold." This was a sweet deal indeed.

The results were immediate. The first Armada Real do Mar Oceano received warning that it might encounter a Dutch blockade of Bahia. But the Bay of All Saints proved clear of the enemy: The Dutch had lifted anchor upon hearing the news that the convoy of the Brazil General Company was on its way. Faith and finance, put into action through the collaboration of a religiously diverse group of investors, helped turn the tide of the war. "One may say that that the Restoration of Pernambuco is due only to God and not the Company," wrote one contemporary, "but it is [through the work of] the Company that this miracle occurred."[92]

Luso–Dutch negotiations may have stalled by 1645, but for Sebastianists, discourse regarding Portugal's future—however it might unfold—took a new turn in support of on-the-ground resistance. Action mattered; words followed. Jesuit António Vieira, for instance, saw in the conflict a vision of Portugal realizing its destiny. Lisbon-born and Bahian-bred, the Jesuit priest-turned-adviser to Dom João IV parsed circumstance for meaning in his roles as preacher and diplomat. The Luso–Dutch war had, after all, marked his life since he was a Jesuit novitiate, in his first encounter with Dutch invaders in Salvador (1624–1625). Years later, with the breakdown in talks and preservation of Portugal on the line, Vieira suggested delivering Pernambuco to the Dutch. After clear Luso-Brazilian victories at Battles of Guararapes and in Angola, the priest divined new survival strategies. These included financial and spiritual collaboration with exiled Jews.

In the battle for Brazil, the guerrilla resistance coordinated and engaged in on-the-ground struggles, as it had since the arrival of the Dutch. Toward the end of 1648, the Portuguese elite—Crown and council, diplomats, merchants, and literati—could only follow. António Vieira and Ambassadors Tristão de Mendonça Furtado and Francisco Sousa Coutinho, loyal servants of Dom João IV, negotiated with the Dutch to save Portugal, and from Paris the Marquis de Nisa brushed up the kingdom's credentials. But the leaders of the guerrilla resistance—all men of marginalized descent—coordinated with each other and trusty "conspirator" António Teles da Silva to expel the Dutch. Beyond the metropole and across the continent, discourse and diplomacy had aimed to shore up the kingdom's reputation with a multi-front strategy. In Europe, exiled Portuguese and other intermediaries hoping to return home tapped informal networks to help secure the legitimacy of Portugal. By 1649 resistance efforts were more directly supported from the metropole by an influx of capital from cross-cultural investors—and manifested in the Brazil General Company.

The Dutch challenge for Brazil, an Exodus-like story as old as Portugal, moved Christians, New Christians, and Jews alike to coordinated action. By the end of 1649, most ports critical to the Lusophone Atlantic had been restored. Interclass, interfaith, and intercultural collaboration coalesced in Brazil during decades in which Brazil might otherwise have gone Dutch. This occurred in fits and starts. So too did an evolving sense of what it meant to be Portuguese—a transformative experience that endured beyond earthly conflict, echoing for centuries in collective Luso memory.

Epilogue

"If we would do so much to live a little more, how much more should we do to live forever?"

—ANTÓNIO VIEIRA,
"SERMÃO DE NOSSA SENHORA DE PENHA DE FRANÇA"

AFTER A NARROW ESCAPE in the 1578 Battle of Alcácer Quiber, António Simões, a woodcarver from Lisbon, fled to North Africa to found what would become the Order of Our Lady of Penha de França (Nossa Senhora da Penha da França). This devotional cult of Mary dated from the earliest days of Portugal's existence.[1] But trauma of defeat, and with it the loss of King Sebastian, infused the order with a new purpose.

The king had disappeared, but Simões survived unscathed—a miracle he attributed to the Virgin Mary. As the enemy approached over a dune, he said, his only recourse was to pray fervently to his Holy Mother. He felt comforted by the image of her protection, surrounded by light, and her hands extended over him; the enemy retreated mysteriously. Simões then swore to God and the Virgin Mary that upon his return he would spread the word of this divine intervention. This he did, spending the rest of his life carving images and statues of Mary, and converting others to her devotion too.[2]

Padre António Vieira knew the story. He chose Simões's church as the site of his final sermon, ahead of his 1652 departure—for the last time—to Brazil. As the Jesuit gazed out over his listeners, he asked them to consider the power of memory and how it lay beyond performed ritual prayer, beyond sacral discourse, in faith and in the power of print. On the eve of his final mission, this time in the aldeias of Maranhão, Vieira urged the Portuguese to collective remembering of what it meant to be Portuguese. In church, in person, and together with his listeners, this included a shared understanding, performance of ritual, and enduring faith.

"Tell me, how [in what way] do you remember?" the Jesuit wondered aloud.[3] Vieira had by this time begun to lay down lines for his *The Hopes of Portugal*, inspired by his encounters with Rabbi Manasseh Ben Israel, in which he would argue that the New World shaped the experiences of the Old.[4] The kingdom was nearing the end of a terrible crisis. After having thrown off and resisted the Spanish, Luso-Brazilians were dislodging the Dutch in Brazil. But would the Portuguese recall this long trial?

For the seventeenth-century Portuguese in Portugal and in Brazil, surviving the Dutch in Brazil meant recalling a divine promise forged in the origin myth of the Battle of Ourique. It meant drawing the prophetic line from Bandarra's *Trovas* to the Dutch attacks on the Portuguese overseas empire. It meant uneasy coordination between Spain and Portugal to reconquer Bahia from the Dutch and emergent alliances between moradores, Jesuits, and their Indigenous allies. For the Sebastianist Father António Vieira, resisting the Dutch meant converting promise into action, remembering the connection between the Old Testament and the New, and moving between and within sacral, diplomatic, and commercial spaces. Vieira wrote and privately circulated *The Hopes of Portugal* in 1659, but promise had been building for decades—both in the kingdom and in Brazil.[5]

Defeating the Dutch required more than hope in recruiting and providing for diverse troops drawn from Portuguese America and around the Lusophone Atlantic. In Brazil, this meant negotiating tradition, which blocked from advancement those with "tainted blood," such as Black and Indigenous commanders Henrique Dias and Felipe António Camarão. They and their men joined forces with Iberian troops against the Dutch, gaining social recognition as honor-worthy, loyal subjects of Portugal.

Celebratory tropes of a multi-ethnic Brazil may have emerged in 1930s scholarship and the early years of Brazil's Estado Novo (1930–1945) but have been stoked, since independence, in the memory of the Dutch challenge.[6] In the context of a weakening and then fully fractured Iberian union, an emergent Luso-Brazilian network drove on-the-ground action in Lisbon, the Atlantic islands, Bahia, and Rio de Janeiro—all across the Portuguese Atlantic world.

During this wide-ranging conflict, and in the decades that followed, chroniclers celebrated the efforts of women and marginalized men. Such attention did not disappear. Friar Santa Rita Durão's eighteenth-century epic poem *Caramaru*, narrated by the Indigenous woman Paraguaçu, highlights how diverse Luso-Brazilians spurred victory over the Dutch. In the modern era, Pernambucan scholars traveled to The Hague, sourcing West India Company documents, translating and transcribing related documents as part of the most important episode of Brazil's colonial history—drawing attention to the contributions of the northeast to the nation.[7]

António Vieira is our only Luso-Brazilian eyewitness from the Dutch invasion of Salvador through the final restoration of Brazil. In him we see an evolution from stunned Jesuit novice to adviser to the king, imagining and arguing for a "transformed world" led by Portugal. The Dutch experience thus inspired him and other literati to an enduring, baroque articulation of the times.[8] The Dutch in Brazil offered unexpected opportunity to those who would see beyond an irregular Portuguese world, to a place where an Afro-descended Henrique Dias, Felipe Camarão of the Potiguar tribe, and Jewish and New Christian merchants, once marginalized for their "tainted blood," rose to prominence by proving their worth to the Crown.[9] Far from the metropole, Luso loyalty and action indicated a polyvalent, situational self-understanding of what it meant to be Portuguese in Brazil.

After a conference panel a few years ago, another researcher lingered to introduce himself; it turned out that we have overlapping interests regarding Portugal's early modern experience. I had just shared my work on the Portuguese reaction to the Dutch and Spanish challenge. He further revealed that he is Portuguese and from Lisbon. "I grew up hearing about Sebastian," he remarked. "That's all my dad talked about at dinner—how Spain took over in 1580 and ruined Portugal, though the king never actually died [in battle]." He had vowed to get as far away from studying the history of Portugal as possible, "and yet here I am." He was in the audience the next day when I discussed the on-the-ground Luso-Brazilian reaction to the Dutch in Brazil. "I'm glad someone is mentioning Henrique Dias," he told me after the session. "He deserves to be remembered."

This exchange confirmed for me not only the enduring memory of trials wrought by the death of the young king but also the improbable Portuguese pushback of the imperial Spanish and Dutch. The vision and efforts of Portuguese subjects on both sides of the Atlantic crystallized in the traumatic moment known as Dutch Brazil. Here, eschatological promise turned to action as Portuguese subjects within Brazil and throughout the Lusophone Atlantic collaborated to save the colony. Portugal's double subsumption—at home by Spain and abroad by the Dutch—sparked emergent, layered discourses regarding sovereign and subject, and an evolution of possibilities in this regard. Vieira's own Sebastianist worldview adapted to the times. For the Jesuit, the restored king Dom João IV served, in the midst of an enduring ordeal, as a reminder of Portugal's expansive, divine mission on earth. On the ground, men and women negotiated the Atlantic war—an effort that resulted in cross-class action and an emergent consciousness unique to the colonial experience. For Vieira and others, the battle for Brazil meant not only reconquest from the Dutch and Portugal's permanent independence from Spain but the restoration, in all of its iterations, of a nearly lost kingdom.

Notes

Introduction

1. Portuguese sailor Diogo Álvares Correia, shipwrecked off the coast of Bahia in the late sixteenth century, lived among the Tupinambá for a decade before reestablishing contact with Europeans. His wife, Paraguaçu was the first Indigenous woman to receive audience in royal courts. Treece, "Caramuru the Myth."
2. Santa Rita Durão, *Caramuru*, 178.
3. On José de Santa Rita Durão's conception of "homeland" and a prenational analysis of his poem, see Garcia, "The Aeneid of Brazil."
4. This is King Sebastian, or Dom Sebastião (1554–1578). Lemos de Faria e Castro, *Jornada de África*.
5. Later known as the Eighty Years War.
6. For instance, Philip II ordered Portuguese men and ships into battle against the English armada (1588). On the "Babylonian captivity," see McAllister, *Spain and Portugal in the New World*, 295.
7. Ittersum, *Profit and Principle*; Borschberg, "Seizure of the Sta. Catarina Revisited," 57.
8. Parker, *Global Calvinism*, 24; on church–company expansionary alliances and entanglements, see also Noorlander, *Heaven's Wrath*; Schalkwijk, *Reformed Church in Dutch Brazil*. For more on the protracted struggle for peace amid the clamor of war, see Israel, *Dutch Republic and the Hispanic World*.
9. Indeed, many WIC directors served actively in Reformed Church consistories. Noorlander, *Heaven's Wrath*, 39.
10. Parker, *Global Calvinism*, 44.
11. Maravall, *Culture of the Baroque*, 20.
12. Vieira, "Sermão pelo bom successo das armas de Portugal contra as de Hollanda."
13. Groesen, *Amsterdam's Atlantic*, 10–11.
14. Nora, "Between Memory and History," 7, 18.
15. On groupness, connectedness, and commonality as a way to grasp self-understanding that comes with "identity," see Cooper, *Colonialism in Question*, 75–77.
16. For example, Tracy, *Rise of Merchant Empires*; Israel, *Empires and Entrepots*; Schmidt, *Innocence Abroad*; Sutton, *Cartography and Capitalism*; Klooster, *Dutch Moment*.

17. Maurits served as West India Company governor-general to Brazil from 1636 to 1644. The literature on his legacy is extensive, first described by his own biographer, Caspar van Baerle, in *The History of Brazil Under the Governorship of Count Johan Maurits of Nassau*. From the twentieth century on, see Boxer, *Dutch in Brazil*, especially "A Humanist Prince in a New World" (112–58). In this particular telling, Portuguese subjects have been rendered flat and inert—at best curious and at worst spiteful actors in the telling. Boxer describes Father Manuel Calado, upon whose account he draws to balance to his rich Dutch sources, as deceitful, unscrupulous, and malicious no fewer than three times by page 71. See also Schmidt, *Innocence Abroad*; Mariana Françozo, "Johan Maurits of Nassau-Siegen's Collection of Curiosities," in Groesen, *Legacy of Dutch Brazil*, 105–6; Sutton, *Cartography and Capitalism*, 85–88; Michiel van Groesen, "Introduction," in Israel and Schwartz, *Expansion of Tolerance*, 9; Ebben, "José Gonsalves de Mello," 133; Pijning, "Paradise Regained."

18. Bruno Miranda, *Gente da guerra: origem, cotidiano e resistência dos soldados do exército da companhia das índias ocidentais do Brasil, 1630–1654* (Recife: Editora UFPE, 2014); Groesen, *Amsterdam's Atlantic*; Klooster, *Dutch Moment*.

19. Oostindie, "Historical Memory and National Canons," 79. The transcribed documents include key Dutch West India Company material, including all of Johan Maurits's letters to the company directors when he was en route to and in Brazil (1636–1644). Such work has been widely commented on and refined in successive generations, particularly by Pernambucan historians. The Instituto Arqueológico, Histórico e Geográfico Pernambucano, founded in Recife in 1862 for the particular purpose of preserving regional history, has such works in its holdings; many are accessible online.

20. By then the Brazilian northeast had long lost its early luster. After the decline of the sugar industry and the late seventeenth-century gold rush that vaulted Minas Gerais to prominence, post-abolition (1888), Pernambuco was eclipsed as well by São Paulo as the economic engine of the country.

21. Mello, *Tempo dos flamengos*, 19–23.

22. Mello's *Tempo dos flamengos* offers a more balanced account but is still weighted heavily on the Nassovian era. See also Ebben, "José Antônio Gonsalves de Mello."

23. Braudel's *The Mediterranean* was to Evaldo Cabral de Mello, Brazil's most prominent historian of Dutch Brazil, "a revelation." When the diplomat-turned-historian was stationed in Europe, he made it a point to attend Georges Duby's weekly seminars at the Collège de France. Suzanne Litrel, "A 'True Liberation.'"

24. Nascimento, "Evocação Pernambucana," 110–11, 118. These works include Calado's *O Valeroso Lucideno*, Albuquerque Coelho's *Memórias diárias de la guerra del Brasil*, Francisco de Brito Freire's *Nova Lusitânia ou história da guerra brasílica*, and Friar Rafael de Jesus's *Castrioto Lusitano*.

25. See, for instance, Lenk, *Guerra e pacto colonial*, and Vainfas, *Traição*. See also the second half of Alencastro, *The Trade in the Living*.

Chapter One

1. Since 1571 Sebastian was determined to retake North African forts that had been abandoned by his grandfather. Brooks, "Military Defeat to Immortality," 42.
2. See Brooks, "From Military Defeat to Immortality," and Tähtinen, "The Intellectual Construction of the Fifth Empire," 415–16.
3. Cardinal Henriques, Sebastian's aging uncle, succeeded Sebastian for a short while. Though there were more than a few pretenders to the throne, Philip's claim in 1580 led to the dual monarchy. Brooks, "Military Defeat to Immortality," 44.
4. Disney, *A History of Portugal and the Portuguese Empire*, 209–10; Newett, *History of Portuguese Overseas Expansion*, 218–21.
5. MacKay, *The Baker Who Pretended to Be King of Portugal*.
6. Sebastian is also referred to as O Adormecido (the Sleeping One). Santis, "A imagem de D. Sebastião em 'O conquistador' e 'Rei Luis de Souza.'"
7. Castro, *Paraphrase et concordancia de algvas prophcias de Bandarra*, 146r.
8. Luis Filipe Silvério Lima and Ana Paula Torres Megiani note that the terms *millenarianism* and *messianism* have been used interchangeably and as "sides of the same coin"—both with an expectant view toward the future. They also remind us that these are modern terms; contemporary sources, including those of the Inquisition, used the term *milenários* to describe their "deviant" practice of faith. Lima, "Prophetical Hopes, New World Experiences and Imperial Expectations."
9. Jonathan Israel, "Dutch Sephardic Jewry, Millenarian Politics, and the Struggle for Brazil (1640–1654)," in David Katz and Jonathan Israel, eds., *Sceptics, Millenarians and Jews* (Leiden: Brill, 1990), 76–97; Luís Filipe Silvério Lima, and Ana Paula Torres Megiani, eds., *Visions, Prophecies and Divinations: Early Modern Messianism and Millenarianism in Iberian America, Spain and Portugal* (Leiden: Brill, 2016).
10. As elucidated by Hugo de Groot (Grotius) and disseminated by the Dutch East India Company. Grotius, a precocious and prolific Dutch jurist, developed theories on international rights and trade contracts, and influenced the development of modern international law. The Dutch East Indies Company commissioned his initial work, which evolved into the enduring 1609 *De Jure Praedae* (On the Law of Prize and Booty) and *Mare Liberum* (The Free Sea). See Martine Julia van Ittersum, *Profit and Principle*.
11. From the eleventh century, Portugal was vassal to the kingdom of León, which ruled over Galicia in what is now northwestern Spain. O'Donnell, "Portugal," 260–61.
12. At one point, the Galicians controlled nearly the entire Iberian Peninsula. At this time, however, Galicia was confined mostly to the northwestern corner. In the Treaty of Tui, Afonso Henriques agreed to cease conquest attempts on Galicia and recognized the suzerainty of Afonso VII, at the time king of Leon, Castile, and Galicia.
13. Lay, *Reconquest Kings*, 78.
14. Jordán, "Empire of the Future and the Chosen People," 49.

15. According to legend, the five shields of the defeated Muslim kings were found strewn upon the battlefield. These Afonso collected, and to this day the five shields decorate the Portuguese national flag as a reminder of the event. Camões, *Os Lusíadas*, cited in Lay, *Reconquest Kings*, 79.

16. Lay, *Reconquest Kings*, 77–79.

17. Lay, *Reconquest Kings*, 79. Toward the end of Afonso's life, poets created verse celebrating his visions and exploits. For the evolution of early modern images of Ourique, see Luís Filipe Silvério Lima, "Imagens e figuras de um rei sonhador: representações do milagre de Ourique e do juramento de Afonso Henriques no século XVII," *História* 26, no. 2 (2007), 311–39, http://www.scielo.br/pdf/his/v26n2/a16v26n2.pdf.

18. Crosby, *Measure of Reality*.

19. Disney, *History of Portugal and the Portuguese Empire*; Newitt, *History of Portuguese Overseas Expansion*; Russell-Wood, *Portuguese Empire*, 1998.

20. Boxer, *The Portuguese Seaborne Empire*, 18–20, 32–35.

21. David Huve, "Spatial Perceptions, Juridical Practices, and Early International Legal Thought Around 1500: From Tordesillas to Saragossa." In *System, Order, and International Law: The Early History of International Legal Thought from Machiavelli to Hegel* (Oxford: Oxford University Press, 2017), 425.

22. Shatzman, *The Old World, the New World, and the Creation of the Modern World*, 30.

23. Muldoon, "Papal Responsibility for the Infidel," 183; Padrón, "Mapping Plus Ultra."

24. Benton, *Search for Sovereignty*, xii, 22.

25. Stuart Schwartz and James Lockhart, *Early Latin America: A History of Colonial Spanish America and Brazil* (Cambridge: Cambridge University Press, 1983), 24–25.

26. Newitt, *History of Portuguese Overseas Expansion*, 72–75.

27. Boxer, "Carreira da India"; Russell-Wood, *Men Under Stress*.

28. Schwartz and Lockhart, *Early Latin America*, 183. On the earliest search for "Emerald Mountain" in Brazil, see, for example, Abreu, *Chapters of Brazil's Colonial History*.

29. Schwartz and Lockhart, *Early Latin America*, 24–26.

30. By all accounts, this was fairly generous: given the uncertain line of the Treaty of Tordesillas, some family grants were larger than whole provinces of Portugal. The practice was first developed under Prince Henry the Navigator. Schwartz and Lockhart, *Early Latin America*, 185; Newitt, *A History of Portuguese Overseas Expansion*, 42–43.

31. The "Everyman" drama made its stage debut about two decades earlier, in 1610. Moises, *A literatura portuguesa através dos textos*, 62–65.

32. Gil Vicente, *Auto da Lusitânia* (1532), in Moises, *A literatura portuguesea através dos textos*, 62.

33. Moises, *A literatura portuguesea atraves dos textos*, 65.

34. See introduction in Scott, *Literature and the Idea of Luxury in Early Modern England* (Burlington: Ashgate, 2015), especially page 5, note 10, regarding medieval roots of this concern in Aquinas; Poley, *Devil's Riches*.

35. Alden, *Making of an Enterprise*.
36. Directed by Duarte Coelho Pereira (Pernambuco) and Martim de Sousa (Bahia).
37. This was Tomé de Sousa, who arrived in Bahia with a retinue of administrators. Lockhart and Schwartz, *Early Latin America*, 190–91.
38. Stohls, "The Expansion of the Sugar Market in Western Europe" 161.
39. Stohls, 162.
40. Lancaster took five English and three Dutch prisoners as well, an indication of ample non-Portuguese competition for the product. Ebert, *Between Empires*, 146.
41. Evaldo Cabral de Mello popularized this term to indicate wealthy sugar producers. For example, see Mello, *Olinda restaurada*, 82. On the European surge in demand for sugar, see, for example, Stols, "The Expansion of the Sugar Market in Western Europe."
42. Alida Metcalf, *Go-Betweens and the Colonization of Brazil*, 112.
43. Schwartz, *Sugar Plantations*, 76, 166.
44. Disney, *A History of Portugal*, 181.
45. António Gonçales Bandarra, cited in Castro, *Paraphrase et concordancia de algvas prophecias de Bandarra*, 37r. De Castro published, commented on, and disseminated Bandarra's work from Paris.
46. António Gonçales Bandarra, cited in Castro, *Paraphrase et concordancia de algvas prophecias de Bandarra*, 34v.
47. Jordán, "The Empire of the Future and the Chosen People."
48. Olson, *Calabrian Charlatan*, 16.
49. António Gonçales Bandarra, cited in Castro, *Paraphrase et concordancia de algvas prophecias de Bandarra*, 35r.
50. Brooks, "Military Defeat to Immortality," 42.
51. MacKay, "The Tragedy of Alcazarquivir," 1–2.
52. Lemos de Faria e Castro, *Jornada de Africa*; MacKay, "The Tragedy of Alcazarquivir."
53. Olsen, *Calabrian Charlatan*, 16.
54. Olsen, 16. Bernhard Klein, "Camoes and the Sea: Maritime Modernity in the Lusiads," *Modern Philology* 111, no. 2 (November 2013): 161.
55. Jordán, "The Empire of the Future and the Chosen People," 49.
56. Camões, *Os Lusíadas*, 1.
57. By most accounts, Dom Sebastião, was hot-tempered and irrational. Brooks, "Military Defeat to Immortality," 42.
58. Lemos de Faria e Castro, *Jornada de Africa*, 20.
59. Brooks, "Military Defeat to Immortality," 43.
60. Lemos de Faria e Castro, *Jornada de Africa*, 24.
61. Lemos de Faria e Castro, *Jornada de Africa*, 29.
62. MacKay, "Tragedy of Alcazarquivir."
63. Though the Book of Daniel, likely written in the second century BCE, was meant "to exhort and console the persecuted Jews," it "must be seen to transcend its

historical situation . . . the vision is presented in symbolic language which never mentions the explicitly historical referents." Collins, *Daniel*, 82.

64. His remains are said to have been joined with those of the other direct descendants of Dom Manuel in the Mosteiro de Belem, outside of Lisbon. Lemos de Faria e Castro, *Jornada de África*, 75.

65. Even before the death of Sebastian, Dom António had been lambasted for insubordination, accused of engaging in spendthrift behavior, and chided for not joining the expedition to retake North Africa. Jacqueline Hermann, "Um rei indesejado."

66. MacKay, *Tragedy of Alcazarquivir*, 18.

67. José I. Suárez, "Portugal's Saudodismo Movement," 129.

68. Boxer, *Portuguese Empire*, 372, 375.

69. Givens, *Judging Maria de Macedo*, 3.

70. João de Castro's prolific textual output included the collection and interpretation of the *Trovas*, which he published complete with analysis in 1603.

71. João de Castro, *Discurso da vida da el-rei D. Sebastião* (Braga: Ediçoes Vercial, 2013): chapter 24.

72. Givens, *Judging Maria de Macedo*, 37.

73. Subrahmanyam, *Portuguese Empire in Asia*, 124.

74. Disney, *History of Portugal*, 209.

75. At the end of the fifteenth century, Spain and Portugal offered Jews the option to convert to Catholicism or risk severe punishment remaining in the Iberian Peninsula. Suspected Judaizers were tortured and put to death. Most Jewish families departed. The terms *converso/a* and *nova cristão*, in Spanish and Portuguese, respectively, mean "New Christian"—one of Jewish heritage who has become a convert to the Catholic Church. Descendants of New Christians were also labeled as such.

76. Subrahmanyam, *Portuguese Empire in Asia*, 125.

77. Israel, *Diasporas Within a Diaspora*, 18–19; Myrup, *Power and Corruption in the Early Modern World*, 116.

78. Israel, "Duarte Nunes da Costa, 16.

79. Israel, *Diasporas Within a Diaspora*, 315–53.

80. Givens, "The St. Paul of Sebastianism," 1–20.

81. "Castro, *Discurso da vida*, chapter 13. For his zeal and prolific written output, he would become known as the "Saint Paul" of Sebastianism.

82. Wilson, *Savage Republic*, 314.

83. Borschberg, "Seizure of the Sta. Catarina Revisited," 34.

84. Borschberg, 38.

85. Borschberg, 31.

86. Borschberg, 57.

87. Ittersum, *Profit and Principle*, xxxix, xxxviii.

88. Benton, *Search for Sovereignty*.

89. Ittersum, *Profit and Principle*, iii.

90. Ittersum, 45.

91. *Mare Liberum* (On the Freedom of the Seas), quickly earned a wide circulation

and entered print in 1609. Wilson, *Savage Republic*. See also Pieter C. Emmer and Wim Klooster, "The Dutch Atlantic, 1600–1800: Expansion Without Empire," *Itinerario* 23 (1999): 48–69. On the development of a Dutch Atlantic, see Benjamin Schmidt, "Dutch Atlantic."

92. Grotius, *Free Sea*, 17.

93. Russell-Wood, *The Portuguese Empire*, 24–25.

94. Grotius's benefactor, Johan Oldebarneveldt, had argued for the truce with Spain. He was routed by Maurits of Nassau on the opposing faction, imprisoned, and executed. His protégé, Grotius, manage to escape certain death when his wife brought a trunk of books to his prison cell; he was then smuggled out and made his way to Paris. Though it would not repair his reputation at home, *Mare Liberum* served, for the Dutch, English, and French, as counter to papal bulls. This opened the door to possession of people and property in the South Atlantic world.

95. João de Castro lived in Paris for more than two decades, until his death in 1628. Piterburg et al., *Braudel Revisited*, 137.

96. Grotius, *De Indis*, cited in Wilson, *Savage Republic*, 313.

97. Request of Antônio Cardoso de Barros to Filipe II, May 28, 1603, Arquivo Histórico Ultramarino (AHU), Bahia Luisa da Fonseca, Cx. 1, Docs. 4–5. AHU documents here may be found through the AHU's Projeto Resgate.

98. Decree of Filipe II, November 2, 1607, AHU, Pernambuco, Cx. 1, Doc. 26; Recommendation of the Conselho da Fazenda to Filipe II, April 5, 1618, AHU Bahia, Cx. 2, Doc. 170.

99. Letter from Filipe II, June 10, 1608, AHU, Pernambuco Cx. 1, Doc. 27.

100. Newitt, *History of Portuguese Overseas Expansion*, 218.

101. Recommendation of the Conselho da Fazenda to Filipe II, April 5, 1618, AHU, Bahia, Luisa da Fonseca, Cx. 2, Doc. 170.

102. Request of Martim de Sá to Filipe II, Lisbon, April 7, 1618, AHU, Rio de Janeiro, Cx. 1, Doc. 9.

103. Israel, *Empires and Entrepots*, 9–11.

104. Israel, *The Dutch Republic: Its Rise, Greatness and Fall*, 498. See Table 26, "The Spanish Ring Around the Republic, 1626–1628."

105. Request of captain-general of Ceará, Martim Soares Moreno, to Filipe II, May 25, 1619, AHU, Ceará, Cx. 1, Doc. 3.

106. Letter of captain-general of Ceará, Martim Soares Moreno, to Filipe II, November 1, 1621, AHU, Ceará, Cx. 1, Doc. 6.

107. Cardoso, "The Conquest of Maranhão."

108. Wilson, *Savage Republic*, 471n13.

109. Schmidt, *Innocence Abroad*, 97.

110. Schmidt, "The Dutch Atlantic and the Dubious Case of Frans Post," 170.

111. Wiesebron, "As muitas facetas da sociedade durante a ocupação neerlandesa do Brasil," 12–13.

112. Schwartz, "Commonwealth Within Itself," 87.

113. Israel, *Empires and Entrepots*, 21.

180   Notes to Pages 31–36

114. Israel, 31. See also David Onnekink, *Reinterpreting the Dutch Forty Years War, 1672–1713* (London: Palgrave Macmillan, 2016), 25–26.

115. Letter from Filipe III to the governor-general of Brazil, August 3, 1622, AHU, Bahia Luisa da Fonseca, Cx. 2, Doc. 242.

116. Letter from Filipe III to governor-general of Brazil, September 28, 1622, AHU, Bahia Luisa da Fonseca, Cx. 2, Doc. 255.

117. Camões, *Os Lusíadas*, Canto X.

118. Boxer, *Portuguese Seaborne Empire*, 375.

119. On the popularity of *Discurso da vida*, see Hermann, *No reino do desejado*, 203–8.

120. These internal challenges included a demographic crisis, slumping consumer demand, rising wages, and a chronic grain shortage. (By the 1620s, Portugal imported nearly a third of its grain.) Disney, *History of Portugal*, 206.

121. Nora, "Between Memory and History," 9.

122. Castro, *Paraphrase et concordancia de algvas prophecias de Bandarra*, 331.

Chapter Two

1. Bartolomeu Guerreiro, *Jornada dos Vassalos*, 6.

2. For a detailed discussion of the conquest, see Edmundson's "Dutch Power in Brazil."

3. For example, see Edmundson, "Dutch Power in Brazil," and Behrens, *Salvador e a invasão Holandesa de 1624–1625*, 28–29

4. Schmidt, *Innocence Abroad*, 250–51. Groesen "Lessons Learned," 167–93; Groesen, *Amsterdam's Atlantic*, 100.

5. That is, serving Philip I, II, and III of Portugal (II, III, and IV of Spain). Edmundson, "Dutch Power in Brazil"; Schwartz, "Voyage of the Vassals," 735n2. Caminietzki and Pastore, "*O fogo e o tinto*"; Lenck, *Guerra e pacto colonial*.

6. Raminelli, *Viagens ultramarinas*, 17–60.

7. Luis Camões, *Os Lusíadas*, 4 (Canto X). A few Portuguese traders—individual operators—remained on the scene, including an unfortunate merchant caught up in the Dutch massacre at Ambon. See John Skinner [1624], *A true relation of the late cruell and barbarous tortures and execution, done vpon the English at Amboyna in the East Indies, by the Hollanders there residing*, 54. On the Luso–Dutch rivalry of the Spice Islands, see Villiers, "Trade and Society in the Banda Islands in the Sixteenth Century."

8. Royal letter of December 3, 1603, cited in Behrens, *Salvador e a Invasão Holandesa de 1624–1625*, 49. At the time, the Dutch targeted Rio but were unsuccessful in their attempt.

9. Philip II of Spain, letter to Diogo Botelho, governor of Brazil, March 31, 1605, Lisbon, in "Correspondência de Diogo Botelho, governador do estado do Brazil (1602–1608)," *Revista do Instituto Histórico e Geográfico Brasileiro* 73 (1910): 8–9.

10. Philip II of Spain, letter to Diogo Botelho, governor of Brazil, May 10 1605, Lisbon, in "Correspondência de Diogo Botelho, governador do estado do Brazil (1602–1608)," *Revista do Instituto Histórico e Geográfico Brasileiro* 73 (1910): 4. https://babel.hathitrust.org/cgi/pt?id=iau.31858027934458;view=1up;seq=38. Note that the letters are slightly out of chronological order.

11. Schmidt, *Innocence Abroad*, 186.
12. Schmidt, 185–88; Israel, *The Dutch Republic and the Hispanic World*, 60–64.
13. "Compendio historial de la jornada del Brasil y suçesos della," 63.
14. "Compendio historial de la jornada del Brasil y suçesos della," 65; Edmundson, "Dutch Power in Brazil," 239. Edmundson notes that the Amsterdam press freely published information on a Dutch invasion of the Iberian South Atlantic.
15. Israel, *The Dutch Republic and the Hispanic World*; Israel, *Dutch Primacy in World Trade*, 105; Moerbeeck, "Motivos porque a companhia das Indias Ocidentais." See also Boxer, *Dutch in Brazil*, 16.
16. Schmidt, *Innocence Abroad*, 170.
17. Noorlander, *Heaven's Wrath*, 165.
18. Moerbeeck, "Motivos porque a companhia das Indias Ocidentais," 32–33.
19. Mello, *O Brasil holandês*, 30.
20. Cassia Trindade de Sá, Helena de, and Maria Isabel de Siqueira, "O Rio de Janeiro na União Ibérica: uma análise da alfândega no contexto e econômico colonial (c. 1580–c. 1640)," *Estudos Históricos* 15 (December 2015), 14, http://www.estudioshistoricos.org/15/eh%201512.pdf.
21. Behrens, *Salvador e a invasão Holandesa*.
22. Moerbeeck, "Motivos porque a companhia das Indias Ocidentais," 32, 34.
23. The Dutch Grand Design, an elaborate plan nurtured from at least the start of the seventeenth century, included conquest of all Portuguese possessions in the South Atlantic. This included Angola, the conquest of which was to secure African labor for the sugar mills of Brazil. Marley, *Wars of the Americas*, 103–34; Meuwese *Brothers in Arms, Partners in Trade*; Donoghue and Jennings, *Building the Atlantic Empires*, 20; Brandon and Fatah-Black. "'For the Reputation and Respectability of the State.'" 84–85.
24. Moerbeeck, "Motivos porque a companhia das Indias Ocidentais," 30.
25. "Westindjen kan syn Nederlands groot gewin/Verkleynt's vyands Macht brengt silver platen in." Cited in Bordo and Cortés-Conde, *Transferring Wealth and Power from the Old to the New World*, 101.
26. Gaspar de Sousa served as viceroy (governor-general) of Brazil from 1612 to 1617.
27. Gadelha, "Conquista e ocupação da Amazônia."
28. The thwarted expansion effort into Maranhão was due also to the lack of funding and shortage of provisions. Gaspar de Sousa to Filipe III (Philip IV of Spain), April 8, 1624, AHU Pernambuco, Cx. 2, Doc. 94, Fols. 1, 4.
29. "Compendio historial de la jornada del Brasil y suçesos della," 65; Edmundson, "Dutch Power in Brazil," 239–40.
30. Abreu, *Chapters of Brazil's Colonial History*, 71.

31. Rumors were that the bishop did not want funds diverted from the construction of his new church. Abreu, *Chapters of Brazilian History*, 71.

32. "Relacion Sumaria de los Avisos, que ha avido en razon de las Prevenciones en Olanda para el Brasil," cited in Edmundson, "Dutch Power in Brazil," 239.

33. The extended (relative to Caribbean competitors) safra season began late July or early August and generally lasted through May. Schwartz, *Tropical Babylons*, 176.

34. Behrens, *Salvador e a invasão Holandesa*.

35. Vieira, "Carta Ânua," 12–13.

36. *Relacion sumaria de los avisos que ha avido en razon de las pretencions que se hacian en olanda para el Brasil*, 1622, Egerton 1131, Fol. 33, BL; *Relation veritable de la prinse de la Baya de todos los santos, & de la ville S. Sauueur au Brasil. par la flotte hollandaise M.DC.XXI*, 1624, John Carter Brown Library, 4.

37. *Relation veritable de la prinse de la Baya*, 9.

38. Guerreiro, *Jornada dos vassalos*, 6r.

39. In particular, those raised on aldeias. See, for example, Vieira's description of the Tupinambá who took down the Dutch. Vieira, "Carta Ânua," 40.

40. Vieira, "Carta Ânua," 12.

41. Aldemburgk, "Relação da conquista e perda da cidade de Salvador pelos holandeses em 1624–1625," 10.

42. "Ordenarão nova companhia de novecentos, mais ladroens, & corsarios, que tratantes, & mercadores, pera infestaram a quarta parte do mundo, Hespanha nova, Perù, & Brazil." This "new company," Guerreiro argued, was formed as a result of Jan Andries Moerbeeck's ("Ioam Andre Mortecan") presentation to the States General on the reasons why the Dutch should conquer Brazil. Guerreiro, *Jornada dos vassalos*, 4v.

43. Guerreiro, *Jornada dos vassalos*, A4.

44. Behrens, *Salvador e a invasão Holanda*, 11n2. The soldiers first used the phrase "Batavian land" as they played a game of passing silver and gold around in a hat.

45. Behrens, *Salvador e a invasão holandesa*, 11. See also note 3: Van Dort was attached to the armada at the island of St. Vicente of Cabo Verde and had arrived in Bahia a month ahead to wait for his companions in the Boipeba inlet, just south of the Bay of All Saints. "When he finally decided to head to Salvador, the city had become "Batavian land"—that is, conquered by the Dutch.

46. Dutra, "Vieira Family and the Order of Christ," 25.

47. Vieira, "Carta Ânua," 14.

48. Vieira, 16.

49. Vieira, 17–18.

50. Vieira, 17.

51. Vieira, 13–14. See also Behrens, *Salvador e a invasão holandesa*, 12.

52. He and his son were sent to the United Provinces and released in 1626, a year after the restoration. "Personal Networks and Circulation in Brazil during the Hispanic Monarchy (1580–1640)," BRASILHIS Database, https://brasilhis.usal.es/en/seccion-contenido/8942.

53. Schalkwijk, *Reformed Church in Dutch Brazil*, 77.

54. Schmidt, *Innocence Abroad*, 212.
55. Guerreiro, *Jornada dos vassalos*, 7r.
56. Guerreiro, *Jornada dos vassalos*, 12r–12v.
57. Vieira, "Carta Ânua," 35–36.
58. Abreu, *Chapters in Brazil's History*, 72.
59. Vieira, "Carta Ânua," 40.
60. Raminelli, "Nobreza e principais da terra," 222.
61. Raminelli, "Nobreza e principais da terra," 218.
62. Russell-Wood, *The Portuguese Empire*, 67–68; Raminelli, "Nobreza e principais da terra"
63. Russell-Wood, *The Portuguese Empire*, 67–68.
64. Raminelli, "Nobreza e principais da terra," 222. For an in-depth discussion of the evolution of Philippine grants to Portuguese subjects in Brazil, see Raminelli, *Viagens ultramarinas*, 17–61.
65. Prior to the invasion, Albuquerque administered Pernambuco. Albuquerque was nominated to the post after Diogo Mendonça Furtado, governor of Bahia (and Brazil), was imprisoned and sent to Amsterdam.
66. Guerreiro, *Jornada dos vassalos*, 13.
67. Abreu, *Chapters in Brazil's Colonial History*, 19, 72–73. Abreu also notes that as he rounded up and coordinated help from Pernambuco, Albuquerque refused being carried about in a hammock, as was typical of men in his station.
68. Those who remained unaware of the invasion of Salvador ended up in Dutch hands. This included nine Jesuits who had the misfortune of poor timing in their trip to Bahia: "And when these priests arrived in Bahia in peace, they found the enemy as masters of the city." They were taken prisoner. Vieira, "Carta Ânua," 31.
69. Vieira, 73.
70. Guerreiro, *Jornada dos vassalos*, 36r.
71. The exact cause of the bishop's death is unclear. Vieira, "Carta Ânua," 33–34; Behrens, *Salvador e a invasão holandesa*, 65.
72. Vieira, "Carta Ânua," 34.
73. Decree of governors, July 23, 1624, AHU, Rio de Janeiro Eduardo de Castro e Almeida, Cx. 1, Doc. 24; Certificate of Luiz Alves de Cubellos, August 2, 1624, Cx. 1, Doc. 25.
74. Oliveira, *Elementos*, 95–96n3.
75. Query of the Conselho da Fazenda to King Felipe III (Philip IV of Spain), August 1, 1624, AHU, Pernambuco, Cx. 2, Doc. 101.
76. Query of the Conselho da Fazenda to King Felipe III.
77. Query of the Consulta da Fazenda, August 19, 1624, AHU, Rio de Janeiro, Eduardo de Castro e Almeida, Cx. 1, Doc. 36; Ordinance nominating head treasurer in charge of armada provisions, August 21, 1624, Doc. 39; Query of the Conselho da Fazenda, August 29, 1624, Doc. 37.
78. Query of the Conselho da Fazenda, October 6, 1624, AHU, Rio de Janeiro, Eduardo de Castro e Almeida, Cx. 1, Docs. 44–45.

79. Guerreiro, *Jornada dos vassalos*, 19; Query of the Conselho da Fazenda, August 29, 1624, AHU, Rio de Janeiro, Eduardo de Castro e Almeida, Cx. 1, Doc. 38.

80. Query of the Conselho da Fazenda, September 3, 1624, AHU, Rio de Janeiro Eduardo de Castro e Almeida, Cx. 1, Doc. 42; Guerreiro, *Jornada dos vassalos*, 21v.

81. Guerreiro, *Jornada dos Vassalos*, 21v.

82. Query of the Conselho da Fazenda, November 8, 1624, AHU Rio de Janeiro, Eduardo de Castro e Almeida, Cx. 1, Docs. 47–48, 49.

83. Schwartz, "Voyage of the Vassals," 744n24.

84. Olival, "Portugal in the Sixteenth and Seventeenth Centuries," 2.

85. Recommendation of the Conselho da Fazenda to the king (Philip IV), November 12, 1624, Lisbon, Bahia Luísa da Fonseca, Cx. 3, Docs. 343–44.

86. Recommendation of the Conselho da Fazenda, October 8, 1624, AHU, Rio de Janeiro, Eduardo de Castro e Almeida, Cx. 1, Doc. 4.

87. Request of Father João Roda Moneteiro, 1624, AHU, Bahia Luísa da Fonseca, Cx. 3, Doc. 345.

88. This never published and heavily redacted account appears to be lifted from Guerreiro, *Jornada dos vassalos*, 236–38. Guerreiro served as the family confessor.

89. It is not known why this version of accounts—which hardly strays from that of Guerreiro—did not make it into print. It is possible that since Ataide was not actually on the expedition, censors "disqualified" his manuscript. It is also possible that this was a relation he never intended to print in the first place.

90. Guerreiro, *Jornada dos vassalos*, 14r.

91. Dom João I threw his weight behind this group, which supported his regnal bid during the crisis of 1370–1380. They proved instrumental in the House of Avis. B. M. Costa, "Os mesteirais e o concelho de Lisboa durante o século XIV: um esboço de síntese (1300–1383)," *Medievalista* 21 (2017): 10.4000/medievalista.1268.

92. "10 d'agosto de 1624—Resposta da Casa dos Vinte e Quatro sobre a contrivuicao que se propunha ao povo para a restauracão da Bahia de Todos os Santos." Oliveira, *Elementos*, 101–3.

93. Oliveira, 103. Of course, such exchanges were not without a cost—if not in the form of elite status then in contracts and set prices.

94. Correia, *Sermam na procissam de graças*.

95. Schwartz, *Voyage of the Vassals*, 740.

96. Guerreiro, *Jornada dos vassalos*, 26, 31, 40r–40v.

97. Camenietzki and Pastore, "O fogo e o tinto," 265.

98. Abreu, *Chapters in Brazil's Colonial History*, 73–74.

99. Guerreiro, *Jornada dos vassalos*, A4–5.

100. I. B., *A Plaine and True Relation*, 3.

101. I.B., *A Plaine and True Relation*, note to reader.

102. Elliot, "Self-Perception and Decline in Early Seventeenth-Century Spain," 42. See especially footnote 4, where Elliot writes, "By 1603 the *visita* (the ordinary form of inquiry) begun in 1590 into the government of a recent viceroy of Peru had so far made use of 49,555 sheets of paper."

103. Guerreiro, *Jornada dos vassalos*, 32r.
104. For example, see Philip's letter, where he makes good on his offer of grants to sons whose fathers died in the rescue. Guerreiro, *Jornada dos vassalos*, 49vr–50v.
105. Maravall, *Culture of the Baroque*, 21.
106. For an excellent accounting of the conflicting record, see Camenietzki and Pastore, "O fogo e o tinto."
107. Camenietzki and Pastore, 272.
108. Camenietzki and Pastore, 274.
109. "Todos los han atribuyd a oraciones y rogativas de Espana." De Castro *Relacion de la jornada del Brasil*.
110. João de Medeiros Correia, "Relaçam verdadeira de tvdo o svccedido na restauração [. . .]," Biblioteca Brasiliana, https://digital.bbm.usp.br/handle/bbm/7218.
111. Guerreiro, *Jornada dos vassalos*, A4v.
112. Guerreiro, 41v.
113. "Dô Ioão de Orelhana." Guerreiro, *Jornada dos vassalos*, 59r.
114. L. L. Tavares in Magalhães, "A jornada dos vassalos," 231.
115. Letter of Manuel do Rego Siqueira to the king (Philip IV), AHU, Bahia, Cx. 1, Docs. 2–5.
116. See Rosenthal, "Plus Ultra," 227.
117. Orso, "Why Maino?" 27.
118. Vieira, "Carta Ânua," 1.
119. See, for instance, the epic poem *Caramaru*.

Chapter Three

1. St. Anthony continued to receive promotions and accompanying pay raises until 1912. He "retired" as a lieutenant colonel. Vainfas, "Saint Anthony," 103–4.
2. St. Anthony, long a presence in Brazil, has had multiple roles and valences; here he extended particular protection to Bahian residents, who ritualized his promotion from the Dutch period until 1912. In colonial Brazil, St. Anthony's prestige among Catholics was matched only by that of Jesus Christ and the Virgin Mary. He was adopted by Afro-Brazilians as well as bounty-hunting white *capitães-do-mato*, who pursued runaway slaves, who knew him as the "divine slave hunter." Vainfas, "Saint Anthony," 102–4.
3. The Dutch would also seize Maranhão in 1641.
4. The Franciscan Fernando Martins de Bulhões of Lisbon, also known Anthony of Padua and "the saint of the people," was born in Lisbon in 1195. Pope Gregory IX, moved by miracles reported at Anthony's tomb, beatified him in 1231, one year after his death. Polzonetti, "Tartini and the Tongue of Saint Anthony Source"; McCloskey, "Saint Anthony Novena Day One."
5. In 1638 Johan Maurits, then governor-general of Dutch-held Brazil (to the north, centered in Pernambuco), launched a monthlong and failed attack on Bahia. The

Dutch were defeated in the second Battle for Bahia (also known as the Siege of Bahia), which lasted for one month in 1638.

6. Conceptismo emerged in late sixteenth-century Spain and with the union of the crowns soon spread to Portugal. This baroque literary style is based on a *concepto* (conceit) underlying "wordplays, paradoxes, antithesis, parellelisms and comparisons which abound in it." Bleiberg et al., *Dictionary of the Literature of the Iberian Peninsula*, 424.

7. Antônio Vieira, "Sermão pelo bom successo das armas de Portugal contra as de Holanda," 49.

8. Svetlana Alpers, *The Art of Describing*, 130.

9. Silva and Alcides, "Collecting and Framing the Wilderness."

10. Neglect of the transatlantic Portuguese reaction to the Dutch in Brazil results, in part, from the accessibility of the well-ordered Dutch West India Company archives (relative to the more fragmented Portuguese language evidence). This includes the records of governor-general of Dutch Brazil Johan Maurits van Nassau-Siegen (1636–1644). Maurits commissioned forty-six artisans, artists, naturalists, and cartographers to accompany him to Pernambuco.

11. Heyn, unable to seize the town for want of manpower, nonetheless chased treasure-laden ships, capturing four and sending them on to Amsterdam. Boxer, *Dutch in Brazil*, 62.

12. Groesen, "Lessons Learned."

13. The expiration of the Twelve-Year Truce in 1621 did not mean the end of peace efforts; these were continued by Dutch and Spanish negotiators throughout the next few strife-ridden decades. See Israel, *Dutch Republic and the Hispanic World*, 201.

14. This included English and other mercenaries. See, for instance, Pudsey, *Journal of a Residence in Brazil*.

15. Albuquerque had been celebrating the birth of the prince of Portugal. Calado, *O valeroso Lucideno*, 42.

16. Calado, 43.

17. Baers, *Olinda conquistada*, 51.

18. Given the hagiographic tendencies of the day, it is likely that the priest's purpose in demonstrating the colonel's proficiency in French was to describe the colonel as a scholar-warrior. Baers, *Olinda conquistada*, 52.

19. T. J. R. Jones, "The Dutch Navy and National Survival in the Seventeenth Century," *International History Review* 10, no. 1 (February 1988): 19; Ozmont, *Three Behaim Boys*, especially 171–83.

20. Baers, *Olinda conquistada*, 22. Cuthbert Pudsey, an English soldier for the Dutch, explained that "160 leagues from Baye lyeth Fernaberke, by land it may be marched to in 25 daies as hath been reported to mee, the Towne is not so strong on the Land side, but by Sea it hath three strong castles." Pudsey, who "sailed under . . . my lord," was part of an English mercenary force that aided the Dutch in Brazil. Pudsey, *Journal of a Residence in Brazil*, 3.

21. Albuquerque et al., "O forte real do Bom Jesus."

22. Calado, *O valeroso Lucideno*, 38.

23. Pudsey, *Journal of a Residence in Brazil*, 43, Fol. 8r.
24. Calado, *O valeroso Lucideno*, 39.
25. Rodrigues, *Relacam verdadeira e breve*, Av.
26. Rodrigues, A2r.
27. Calado, *O valeroso Lucideno*, 42.
28. Calado, 43.
29. Colonel van Dorth's replacement as garrison commander drank himself to death; his brother nearly did the same. Groesen, "Lessons Learned."
30. Oliveira et al., *Ensaios sobre a América portuguesa*, 40n7.
31. Groesen, "Lessons Learned," 182–83.
32. Ambrosio Richshoffer, *Diário de um soldado da Companhia das Indias Occidentais (1629–1632)*. Translated by Alfredo de Carvalho (Recife: Instituto Arqueológico, Histórico e Geográfico Pernambucano, 1897), 57–59. Calado also writes of how the men broke into merchants' stores and helped themselves to flasks of wine, so the street was strewn with drunks. Calado, *O valeroso Lucideno*, 51.
33. Miranda, "Doentes e incapazes para marchar."
34. Richshoffer, *Diário de um soldado*, 83.
35. Richshoffer, 82.
36. Richshoffer, 99.
37. Richshoffer, 82. Desertion was a major problem for the Dutch, who had trouble rounding up troops in the first place. While the West India Company offered a three-year contract to Brazil, which seemed a better choice than the East India Company offer of five years to the Indies, the odds against the soldiers were grim indeed. Most of these men were aimless. They included Stephen Behaim, a one-time "scamp" who had been hustled out of Texel by his brothers and caretaker for his troublesome ways. After a year of no contact, he was found with rotting toes and delirious, and he died from infection. Ozment, *Three Behaim Boys*.
38. Not much is known about his origins and why or how he went to northeastern Brazil in 1618 or 1620—well ahead of the Dutch invasion of Bahia in 1624. See Richshoffer, *Diário de um soldado* 95.
39. Verdonck and Carvalho, "Descripcão das capitanias de Pernambuco."
40. On the use of the term *mouro* in this translation of Verdonck's account from Dutch, note that Portuguese racial and cultural classifications were in flux through the early modern period and throughout the kingdom. Havik and Newitt, *Creole Societies in the Portuguese Empire*, 148.
41. Brabanders hail from the Dutch province of Brabant. Richshoffer, *Diário de um soldado*, 95.
42. Richshoffer, *Diário de um soldado*, 103.
43. Richshoffer, 103.
44. Ronaldo Vainfas says that Portuguese accounts all point to the exact date of Calabar's desertion: April 20, 1632. The Portuguese term *mulato* refers to someone of European and African heritage; *mameluco* refers to a person of Indian and European descent. Vainfas notes that Calabar was cast as both terms but that given his fluency

in Tupi, he is best described as mameluco. Calado describes him as "Hum mancebo mameluco" (a young mameluco). Pudsey, *Journal of a Residence in Brazil*, 69; Regina de Carvalho, "Calabar: um intermediário cultural no Brasil Holandês," *Revista 7 Mares*, no. 3 (October 2013), 68; Vainfas, *Traição*, 86; Calado, *O valeroso Lucideno*, 1:12–15.

45. Albuquerque Coelho, *Memórias diárias da guerra do Brasil*, 84.

46. Vainfas, *Traição*, 90. Cuthbert Pudsey, an English eyewitness and soldier for the Dutch, notes that the traitor had committed a terrible crime that forced him to desert or die at the hands of the Portuguese: he had "ravished" a woman and cut out her tongue lest she betray him. Pudsey, *Journal of a Residence in Brazil*, 69.

47. Pudsey, *Journal of a Residence in Brazil*, 69.

48. Quotes from Pudsey, *Journal of a Residence in Brazil* 69; see also Albuquerque Coelho, *Memórias diárias*, 212.

49. Albuquerque Coelho, *Memórias diárias*, 212.

50. Calado, *O valeroso Lucideno*, 48.

51. Albuquerque Coelho, *Memórias diárias*, 84.

52. Meanwhile, a fair number of Dutch West India Company soldiers crossed over to the Portuguese, especially in the brutal early years.

53. The strategic location of the fortification, built early on in the war between Olinda and Recife, enabled the resistance to harass the Dutch, greatly impeding their progress in settling the area and establishing a more permanent presence. The fort's destruction five years later led to the southward retreat of the Luso-Brazilian-Spanish army. Calado, *O valeroso Lucideno*, 52.

54. Albuquerque Coelho, *Memórias diárias*, 84.

55. Vainfas, *Traição*, 90.

56. Vainfas, 90.

57. Albuquerque Coelho, *Memórias diárias*, 212; Calado, *O valeroso Lucideno*, 59–63.

58. Bandeirantes were early bounty and fortune hunters, the most famous of whom hailed from the region of São Paulo (originally known as the captaincy of São Vincente). The purpose of their expeditions, known as *bandeiras* ("flags"), was to capture Indigenous people for slave labor. While most bandeirantes were first-generation Portuguese, by the seventeenth century some groups included mamelucos.

59. Vainfas, *Traição*, 58.

60. This title was later granted to one of de Moraes's proteges, the Poti Antônio Felipe Camarão. Alden, *Making of an Enterprise*, 208.

61. Vainfas, *Traição*, 15.

62. Competing theories obscure Manoel de Moraes's reasons for switching to the Dutch side. It is widely accepted that he surrendered during the Portuguese defeat at the 1634 Battle of Paraíba. However, this may not have been a decision to simply save his skin. Irishman Bernard O'Brian del Carpio told his Spanish friend Fernando Ruiz de Contreras that de Moraes felt that Portuguese ground commander Matias de Albuquerque had been disrespectful to him. He had also been concerned about back pay for services rendered to the Portuguese. At that time, O'Brien reported, the Jesuit had

given up attending Mass. This encounter is described in McGinness, "Negotiating the Confessional Divide Between Dutch Brazil and the Republic," 236–37; see especially footnotes 40–43.

63. Vainfas, *Traição*, 76–79.
64. Boxer, *Dutch in Brazil*, 267.
65. Alden, *Making of an Enterprise*, 210.
66. Baerle, *History of Brazil*, 102.
67. Boxer, *Dutch in Brazil*, 67–68.
68. Baerle, *History of Brazil*, 102–19. See chapter 5, "The Affair Arciszewsky" See also the translator's note, xvii–xix.
69. Schmidt, *Innocence Abroad*, 250–51.
70. Groesen, *Amsterdam's Atlantic*, 5.
71. Samuel van Hoogstraten, a seventeenth-century Dutch painter, poet, and theorist, composed a treatise on the nature of Dutch art in which he "introduced drawing as linked to letters formed in writing, to planning war maneuvers, to medicine, astronomy, natural history and surveys." Alpers, *Art of Describing*, 122, 142.
72. Corrêa do Lago and Corrêa do Lago, *Frans Post*, 26–27.
73. Maurits's artistic entourage included Latin poet and personal chaplain Franciscus Plante and aspiring artists Albert Eckhout and Frans Post. The expenses of his physician, his secretary, and Plante, his chaplain, were covered by the WIC. Boxer, *Dutch in Brazil*, xii, 69.
74. Cleveland, "Mapping the Landscaped Brazilian Body," 44.
75. Phaf-Reinberger, "Science and Art in the 'Dutch Period,'" 43n19.
76. Brienen, "Albert Eckhout and Frans Post," 65.
77. The Portuguese colonialists divided the Indigenous people of Brazil into two groups: the Tupinambá, for their Tupi-derived language, and the Tapuya/Tapuia, a non-Tupi-speaking group that lived in the interior. The Tarairu inhabited the sertão of Rio Grande do Norte. The first group was in reality comprised of several different and at times warring tribes, including the Potiguara, the Tupiniquim, and the Caeté. These the Portuguese named *índios mansos* (tame Indians); many were also *índios* aldeados. See, for example, Anderson, "Mapping Colonial Interdependencies in Dutch Brazil," 57–59; Meuwese, *Brothers in Arms*, 126–32.
78. Vieira, "Carta ânua da provincia do Brasil," 40.
79. The Indigenous left in Bahia at the time of Dutch withdrawal in 1625 bore the brunt of Portuguese wrath for serving the Dutch. According to a WIC officer, this was actually due to neglect by the Dutch: in their surrender at Bahia, the Dutch "forgot to include them [Indian allies] in the treaty, the result of which was cruel treatment by the Spanish [Portuguese]." Richshoffer, *Diário de um soldado*, 84.
80. Later, the High Council lamented funds spent on Pieter Poti and his cousin Antonio Parawba, who were "more perverse and wild," went the complaint, "in their way of life than other *brasilienses*." Hemming, *Ouro vermelho*, 223.
81. *Tempo dos flamengos*, 223–25.
82. Meuwese, *Brothers in Arms*.

83. Brazilienses was a Dutch name for Tupi who were loyal to the Portuguese. Richshoffer, *Diário de um soldado*, 92–93.
84. Richshoffer, *Diário de um soldado*, 93.
85. Alpers, *Art of Describing*, xxiv.
86. Pereira Fagundes, "Felipe Camarão," 201.
87. As an *índio* aldeiado, Camarão, a member of the Poti tribe, was raised on an aldeia.
88. Diogo Lopes Santiago, cited in Pereira Fagundes, "Felipe Camarão," 203.
89. Felipe Camarão to the Dutch, Recife, April 1638, in "Carta dos holandeses, oferecendo o perdão a todos os rebeldes que se renderem a seu domínio e respostas dos brasileiros [. . .]," BNDB, Mss. II-31, 28, 003, Fol. 5.
90. Albuquerque Coelho, *Memórias diárias*, 275–83.
91. Francisco d'Angola and Juse d'Angola are examples of free Black soldiers fighting for the Dutch in Brazil. Mark Meuwese, *Brothers in Arms*, 183.
92. Cleveland, "Mapping the Landscaped Brazilian Body," 5.
93. Palmares is often referred to as a *quilombo*, but that word did not exist in seventeenth-century literature. *Mocambo* was the term most frequently used to discuss such settlements.
94. Nieuhof, *Memorável viagem marítima e terrestre ao Brasil*.
95. Baerle, *History of Brazil*, 236.
96. Kent, "African State in Brazil."
97. In Ambundo, *mu-kambo* literally means "hideout." The term *quilombo* was first used after the departure of the Dutch; the first official use was in 1692, in a letter to Lisbon. Kent, "African State in Brazil," 163.
98. Kent, "An African State in Brazil,"169.
99. Diggs, "Zumbi and the Republic of Os Palmares." On the failed Dutch expeditions, see Kent, "An African State in Brazil," 161, 166–67.
100. Schwartz, *Early Brazil*.
101. N. N., *A Little True Forraine Newes*. According to his WIC contract, Maurits was guaranteed a percentage of the sugar profits, but monoculture proved less than successful.
102. Corrêa do Lago and Corrêa do Lago, *Frans Post*, 109.
103. Calado, *O valeroso Lucideno*, 1:301.
104. Albuquerque Coelho, *Memórias diárias*, 109.
105. Henrique Dias to the Dutch. Recife, April 1638, "Carta dos holandeses oferecendo o perdão a todos os rebeldes que se renderem a seu domínio e respostas dos brasileiros [. . .], BNDB, Mss. 31, 28, 003, Fol. 3.
106. Albuquerque Coelho, *Memórias diárias*, 109.
107. Kent, "An African State," 161.
108. Quoted in Harmsen, "Barlaeus' Description of the Dutch Colony in Brazil," 159.
109. OWIC listings on Brazil are primarily housed in the Nationaal Archief at The Hague.
110. Mello, *Gente da nação*, 273–74.
111. Ronaldo Vainfas and Jacqueline Hermann, "Judeus e conversos na Ibéria no

século XV: sefardismo, heresia, messianismo," in *Os Judeus no Brasil*, ed. Keila Grinberg (Rio de Janeiro: Civilização Brasileira, 2005), 47.

112. Arnold Wiznitzer, "Jewish Soldiers in Dutch Brazil (1630–1654)," *Publications of the American Jewish Historical Society* 46, no. 1 (1956): 42, http://www.jstor.org/stable/43059884.

113. Jaqueline Hermann, "As metamorfoses da espera," 339; Mello, *Gente da nação*.

114. Hermann, "As metamorfoses da espera," 347.

115. Novinsky, *Cristãos novos na Bahia*, chapter titled "O Homem Dividido."

116. Some contemporary chroniclers—generally Portuguese but a few Dutch—termed the colony New Holland or Nova Holanda. Mello, *Tempo dos flamengos*, with thanks to Bruno Ferreira Miranda for clarifying the source of this term.

117. Wiznitzer, *Jews in Colonial Brazil*, 73.

118. Mello, *Tempo dos flamengos*, 308. By 1637, however, the West India Council had expressed concern about the "flood" of Jews out of Amsterdam into the colony. The legislative assembly set up by Governor-General Johan Maurits included Portuguese, Luso-Brazilian, and Indigenous representatives—none were Jewish. Wiznitzer, *Jews in Colonial Brazil*, 74. See also Anita Novinsky, *Cristãos novos na Bahia*; Kagan and Morgan, *Atlantic Diasporas*; Israel, *Diasporas Within a Diaspora*.

119. In 1642, two hundred Jews under the auspices of Rabbi Isaac Aboab migrated to Recife. Arnold Wiznitzer, *The Minute Book of Congregations Zur Israel of Recife and Magen Abraham of Mauricia, Brazil* (New York: American Jewish Historical Society, 1953), 214, 235; George Alexander Kohut and John Parry, "Early Jewish Literature in America," *Publications of the American Jewish Historical Society* 3 (1895): 103.

120. Israel, *Diasporas Within a Diaspora*, 383.

121. Calado, *O valeroso Lucideno*, 114.

122. Among other such advice, he came to influence Maurits in terms of military strategy—strongly advising him to pursue a maritime-based attack on the rebel Portuguese. The Luso-Brazilian resistance would not be overcome, he argued, with a devastating land campaign. Mello, *Olinda restaurada*, 65.

123. Calado, *O valeroso Lucideno*, 114.

124. Schwartz, "Prata, açúcar e escravos: de como o império restaurou Portugal," 219.

125. Araujo-Jorge, "História diplomática do Brasil Frances no século XVI," 820.

126. Vieira, "Sermão pelo bom successo das armas de Portugal contra as de Hollanda," 50.

127. Corrêa do Lago and Corrêa do Lago, *Frans Post*, 28.

128. In pre-abolition Brazil, bare feet, rather than skin tone, indicated status as an enslaved person.

Chapter Four

1. Rosemeri Moreira, "Heroínas, gênero e Guerras," 218–19. In popular print see Galvão, "Heroínas de Tejucupapo." Souza Silva, *Brasileiras celebres*, 84–86.

2. Tavares, "Dia internacional da mulher."
3. Mention of female participation in the Battle of Tejucupapo is notably absent in the Portuguese Overseas Council records and does not appear in Dutch West India Company records.
4. Calado, *O valeroso Lucideno*, 249.
5. Santiago, *História da guerra de Pernambuco*, 396.
6. The manuscript, referenced several times in the seventeenth century, was finally uncovered in the municipal library of Porto.
7. Souza Silva, *Brasileiras celebres*, 86.
8. Carrega, *Breve história socioeconómica de Faro*, 19–20.
9. Mackay, *The Baker Who Pretended to Be King of Portugal*, 50.
10. Herculano, "A padeira d'Aljubarrota," 414. Francisco Brandão hailed from Alcoçaba, the municipality in which Aljubarrota is located.
11. The extent to which women enjoyed and deployed those rights varied. See, for example, Abreu-Ferreira, "Work and Identity in Early Modern Portugal."
12. Poska, "The Case for Agentic Gender Norms for Women in Early Modern Europe," 356.
13. Wiesner-Hanks, *Challenging Women's Agency and Activism in Early Modernity*, 22.
14. Abreu-Ferreira "Women's Property, Women's Lives"; Abreu-Ferreira, "Women, Law and Legal Intervention in Early Modern Portugal"; Abreu-Ferreira, "Work and Identity in Early Modern Portugal."
15. Abreu-Ferreira, "Fishmongers and Shipowners," 13.
16. Abreu-Ferreira, "Women, Law and Legal Intervention in Early Modern Portugal," 295.
17. Coates, *Convicts and Orphans*, 142.
18. Coates, 142; Rosenthal, "As órfãs d'el rei," 78.
19. Coates, 144–45.
20. Portuguese women could and did own ships, likely inherited from their fathers or husbands. Abreu-Ferreira, "Fishmongers and Shipowners," 7.
21. Dutra, "Duarte Coelho Pereira," 440–41.
22. Portuguese women's ability to own property and conduct business is evidenced in Silva, "Sesmarias." The size of sesmarias granted by the donatary varied, though in the northeast captaincies, they generally were about three leagues long by one league wide.
23. List of female engenho owners and lavradors are in Silva, "Sesmarias." These documents confirmed identity, confirmed legitimacy, and signaled permanent stakes in settlement.
24. Plataforma S.I.L.B, "Informações sobre a sesmaria," http://www.silb.cchla.ufrn.br/sesmaria/RN%200190.
25. A close read of this document indicates the roles and ownership status of women in the captaincy. Dussen, *Relatório sôbre as capitanias*, 31–87.
26. Dussen, 37–81.
27. Schwartz, *Sugar Plantations in the Formation of Brazilian Society*, 298n89.

28. Pudsey, *Journal of a Residence in Brazil*, 45.
29. Note likely written by WIC officer Zacharias Wagener, in Ferrão and Soares, *Dutch Brazil*, 190.
30. I. B., *A Plaine and True Relation*, 3.
31. Pudsey, *Journal of a Residence in Brazil*, 67.
32. Hamer, "'Our Dutchmen Run After Them Very Much.'"
33. Groesen, *Amsterdam's Atlantic*, 154.
34. Ana Paes to the High Council, August 27, 1637, in *Revista do Instituto Arqueológico, Histórico e Geográfico Pernambucano* 34 (December 1887): 59–60.
35. Frazão, "Anna Paes."
36. Mello, *Olinda restaurada*, 438.
37. Pudsey, *Journal of a Residence in Brazil*, 43.
38. Pudsey, 43.
39. Pudsey, 43–45.
40. I. B., *A Plaine and True Relation*, 3.
41. I. B., *A Plaine and True Relation*, 11.
42. *Chapins* were elevated shoes in fashion among Iberian elites of the seventeenth century. Mello, *O Brasil holandês*, 260.
43. Albuquerque Coelho, *Memórias diárias*, 194–95.
44. Albuquerque Coelho, *Memórias diárias*, 194–95.
45. Albuquerque Coelho, *Memórias diárias*, 195.
46. Alternate spellings include "Geronimma" and "Geronima" (Dutch) for the first name and "d'Almeida" (Portuguese and Dutch) for the surname.
47. Calado, *O valeroso Lucideno*, 127–28.
48. Santiago notes that the Rodrigo Barros Pimentel family was among the most elite in town. Santiago, *História da guerra*, 321.
49. "Extract from the tax roll concerning the case against Gerrit Crajesteijn," March 25, 1641, Nationaal Archief (NA), Old West India Company (OWIC), 56, no. 69.
50. "Extract from the tax roll." See also "Letter (copy) in Portuguese from Gerrit Crajesteijn to Donna Jeronima d'Almeida, housewife of Rodrigo de Barros Pimentel, owner of the ingenho Morro," March 1641, NA OWIC 56, no.75. I thank Deborah Hamer for her translations of Dutch-language documents regarding Gerrit Craeijesteijn and Jerônima de Almeida.
51. "Deposition (copy) of Donne Jeronima and Bartholomeus Luis de Almeida," March 11, 1641, NA OWIC 56, no. 76. Note: the document is dated March 9, 1641.
52. "Deposition," Fol. 2.
53. Calado, O *valeroso Lucideno*, 1:125.
54. Calado, O *valeroso Lucideno*, 1:127–28.
55. Given the scanty record, Brazilian scholars have tracked down, elaborated on, and questioned Maria Ortiz's existence. That said, the area of town where she was reputed to have lived has been renamed in her honor, and she is recognized as a national heroine. Her existence is confirmed in França, "Maria Ortiz." See also Brito Freire, *Nova Lusitania*, 95.

56. Maria de Lourdes Correia Fernandes, "Cartas de sátira e aviso: em torno dos folhetos Malícia das mulheres e Conselho para bem casar de Baltasar Dias," *Revista de Estudos Ibéricos* 1 (2004): 161–81.
57. Dias, *Malícia das Mulheres*, Fol. 8.
58. Printed by António Alvares. Subsequent editions ensued; the earliest surviving copy was published in 1659. Anastácio Vanda, "Notes on the *Querelle des Femmes* in Eighteenth-Century Portugal." *Portuguese Studies* 31, no. 1 (2015), 55.
59. With the 1668 treaty between Portugal and Spain.
60. Brito Freire, *Nova Lusitania*, 250.
61. Silva, *Brasileiras celebres*, 54.
62. Silva, *Brasileiras celebres*, 88.
63. This is excerpted from the work of eighteenth-century Benedictine monk Domingos Loreto Couto, which remained unpublished until 1904. Couto, *Desagravos do Brasil*.
64. Couto, *Desagravos do Brasil*, 525–27.
65. It is not known when he completed his work. His manuscript was discovered in the municipal library of Porto sometime between 1871 and 1876. Santiago, *História da guerra de Pernambuco*, 118.
66. Santiago, *História da guerra de Pernambuco*, 391.
67. Calado, *O valeroso Lucideno*, 2:255.
68. Calado, 2:255.
69. Calado, 2:257.
70. Santiago, *História da guerra de Pernambuco*, 394.
71. Calado, *O valeroso Lucideno*, 1:301.
72. Calado, 2:53.
73. Dutra, "A Hard-Fought Struggle for Recognition," 93.
74. José Antônio Gonsalves de Mello, *Restauradores de Pernambuco*, 21.
75. Ronaldo Raminelli, "Impedimentos da cor: mulatos no Brasil e em Portugal," *Varia Historia*, 28 no. 48 (July–December 2012): 711.
76. Raminelli, 700.
77. Raminelli, 713.
78. Brandão, "Tejucupapo."
79. See, for example, Tavares, "Dia internacional da mulher."
80. Tavares, "Dia internacional da mulher."
81. Brandão, "Tejucupapo."
82. GV News, "Escadaria Mariz Ortiz é Reformada Por Detentos," January 10, 2018, https://gvnews.com.br/escadaria-mariz-ortiz-e-reformada-por-detentos/.
83. The memory of Maria Ortiz has been contested over the years. Some writers have reduced her role to that of a prostitute; others contend that she never existed at all. See, for example, Walter de Aguiar, "Maria Ortiz: Mea Culpa," Morro do Moreno, April 26, 2013, http://www.morrodomoreno.com.br/materias/maria-ortiz-mea-culpa.html. See also Almeida Teles, *Breve história do feminismo no Brasil e outros*.
84. Soares da Silva, *Memórias para a historia de Portugal*, 1276–77.

Chapter Five

1. Albuquerque Coelho, *Memórias diárias*, 200.
2. At the end of their three-year contract with the Dutch West India Company, soldiers could and did opt to stay and settle in Dutch-held Brazil. In addition, given Dutch religious tolerance, the Jewish population swelled to nearly half of all Europeans in Pernambuco. In 1642 Rabbi Isaac Aboab de Fonseca and *hakham* (scholar) Moses Raphael e Aguilar of Amsterdam migrated to Recife with a few hundred members of the Congregation Talmud Torah of Amsterdam. See, for example, Wiznitzer, *Jews in Colonial Brazil*, 86.
3. It is estimated that the Dutch West India Company sustained casualties of up to 40 percent within a month of invading Pernambuco in 1630; about 30 percent had been afflicted with sickness during the crossing. Company men remained without ready access to provisions for the next two years. Miranda, "'Doentes e incapazes para marchar.'" See also Stephen Behaim's 1635 letter to his brothers in Ozment, *Three Behaim Boys*, 273.
4. For instance, in 1624 Manuel Severim de Faria, the influential and lettered canon and precentor of the Cathedral of Evora, reminded Philip IV that the "Province of Spain" was very nearly an island, all but disconnected by hundreds of leagues from principal states such as Flanders, Naples, and Milan—not to mention possessions on the coasts of the New World, Asia, Africa, and the "islands of the Ocean Sea." He argued in favor of strengthening the maritime power of the Spanish, the Portuguese, and the Biscaynes to keep the vast kingdom intact. Faria, *Discursos varios políticos*, A2r–A3v.
5. Men recruited for the Spanish-led rescue armadas hailed from Spain and its dominions—primarily Portugal and Naples. On rationing during the transatlantic crossing, see Mello, *Olinda restaurada*, 25.
6. See, for example, Albuquerque, *A remuneração de serviços da guerra holandesa*, 32–34.
7. Henrique Moniz Telles, cited in Magalhães, "A jornada dos vassalos," 261.
8. Philip II, primarily concerned with access to Lisbon ports, promised at Tomar that he would accept Portugal's autonomy in exchange for this and recognition of him as king of both crowns. As such, he would only be represented in Portuguese affairs by a Portuguese noble, and the Cortes could only be summoned in Portugal. All current church and official posts would remain in the hands of the Portuguese elite, though they could be eligible for posts in Spanish dominions. Malyn Newitt, *Portugal in European and World History* (London: Reaktion Books, 2009), 96–97; Disney, *History of Portugal*, 199–202. In 1619 Philip III needed Cortes approval to ensure succession of his heir to the Portuguese throne and made the journey to Lisbon in time of unrest.
9. Guerreiro, *Relação das festas*, scan 26/130.
10. Guerreiro, scan 15/130, referencing the loss of Sebastian; scan 26/130, praising the spectacle.
11. Guerreiro, scan 59/130; Disney, *History of Portugal*, 199.
12. Malyn Newett, *Portugal in European and World History*, 174.
13. The Mesa da Consciência e Ordens (Board of Conscience and Orders), formed

in 1532, was a "royal council of theologians devoted to issues like war, commerce, conversion, and slavery." Giuseppe Marcocci, "Conscience and Empire: Politics and Moral Theology in the Early Modern Portuguese World," *Journal of Early Modern History* 18, no. 5 (2014): 473–94; Elliot, *Imperial Spain: 1469–1716*, 257.

14. See chapter 2 on preparations for and the restoration of Bahia, 1624–1625. However, as the Carreira da Índia provided the bulk of overseas revenue to the Crown at this time, Spain also directed efforts to protect Portugal's holdings to the east.

15. The Conselho da Fazenda, enacted by statute on November 20, 1591, built upon existing administrative structure centered primarily on Portugal's Regimentos e Ordenações da Fazenda, of October 17, 1516. This unit oversaw revenues and rents from the Portugal and its overseas claims. One decade into the union of the Iberian crowns, the creation of the Conselho da Fazenda was meant to streamline and centralize administration of Portugal's overseas possessions. In theory, each of the above-mentioned dominions, governed by individual viceroys, operated by its own laws. In Associação dos Amigos do Torre do Tombo, "Conselho da Fazenda."

16. Kagan, *Clio and the Crown*, 202.

17. Moerbeeck, "Motivos porque a companhia das Indias Ocidentais"; Moerbeeck, *Lista de tudo que o Brasil*, 29.

18. Moerbeeck, 31.

19. Moerbeeck, 33.

20. Abreu, *Chapters in Brazil's Colonial History*, 73.

21. Albuquerque Coelho, *Memórias diárias*, 6–8. The Portuguese installed a garrison in the wake of pirate James Lancaster's 1595 pillage of Recife—220 musketeers and harquebusiers divided in two companies between Olinda and Recife. But the number of soldiers declined from 1609, the start of the Twelve-Year Truce, to sixty men. Mello, *Olinda restaurada*, 183–84.

22. This occurred with the en masse departure of Spanish and Italian troops from Brazil, for instance, resulting from the 1641 restoration of Portugal. Mello, *Olinda restaurada*, 189; Lenk, *Guerra e pacto colonial*. For a more general discussion, see Parker, *Army of Flanders*, 23–30.

23. Parker, *Army of Flanders*, 25.

24. Geoffrey Parker, *The Military Revolution: Military Innovation and the Rise of the West, 1500–1800* (Cambridge: Cambridge University Press, 1996), 48–49.

25. Mello, *Olinda restaurada*, 186–88, 211.

26. During the reign of Philip IV, financial contributions were expected across all classes of society in Portugal. This was to offset the cost of the continuing, multi-front war effort against the Dutch. By 1633 government officials were expected to donate half of their emoluments. Newett, *Portugal in European and World History*, 103.

27. Portuguese served Spain on the European front. Costas, Lains, and Miranda. *Economic History of Portugal (1143–2010)*, 113. Newett, *Portugal in European and World History*, 102.

28. Robert Southey, *History of Brazil*, Part I (London: Longman, Hurst, Rees, and Orme, 1810), 526.

29. Requerimento of Manuel Pires Bizerra, September 18, 1633, AHU, Bahia Avulsos, Cx. 1, Doc. 17, Fol. 1r.

30. Mello, *Olinda restaurada*, 187–88.

31. Up to 13 percent of the total fighting force at the time. Dias has been described as a *crioulo forro*, or free Black man of Brazilian descent. He commanded what was known as the Terço da Gente Preta (Tertia of Black People) or the Terçia de Henrique Dias. Terços were called legions during Roman times; the French and Germans called them regiments. Mattos, "Da guerra preta," 1, 9–10, 10n22; *Olinda restaurada*, 193.

32. According to Mello, the number ranged from 10 to 15 percent of the fighting force. Mattos "Da guerra preta," 10; Mello, *Olinda restaurada* 193, 236–37.

33. Mattos, "Da guerra preta,"12.

34. Brásio, *Monumentá missionária Africana*, 8:403–4.

35. Brásio, 8:419.

36. In Brazil, aldeias were Jesuit-run Indigenous villages, but in Portuguese West Africa, aldeias were villages. Brásio, *Monumenta missionária Africana*, 8:416–19.

37. Lamego was also the site of civil unrest in 1629, brought on by increased levies on the townspeople. João Rodrigues de Sousa to Philip III of Portugal, January 10, 1635, AHU, Pernambuco, Cx. 2, Doc. 146; Newett, *Portugal in European and World History*, 103.

38. Conselho da Fazenda to King Philip IV, November 22, 1636, AHU, Pernambuco, Cx. 3, Doc. 249.

39. Conselho da Fazenda, April 28, 1638, AHU, Eduardo de Castro e Almeida, Cx. 1, Doc. 172.

40. Given their tenuous hold on the Brazilian hinterlands, Dutch West India Company ground troops were almost wholly dependent on transatlantic shipments of supplies. Miranda, "'Doentes e incapazes para marchar,'" 346.

41. Vasconcelos, *Arte militar*.

42. Oliveira, *Elementos*, 350.

43. Oliveira, 356.

44. Oliveira, 354–55, 357.

45. "Letter of Philip III about the provisioning of bread to the city," June 29, 1630, Arquivo Municipal de Lisboa (AML), Livro 3º do provimento do pão, Fols. 67, 67v.

46. Oliveira, *Elementos*, 357.

47. Oliveira, 359–60.

48. Oliveira, 366.

49. Oliveira, 367.

50. Ozment, *Three Behaim Boys*, 273–74.

51. Chaunu, "Brésil et Atlantique au XVII siècle," 1204.

52. Request of Margarida Vareira to King Philip III, November 29, 1634, AHU, Avulsos, Cx. 1, Doc. 7; Schwartz, "Commonwealth within Itself," 175. Along with Lisbon, Viana do Castelo served as a major port for ships bound to international destinations. In the first decades of the seventeenth century, at least seventy Brazil-bound ships were dedicated to provisions and supplies.

53. Request of Margarida Vareira to King Philip III, November 29, 1634, AHU, Avulsos, Cx. 1, Doc. 7.
54. Also known as the Arraial do Bom Jesus, Forte Real, or simply the Real.
55. Albuquerque et al., "O Forte Real do Bom Jesus."
56. Albuquerque Coelho, *Memórias diárias*, 202.
57. Albuquerque Coelho, 200.
58. Albuquerque Coelho, 206.
59. By the time of his writing, the Spanish had arrived. He was en route to the Low Countries aboard the *Overjissel* on December 10, 1639. Dussen, *Relatório*, 137.
60. On the conquest of Pernambuco, see chapter 3.
61. Dussen, *Relatório*, 137–38.
62. WIC letter to the States General, 1649. Mello, *Olinda restaurada*, 212.
63. Mello, *Olinda restaurada*, 211.
64. Mello, *O Brasil holandês*, 187.
65. Mello, 188.
66. Mello, 189.
67. Albuquerque Coelho, *Memórias diárias*, 275.
68. Albuquerque Coelho, 276.
69. Bispo D. Juan de Palafox y Mendoza, "Guerra en la parte del Brasil," in Magalhães "A relacion de la vitoria," 58.
70. It is not known how or why they sank. Albuquerque Coelho, *Memórias díarias*, 275.
71. Bispo D. Juan de Palafox y Mendoza in Magalhães, "A relacion de la vitoria," 59.
72. Albuquerque Coelho, *Memórias diárias*, 275.
73. Albuquerque Coelho, 276.
74. Albuquerque Coelho, 293; Francisco Martinez, *Relacion de la vitoria que alcanzaron las armas catolicas en la Baía de Todos Santos, contra ola* [. . .], 1638, 2r, John Carter Brown Library.
75. Albuquerque Coelho, *Memórias diárias*, 277.
76. Albuquerque Coelho, *Memórias díarias*, 278. A terço, evolved from the Spanish tercio in the late sixteenth century, was a military formation of one thousand to three thousand men. Christon I. Archer, John R. Ferris, Holger H. Herwig, and Timothy H. E. Travers, *World History of Warfare* (Lincoln: University of Nebraska Press, 2008), 239.
77. Albuquerque Coelho, *Memórias diárias*, 278–79.
78. Mello, *Olinda restaurada*, 240.
79. Albuquerque Coelho, *Memórias diárias*, 288.
80. Albuquerque Coelho, 287. The author notes the delivery of thirteen hundred "fangas de farinha." A *fanga* is an early modern Portuguese measurement of dry goods. The conversion from *fangas* to bushels may be calculated here: https://www.convert-me.com/en/convert/history_volume/ptfanga.html?u=ptfanga&v=1%2C300.
81. Albuquerque Coelho, *Memórias diárias*, 288.
82. "Holandeses na Bahia," Fol. 1.

83. "Holandeses na Bahia," Fol. 2.
84. Albuquerque Coelho, *Memórias diárias*, 285–88.
85. Albuquerque Coelho, *Memórias diárias*, 288.
86. Johan Maurits, letters to the States General, BNDB, "Documentos para a história do Brasil," http://objdigital.bn.br/objdigital2/acervo_digital/div_manuscritos/mss1452501/mss1452501.pdf. See also Albuquerque Coelho, *Memórias diárias*, 293; Martinez, *Relacion de la vitoria*, 5r.
87. Albuquerque Coelho, *Memórias diárias*, 293; Martinez, *Relacion de la vitoria*, 5v.
88. Albuquerque Coelho, *Memórias diárias*, 295.
89. "Holandeses na Bahia," Fols. 6–8.
90. "Holandeses na Bahia," Fol. 8
91. Albuquerque Coelho, *Memórias diárias*, 284, 295.
92. Mello, *O Brasil holandês*, 193.
93. Marcos Galindos, ed., *Episódios Baiános* (Recife: Nectar, 2010), 272.
94. "Holandeses na Bahia," Fol. 10.
95. Albuquerque Coelho, *Memórias diárias*, 295.
96. Henrique Moniz Telles, citied in Magãlhaes, "A jornado dos vassalos," 261.
97. Albuquerque Coelho, *Memórias diárias*, 293, 295; Martinez, *Relacion de la vitoria* 5rv.
98. Henrique Moniz Telles, citied in Magãlhaes, "A jornado dos vassalos," 261.
99. Salas Almela, *Conspiracy of the Ninth Duke of Medina Sidonia*, 30.
100. For more on the restoration of Portugal, see Hespanha, "Revoltas e revoluções"; Costa, "Interpreting the Portuguese War of Restoration"; Cunha, "Elites e mudanca politica."
101. Séyner, 'Historia del levantamiento de Portugal," 206.
102. Cunha, "Elites e mudança," 325–43.
103. Costa, "Interpreting the Portuguese War of Restoration," 394.
104. "Colecção Chronologica da Legislação Portugueza 1640–1647," ANTT, CGH, consulta 153, 1649, pp. 151–53.
105. Mello, *Olinda restaurada*, 189.
106. Mattos, "Guerra Preta," 10n26; Mello, *Olinda restaurada*, 14, 190–92.
107. Mello, *Olinda restaurada*, 190.
108. For example, Jorge de Mascarenhas, Marquês de Montalvão, "Parecer do Conselho Ultramarino ao rei de Portugal, a respeito das cartas enviadas a André Vidal de Negreiros e João Fernandes Vieira," October 10, 1647, BNDB.
109. Consulta of the Overseas Council, October 27, 1645, Rio de Janeiro, Eduardo de Castro e Almeida, Cx. 3, Doc. 403; Consulta of the Overseas Council, March 14, 1646, AHU, Rio de Janeiro, Eduardo de Castro e Almeida, Cx. 3, Doc. 434.
110. Consulta of the Overseas Council, March 14, 1646, AHU, Rio de Janeiro, Eduardo de Castro e Almeida, Cx. 3, Doc. 434.
111. Beatriz Nizza da Silva, *Ser nobre na colônia* (São Paulo: Editora UNESP, 2005), 154–55.
112. *Archivo dos Açores*, 214.

113. For the story of Sebastião Correa de Carvella from Ilha Terceira in the Azores, another soldier who was awarded the Order of Christ for his service in Brazil, see *Archivo dos Açores*, 212.

114. Letter to the king, 1640, AHU, Bahia Avulsos, Cx. 1, Doc. 32.

115. Parecer of the Conselho da Fazenda, October 19, 1639, AHU, Bahia Avulsos, Cx. 1, Doc. 30.

116. Parecer of the Conselho da Fazenda, ant. 1640, AHU, Bahia Avulsos, Cx. 1, Doc. 33.

117. Brásio, *Monumenta missionária Africana*, 8:418.

118. Brásio, 8:419.

119. Gade, Daniel W., "Names for Manihot Esculenta: Geographical Variation and Lexical Clarification," *Journal of Latin American Geography* 1, no. 1 (2002): 43–57. http://www.jstor.org/stable/25765027.

120. Mello, *Olinda restaurada*, 221.

121. Marcena, *Mexendo o pirão*, 118.

122. Some petitions, like Barbosa's, were turned down flat. But generally a petitioner who had strong supporting letters had an easier time gaining part of his requests. Petitioners could also resubmit. Albuquerque, *Remuneração de serviços da guerra holandesa*, 32.

123. Albuquerque, *Remuneração*, 33.

124. Albuquerque *Remuneração*, 35. With the Pernambucan uprising of 1645, Dom João IV suspended the grant of such requests lest it appear that he favored rebel activity over peace with the Dutch. This changed after the second Battle of Guararapes (1649), when it seemed the Dutch were losing their hold in Brazil. Albuquerque, *Remuneração*, 37.

125. Sadlier, *Brazil Imagined*, 88.

126. Schwartz, *Sugar Plantations*, 31.

127. Soares, "Engenho sim," 79.

128. Gabriel Soares de Souza, *Tratado descriptivo do Brasil em 1587*, in Soares, "Engenhos sim," 79.

129. Brandão, *Diálogos das grandezas do Brasil*, 112.

130. Marcena, *Mexendo*, 9–10.

131. Marcena, 107, 112–13.

132. Bahia had policies and regulations on planting, but this was not enforced. Marcena, 347.

133. Lenk, *Guerra e pacto colonial*, 430. The literal translation is "flour of the land."

134. In times of extreme crisis, as in the case of imminent Dutch attack, farinha was drawn from farther south, in São Vicente. This option was less dependable and less desirable, in no small part due to the lower quality of the farinha and local political tensions that made for unreliable shipping. Lenk, *Guerra e pacto colonial*, 433–35.

135. Albuquerque Coelho, *Memórias diárias*, 202.

136. Farinha is integral to Bahian cuisine as well. In late seventeenth-century Bahia, legislation to compel sugar producers to grow enough manioc to feed their enslave workers (the surplus was to be sold on the market) was introduced. This may indicate that

Chapter Six

1. Spilbergen, *East and West Indian Mirror*, 66.
2. Regarding the Rio de la Plata region, between 15 and 30 percent of Potosí silver was exchanged for slaves transported from West Africa to Rio de Janeiro. Flynn and Giráldez, "Born with a 'Silver Spoon,'" 217.
3. Valladares, *A Independência de Portugal*, 43–44.
4. These included protests at Évora, which nearly derailed Spanish rule as the unrest spread through the south of Portugal. Valladares, *A Independência de Portugal*, 40–41.
5. Olival, "Portugal in the Sixteenth and Seventeenth Centuries," 2.
6. Known today as the Praça do Comercio.
7. Oliveira, *Elementos para a história munícipio de Lisboa*, 411–12.
8. Flecknoe, *A Relation of Ten Years in Europe, Asia, Affrique, and America*.
9. Oliveira, *Elementos para a história munícipio de Lisboa*, 417.
10. Oliveira, 421.
11. Oliveira, 419.
12. Myrup, "Kings, Colonies, and Councilors," 188–89.
13. Costa, "Interpreting the Portuguese War of Restoration," 394.
14. "Colecção Chronologica da Legislação Portugueza 1640–1647," ANTT, CGH, consulta 153, 1649, pp. 151–53.
15. Sá joined the Overseas Council in 1645. Boxer, *Salvador de Sá*, 214.
16. Jorge de Mascarenhas, Marquês de Montalvão, "Parecer do Conselho Ultramarino a respeito da carta inclusa de João Fernandes Vieira, que trata das vitórias contra os holandeses O Conselho Ultramarinho," August 7, 1649, BNDB.
17. The viceroy's distinguished career ended in the prison at the Castle of St. Jorge, located atop the highest hill in Lisbon. Myrup, *Power and Corruption in the Early Modern World*, 36.
18. Valladares, *A Independência de Portugal*, 47.
19. The real instigator of this treason, alleged one contemporary, was their Spanish-born mother. Lenk, *Guerra e pacto colonial*, 263–64.
20. Cunha, "Elites e mudanca politica," 343.
21. Tutino, *Making a New World*; Flynn and Giraldez, "Born with a 'Silver Spoon,'" 202.
22. Hanke, "Portuguese in Spanish America," 7.
23. O'Malley and Borucki, "Patterns in Intercontinental Slave Trade," 321. Through 1698, enslaved people trafficked to the east coast of South America disembarked at Rio, Recife, and Bahia only.

24. Boxer, *Salvador de Sá*, 254n50. Esteves, "Para o estudo das relações comerciais," 30.

25. Letter of Diogo Soares to D. Diogo de Meneses, December 16, 1619, AHU, Rio de Janeiro Avulsos, Cx.1, Doc. 4.

26. Sá married Catarina Ugarthe, a wealthy widow to whom her late husband had bequeathed his vast estate. This was not unusual; intermarriage between Portuguese merchants and Spanish elites had long facilitated family wealth-building—in this case, the slave-for-silver exchange. Alex Borucki, "Trans-imperial History in the Making of the Slave Trade to Venezuela, 1526–1811," *Itinerario* 36, no. 2 (2012): 33.

27. Valladares, *A Independência de Portugal*, 48.

28. The Spanish and Portuguese had collaborated, for example, in the hunt for gold and silver on the Brazilian frontier. Hanke, "Portuguese in Spanish America," 4, 433n2.

29. Valladares, *A Independência de Portugal*, 51–52.

30. Valladares, 52.

31. Salvado and Miranda, *Cartos do 1º*, 1:436.

32. The count's ill-fated crossing in 1639 led to the deaths of three thousand men. Torre then decided that the armada would recover in Bahia rather than directly engage the Dutch in Pernambuco. His delay of a year afforded the Dutch West India Company time to prepare for battle. It would be the last such Luso–Spanish venture—and end with most of his fleet scattered to Cartagena de Indias. Post-restoration, he was suspected of colluding with the Dutch and imprisoned for life. Miranda and Salvado, "Struggling for Brazil"; Fernández Duro, *Armada española*, 134.

33. Esteves, "Para o estudo das relações," 35.

34. Letter from Domingos Correia to the king, November 29, 1642, AHU, Rio de Janeiro Avulsos, Cx. 2, Doc. 106, Fols. 2, 6.

35. Esteves, "Para o estudo das relações," 32.

36. Borucki et al., "Atlantic History and the Slave Trade to Spanish America," 433.

37. Borucki, "Trans-imperial History," 33–34.

38. Newson and Minchin, *From Capture to Slave*; see also Borucki et al., "Atlantic History and the Slave Trade to Spanish America," 45.

39. Ferry, "Encomienda, African Slavery, and Agriculture," 613, 623.

40. Cartagena, the most important port city in Spanish America, also received routine arrivals of enslaved persons. Restoration led to an open hatred of Luso merchants, most of whom were New Christians. Valladares, *A Independência de Portugal*, 51.

41. "Requerimento de António Abreu de Lima ao Conselho Ultramarino," April 21, 1641, in Brásio, *Monumento missionária Africana*, 8:499.

42. Alencastro, *Trade in the Living*, 237.

43. N. N., *A Little True Forraine Newes*, 4.

44. Johan Maurits to the Heeren XIX, August 12, 1641, in *Officios de Conde Maurício de Nassau*, 142–44.

45. Esteves, "Para o estudo," 30. The Intra-American Slave Trade Database indicates continued movement, from the late sixteenth century, of captives transported from Brazil, most often from Rio de Janeiro or (before the Dutch era) Pernambuco, Bahia, or

an unspecified place, to Buenos Aires. During the Dutch challenge for Brazil and through the union, brisk trade continued, mostly out of Rio de Janeiro. This did not completely halt after the dissolution of the dual crown and the reconquest of Angola. For example, in 1649, the *S. Pedro* transported 303 enslaved Africans from Rio de Janeiro to Buenos Aires.

46. Esteves, "Para o estudo," 30. Alencastro, *Trade in the Living*, 100.
47. Albuquerque Coelho, *Memórias diárias*.
48. Loyalists to the House of Braganza uncovered and quelled a conspiracy against the Crown designed to deliver Portugal back to Philip IV in 1661. Eight involved in the plot were executed in a bloody spectacle attended and applauded by thousands of Portuguese. Cunha, "Elites e mudanca politica," 343.
49. Mascarenhas served under both Philip III and Philip IV of Spain (II and III of Portugal), enjoying a meteoric rise especially from 1624. Lorraine White, "Dom Jorge Mascarenhas: Family Tradition and Power Politics in Habsburg Portugal." *Portuguese Studies* 14 (1998): 65–83. See also Myrup, *Power and Corruption*, chapter 1.
50. Calado, *O valeroso Lucideno*, 202.
51. Mello, *Olinda restaurada*, 189.
52. Calado, *O valeroso Lucideno*, 203.
53. Calado, 203–4.
54. Calado, 213; Cunha, "Elites e mudança política," 343.
55. Coroacy, "O Rio de Janeiro," 103.
56. Coroacy, 103–4.
57. The captaincy of São Vicente was also under Sá's jurisdiction.
58. In 1624 the legitimacy of the Countess of Vimieiro, Mariana de Sousa Guerra, the fourth donatary of São Vicente, was contested, and she was forced to relinquish her claim. In reaction, she secured backing and support to create Itanhaém, a southerly section of the captaincy. Lana Sato, "Capitania de Itanhaém," *Atlas digital da América Lusa*, October 6, 2017, http://lhs.unb.br/atlas/Capitania_de_Itanhaém.
59. Fraga and Krause, *1640*, 72–73.
60. Alden, "Some Reflections on Antonio Vieira," 8.
61. Cohen, "Millenarian Themes," 28–29.
62. In North Africa, word of the December 1 uprising came as a shock. But between the high cost of maintaining what was left of the colony and its declining commercial importance, North Africa was less of a priority for the Braganzas. North African Iberian outposts depended heavily on supplies, which had come mainly from Sevilla. So Ceuta and Tangier declared for King Philip Fraga and Krause, *1640*, 5.
63. Salvado and Miranda, *Cartos do 1°*, 2:485.
64. Fraga and Krause, *1640*, 63
65. Johan Maurits, "A Brief Report on the State That Is Composed of the Four Conquered Captaincies: Pernambuco, Itamaracá, Paraíba and Rio Grande, Situated in the North of Brazil," in Schwartz, *Early Brazil*.
66. Simão de Vasconcellos, *Vida do P. Joam d'Almeida da Companhia de Iesu* [. . .] (Lisbon: Oficina Craesbeeckiana, 1658), 220.
67. Alencastro, *Trade in the Living*, 219.

68. Alencastro, 218–19.
69. Lenck, *Guerra e pacto colonial*, 125.
70. Boxer, *Salvador de Sá*, 217.
71. Alencastro, *Trade in the Living*, 220.
72. Alencastro, 222–23.
73. Alencastro, 218–25.
74. Boxer cites personal enmity between the two governors-general. Sá would later talk his way out of this betrayal to the king. After sitting on the Overseas Council, he applied for—but did not receive—governorship of Macao, though he had full support of his peers on the council. Boxer indicates that this was because of Sá's connections to Spain. Boxer, *Salvador de Sá*, 212–13.
75. Boxer, *Salvador de Sá*, 214.
76. Sa served as governor-general of Angola from 1647 to 1652. Russell-Wood, *Portuguese Empire*, 67–68.
77. Alencastro, *Trade in the Living*, 230.
78. Vasconcellos, *Vida do P. Joam d'Almeida da companhia de Iesu*, 221. See also Boxer, *Salvador de Sá*, 404–5.
79. Valladares, *A Independência de Portugal*, 220–21.
80. Almeida and fellow priests of the Company of Jesus encouraged African labor as a means of pursuing a particular colonialist agenda: saving souls and expanding Portugal's reach. Alencastro, *Trade in the Living*, 232–36.
81. As Sá remained in Angola, the Overseas Council petitioned Dom João IV to name a new governor of Rio de Janeiro, as well as supply munitions and other help to guard against the Dutch. Consulta of the Conselho Ultramarino to King D. João IV, August 19, 1648, AHU, Rio de Janeiro, Cx. 2, Doc. 193, Fol. 2.
82. Alencastro, *Trade in the Living*, 236.
83. Alencastro, 100–1.
84. Consulta da Conselho Ultramarino, June 16, 165l, AHU, Angola, Cx. 6, Doc. 14; Esteves, "Para o estudo," 38–39.
85. Esteves, 36–37.
86. Esteves, 35–36.
87. Zimbo was also harvested off the island of Luanda. "Relação de Fernão de Sousa a el-rei," June 14, 1633, in Brásio, *Monumenta missionária Africana*, 8:233; "Parecer de Francisco Leitão sobre a missão dos Capuchins," December 4, 1643, in Brásio, *Monumenta missionária Africana*, 9:95.
88. The other 6 percent of cowries originated in Asia. M. Florentino, "The Slave Trade, Colonial Markets, and Slave Families in Rio de Janeiro, Brazil, ca. 1790–ca. 1830," in *Extending the Frontiers: Essays on the New Transatlantic Slave Database*, edited by David Eltis and David Richardson (New Haven: Yale University Press, 2008), 286, Figure 10.1.
89. Alencastro, *Trade in the Living*, 241.
90. Alencastro, *Trade in the Living*, 263.

Chapter Seven

1. Craigwood, "Place of the Literary in European Diplomacy."
2. Sousa Coutinho, *Correspondência diplomática*, 5.
3. Sousa Coutinho, 5.
4. Sousa Coutinho, 4.
5. Boxer, *Dutch in Brazil*, 104–5.
6. Such as the conspiracy of 1641 and the threat to the Portuguese throne. Cunha, "Elites e mudança política."
7. Israel, *Dutch Republic and the Hispanic World*, 349.
8. "Conselho da Guerra," ANTT, https://digitarq.arquivos.pt/details?id=4411624.
9. Fernando Dores Costa, "Governadores das armas," https://doi.org/10.4000/books.cidehus.4401.
10. Angelo Ribeiro, *História de Portugal*, Vol. 5, *A restauração da independência: o início da dinastia de Bragança* (Matosinhos: Quidnovi, 2004), 69.
11. *Boletim do Conselho Ultramarinos*, Legislação Antiga, Vol. I (1446–1754): 239. Lisboa: Imprensa nacional, 1867; on the formation of the Overseas Council, see Myrup, "Kings, Colonies, and Councilors."
12. Myrup, 188.
13. Costa, "O conselho de guerra como lugar de poder," 400.
14. Myrup, *Power and Corruption*, 191.
15. Stuart Schwartz, *Sovereignty and Society in Colonial Brazil: The High Court of Bahia and Its Judges 1609–1751* (Berkeley: University of California Press, 1976), 69.
16. Schwartz, 69.
17. Myrup, "Kings, Colonies, and Councilors," 188.
18. Myrup, 190.
19. Evaldo Cabral de Mello, *O negócio do Brasil: Portugal, os Paises Baixos e o nordeste (1641–1649)* (Lisbon: Comissão Nacional para Comemoracões dos Descobrimentos Portugueses, 2001), 29.
20. Silva, *Dutch and Portuguese in Western Africa*, 33; Sousa Coutinho, *Correspondência diplomática*, ix.
21. Sousa Coutinho, *Correspondência diplomática*, x.
22. Sousa Coutinho, 1; Prestage, "O papel da diplomacia," 10.
23. Pinto, "Captains, Sultanas and Liaisons Dangereuses," 13.
24. Sousa Coutinho, *Correspondência diplomática*, xiii.
25. *Civil War*, or *Pharsalia*, described Julius Caesar's conflict with Pompey. In Book I, from which this quote is drawn, he crosses the Rubicon. In the seventeenth century, Englishman Thomas May's translation of *Pharsalia* was particularly popular, with the first English printing in 1626. By 1640 May's translation to Latin was available in Leiden too. Lucan, *Civil War*, 1:81; Brian Lockey, *Early Modern Catholics, Royalists, and Cosmopolitans: English Transnationalism and the Christian Commonwealth* (London: Routledge, 2016).
26. Sousa Coutinho, *Correspondência diplomática*, 319.

27. Montcher, *Mercenaries of Knowledge*, 222–23.
28. On "biblipolitics," see Montcher, "Early Modern Bibliopolitics."
29. The much-lauded scholar had run afoul of the Inquisition and had been banished from Portugal for life. While exiled to São Tomé, he ended up in Paraíba and was nearly caught in disguise on an engenho. With the Inquisition hot on his heels, he managed to escape and find his way to Rome.
30. Lima, "Prophetical Hopes," 376–78. See also ANPUH, "Devotos do 'encuberto': O Marques de Niza- primeiras impressões de uma longa pesquisa," https://www.encontro2016.rj.anpuh.org/resources/anais/42/1466974412_ARQUIVO_trabalhoanpuh.pdf.
31. Saraiva, *História e utópia*, 87.
32. Instead, Dutch expansion continued apace.
33. Calado, *O valeroso Lucideno*, 1:224.
34. Costas, "Pernambuco e a companhia geral do comércos do Brasil," 41.
35. Mello, *O Brasil holandês*, 348; Nieuhof, *Memorável viagem*, 110.
36. Nieuhoff, 110.
37. Nieuhoff, 112–13.
38. Nieuhoff, 136–38.
39. The accusations were in fact quite accurate. Henrique Dias, Felipe Camarão, and their respective regiments had at this time crossed the São Francisco River and were en route to Recife. Mello, *O Brasil holandês*, 352; Nieuhoff, *Memorável viagem*, 161.
40. Gouvêa, *Maurício de Nassau e o Brasil Holandês*, 151. Gaspar, "Anna Paes."
41. Boxer, *Dutch in Brazil*, 215.
42. Silva and Alcides, "Collecting and Framing the Wilderness," 170.
43. Cabral de Mello, citing in full a translated (to Portuguese) account by Michiel van Goch, a member of the Dutch Supreme Council. Van Goch accompanied the Dutch army and offers the most complete narrative of this second Battle of Guararapes, which began the night of February 17, 1649. Mello, *O Brasil holandês*, 452–57.
44. Prestage, "O papel da diplomacia," 11–12.
45. Sousa Coutinho, *Correspondência diplomática*, 330.
46. Sousa Coutinho, 341.
47. Sousa Coutinho, 330.
48. Sousa Coutinho, 342.
49. Sousa Coutinho, 335.
50. Sousa Coutinho, 334.
51. Sousa Coutinho, 335.
52. Sousa Coutinho, 370.
53. Evaldo Cabral de Mello, *O negócio do Brasil: Portugal, os paises baixos e o nordeste (1641–1649)* (Lisbon: Comissão Nacional para Comemoracões dos Descobrimentos Portugueses, 2001), 127.
54. "Diário ou breve discurso acerca do rebellião do perfidios designios dos Portuguezes do Brazil," 172.
55. Wiznitzer, "Jews in the Sugar Industry of Colonial Brazil."
56. Sousa Coutinho, *Correspondência diplomática*, 310–16. For more on Moniz's

role, see; Iñurritegui Rodríguez, José María, and David Martín Marcos, "Literatura política Portuguesa do século XVII: António Moniz de Carvalho e a soberania do interesse," *Ler Historia* 77 (July 2020): 61–81. doi:10.4000/lerhistoria.7322.

57. "António Vieira to D. João," 1644, Manuscritos da Livraria, no. 1098, Fol. 3, ANTT.

58. Alden, "Some Reflections on Antonio Vieira," 10.

59. Costa, "Redes Mercantis na Companhia Geral," 5.

60. Lima, "Prophetical Hopes," 377.

61. Boxer, "Padre António Vieira," 481.

62. Saraiva, "António Vieira," 25. Vieira joined forces with Sousa Coutinho in his first visit, which lasted three months, before he was called away to other duties.

63. Jonathan Israel, *The Diplomatic Career of Jeronimo Nunes da Costa*, 173–74.

64. As in other stories, such as that of the recent martyrdom of Isaac de Castro, a nineteen-year-old burned alive in Lisbon for openly Judaizing in Bahia. Saraiva, "Antonio Vieira," 36.

65. His older brother Abraham Farrar described the situation of the "exiled Jew" in the frontispiece of his 1627 *Declaracao das 613 encomendancas*. Saraiva, *Historia e utopia*, 85.

66. Saraiva, "António Vieira," 36.

67. It is not known with certainty that Vieira ever met with Menasseh Ben Israel, as the only documents regarding their encounter are from Vieira's inquisitorial testimony as well as references to the meetings in his letters. From these we can gather that he met Menasseh Ben Israel with an unidentified Jew at an Amsterdam inn and that he attended synagogue and heard the rabbi speak. Saraiva, "Antonio Vieira," 44.

68. Cohen, "Millenarian Themes," 23.

69. Inspired by the exchange, Vieira wrote the first lines of his *Hopes of Portugal, Fifth Empire of the World* before he was called to supervise missions in the Amazon. Saraiva, "Antonio Vieira," 50.

70. Israel, *Diaspora Within a Diaspora*, 366.

71. Livermore, *History of Portugal*, 298.

72. *Parecer a favor da entrega de Pernambuco aos Holandeses*, in Doré, "Ásia no papel forte do Padre António Vieira."

73. Vieira, "Papel que fez o Padre Antonio Vieira a favor da entrega de Pernambuco aos holandeses," *Escritos históricos e políticos* (São Paulo: Martins Fontes, 1995), 368.

74. Vieira, "Papel que fez o Padre António Vieira," 312.

75. Boxer, "Padre António Vieira," 481, 487.

76. Alencastro, *Trade in the Living*. For an accounting of diplomatic intrigues regarding Angola, see pp. 218–26.

77. Beckhoe, *A Relation of Ten Years in Europe, Asia, Affrique, and America*, 56.

78. "Proposta feita a El-Rei Dom João IV, em que se lhe representava o miserável estado do reino e necessidade que tinha de admitir os judeus mercadores que andavam por diversas partes da Europa. 3 de julho de 1643, Lisboa." Antônio Vieira, *Obras escolhidas*, Vol. 4 (Lisbon: Livraria Sá da Costa, 1951), 7–8.

79. Rodrigo Ricupero, "O exclusivo metropolitano no Brasil e os tratados diplomáticos de Portugal com a inglaterra (1642–1661)," *Revista de História* 176 (June 5, 2017): 10–11.
80. Alden, "Some Reflections on Antonio Vieira," 10.
81. Mello, *Olinda restaurada*, 26.
82. Israel, *Empires and Entrepots*, 342.
83. Israel, *Conflicts of Empires*, 174; Israel, "Duarte Nunes da Costa."
84. Israel, *Conflicts of Empires*, 175.
85. Costas, *O transporte no Atlântico*, 493.
86. Costas, "Merchant Groups," 2.
87. Costas, 4.
88. Antúnes, "Free Agents and Formal Institutions," 183.
89. Article XV of the charter proposed by investing merchants on March 8, 1649, and confirmed by Dom João on March 10, 1649. Silva, "Instituição da companhia geral para," 36.
90. Parecer do Pedro Fernandes Monteiro a Duas Consultas do Conselho de Estado, n.d., BA, 50-V-35.
91. Boxer, "Padre António Vieira," 495.
92. "Parecer do Pedro Fernandes Monteiro a Duas Consultas do Conselho de Estado," n.d., BA, 50-V-35.

Epilogue

1. Pimentel, *História do culto de nossa senhora em Portugal*, 1.
2. Pimentel, 193–95.
3. Vieira, "Sermão de nossa senhora de Penha de França," 182.
4. Cohen, "Millenarian Themes," 23.
5. Cohen, 23–46.
6. For instance, sociologist Gilberto Freyre's 1933 *Masters and Slaves* (A Casa Grande e Senzala). See Kim Baker, *Freedoms Given, Freedoms Won: Afro-Brazilians in Post-Abolition São Paulo and Salvador* (New Brunswick, NJ: Rutgers University Press, 2000), 10.
7. Transcriptions and translations (to Portuguese) of key Dutch documents have, since Brazil's independence from Portugal, helped build a national narrative. The documents include key Dutch West India Company material, including Johan Maurits's letters to company directors when he was en route to and from Brazil (1636–1644). Such work has been commented on and refined in successive generations, particularly by Pernambucan historians.
8. The term *baroque*, derived from the Portuguese/Spanish word *barreuco*, indicates an irregular geographical protuberance and/or the Portuguese *barroco*, used to describe an irregular pearl. It has been deployed here and throughout simply as

a "metaphor for irregularity in form and function." Walter Moser, "The Concept of Baroque," *Revista Canadiense de Estudios Hispánicos* 33, no. 1 (2008): 11–37; Joan E. Meznar, Thomas Cohen, and Stuart B. Schwartz, "António Vieira: Word and Power in the Portuguese Baroque," *Luso-Brazilian Review* 40, no. 1 (2003), 116–22; Molly Warsh, *American Baroque: Pearls and the Nature of Empire, 1492–1700* (Chapel Hill: University of North Carolina Press, 2018), 11.

9. Ronaldo Raminelli, *Viagens ultramarinas*, 49–51.

Bibliography

Archives

AHN Archivo Histórico Nacional
AHU Arquivo Histórico Ultramarino
AML Arquivo Municipal de Lisboa
ANTT Arquivo Nacional Torre do Tombo
BA Biblioteca de Ajuda
BL British Library
BNE Biblioteca Nacional España
BM Biblioteca Madrid
LL Lilly Library, Indiana University
LOC Library of Congress
NYPL New York Public Library

Digital Archives

NA. Nationaal Archief. http://www.gahetna.nl
BBM. Biblioteca Brasiliana Mindlin. https://www.bbm.usp.br
BNDB. Biblioteca Digital Nacional Brasil. http://bndigital.bn.gov.br/
BNP. Biblioteca Nacional Portugal. http://www.bnportugal.gov.pt/
EEBO. Early English Books Online. http://eebo.chadwyck.com
GO. Governo dos Outros. http://www.governodosoutros.ics.ul.pt/
SILB. Plataforma Sesmaria do Império Luso-Brasilieiro. http://www.silb.cchla.ufrn.br/

Primary Source Collections

Archivo dos Açores. Vol. 5. Ponta Delgada: Typ. do Archivo dos Açores, 1883.
Brásio, António, ed. *Monumenta missionária Africana: Africa Ocidental*. Vols. 8 and 9. Lisbon: Centro de estudios africanos da faculdade de letras da Universidade de Lisboa, 2004.

Oliveira, Eduardo Freire de, ed. *Elementos para a história munícipio de Lisboa.* Vol. 3. 1621–1633. Reprint, Lisbon: Typographia Universal, 1888.
Salvado, João Paulo, and Susana Münch Miranda. *Cartas do 1.º Conde da Torre.* 4 vols. Lisbon: CNCDP, 2001.
Sousa Coutinho, Francisco de. *Correspondência diplomática de Francisco de Sousa Coutinho durante a sua embaixada em Holanda.* Edited by Edgar Prestage and Pedro deAzevedo. Coimbra: Imprensa da Universidade, 1920.

Published Primary Sources

Adams, Edward. *A Brief Relation of the Surprizing Several English Merchants Goods by Dvtch Men of Warre.* London, 1664.
Albergaria, António Soares de. *Tropheos Lusitanos.* Part 1. Lisbon, 1632.
Albernaz, João Teixeira. *Atlas do estado do Brasil, coligido das mais sertas noticias q̃ pode aiuntar Dõ Ieronimo de Ataide,* 1631. Geography and Map Reading Room, LOC.
Albuquerque Coelho, Duarte de. *Memórias diárias da guerra do Brasil (1630–1638).* 1654. Reprint, Recife: Secretaria do Interior, 1944.
Aldemburgk, Hohann Gregor. "Relação da conquista e perda da cidade de Salvador pelos holandeses em 1624–1625," In *Documentos Holandeses.* Vol. 1, *Serviço de documentação,* edited by Ricardo Behrens. Rio de Janeiro: Ministério da Educação e Saúde, 1945.
Andrade, Miguel Leitão de. "Batalha de Alcácer-Quibir." In *Miscelânea.* Lisbon: Mattheus Pinheiro, 1629.
Baers, João. *Olinda conquistada: narrativa do padre Joao Baers, capelao do Cel. Theodoro Waerdenburch.* Translated by Alfredo de Carvalho. 1630. Reprint, São Paulo: Ibrasa, 1978.
Baerle, Caspar van. *The History of Brazil Under the Governorship of Count Johan Maurits of Nassau, 1636–1644.* Translated by Blanche T. van Verckel-Ebeling Koning. Gainesville: University of Florida Press, 2011.
Beckhoe, Richard. *A Relation of Ten Years in Europe, Asia, Affrique, and America.* London, 1656. EEBO.
Brandão, Ambrósio Fernandes. *Diálogos das grandezas do Brasil.* 1618. Reprint, Curitiba: Positivo, 2005.
Brito Freire, Francisco de. *Nova Lusitânia, historia da guerra Brasilica: A purissima alma e saudosa memoria do serenissimo principe Dom Theodosio, principe de Portugal, e principe do Brasil.* Vol. 2. Lisbon: Officina de Joam Galram, 1675.
Burgos, Bartolome Rodrigues de. "Relacion de La iornada del Brasil escrita a Juan de Castro escriviano publico de Cadiz [. . .]." 1625. Diversos-Colecciones 26, no. 40. AHN.
Calado, Manuel. *O valeroso Lucideno e triunfo da liberdad.* Vols. 1 and 2. Edited by Leonardo Dantas Silva. 1648. Reprint, Recife: Companhia Editora de Pernambuco, 2004.

Camões, Luis de. *Os Lusíadas*. 1572. Reprint, Sydney: Wentworth Press, 2016.
Castro, João de. *Paraphrase et concordancia de algvas prophecias de Bandarra, capateiro de Trancoso*. 1603. Reprint, Porto: Scholar Select, 1603.
Castro, Juan de. *Relacion de la jornada del Brasil*. 1625. Diversos-Colecciones 26. no. 40, AHN.
"Compendio historial de la jornada del Brasil y suçesos della [. . .]." 1626. Reprinted in *Colección de documentos inéditos para la historia de España*. Madrid: Imprensa de la Vicida de Calero, 1842.
Correia, Simão. *Sermam na procissam de graças que a muito nobre villa de Villa Real fez pella restauração da cidade do Salvador da Bahia* [. . .]. Biblioteca Brasiliana. https://digital.bbm.usp.br/handle/bbm/7308.
Couto, Domingos Loreto. *Desagravos do Brasil e glórias de Pernambuco*. Rio de Janeiro: Officina Typographica da Bibliotheca Nacional, 1904.
"Diário ou breve discurso acerca do rebelião so perfísios designos dos Portuguezes do Brazil, sedcobertos em junho de 1645, e do mais que se passou até 28 de Abril de 1647." In *Papeis concernentes a Gaspar Dias Ferreira*, pp. 73–175. Recife: Instituto Archeológico Geográfico Histórico Pernambucano, 1887.
Dias, Baltasar. *Malícia das mulheres*. Lisbon, 1738.
Dussen, Adriaen van der. *Relatório sôbre as capitanias conquistadas no Brasil pelos Holandeses (1639): Suas condições econômicas e sociais*. Translated by José Antonio Gonsalves de Mello. Rio de Janeiro: Instituto do Açúcar e do Álcool, 1947.
"The Dutch Boare Dissected, or a Description of Hog Land." London, 1665. EEBO.
Faria, Manuel Severim de. *Discursos varios políticos*. Evora: Manoel Carvalho, 1624. BNP.
Feltham, Owen. *A Brief Character of the Low-Countries Under the States Being Three Weeks Observation of the Vices and Vertues of the Inhabitants*. London, 1659.
Flecknoe, Richard. *A Relation of Ten Years in Europe, Asia, Affrique, and America All by Way of Letters Occasionally Written to Divers Noble Personages, from Place to Place, and Continued to this Present Year*. London, 1656.
Grotius, Hugo. *The Free Sea*. Edited by David Armitage. Translated by Richard Hakluyt. 1609. Reprint, Indianapolis: Liberty Fund, 2004.
Guerreiro, Afonso. *Relação das festas que se fizeram na cidade da Lisboa na entrada del Rey D. Philippe primeiro do Portugal*. Lisbon, 1581.
Guerreiro, Bartolomeu. *Jornada dos Vassalos da coroa de Portugal* [. . .]. Lisbon: Mattheus Pinheiro, 1625.
I. B. *A Plaine and True Relation, of the Going Forth of a Holland Fleete the Eleuenth of Nouember 1623, to the Coast of Brasile*. Rotterdam, 1626. EEBO.
Lemos de Faria e Castro, Damião António de. *Jornada de Africa* [. . .]. 1625. Reprint, Lisbon: Livro Aberto, 2004.
May, Thomas. *Pharsalia: Or, The Civill Vvarres of Rome, between Pompey the Great, and Iulius Caesar*. London: Augustine Mathewes, 1635.
Moerbeeck, Jan Andries. "Lista de tudo que o Brasil pode produzir anualmente." Translated by José Honorio Rodrigues and Agostinho Kelzjers. 1625. Reprinted in *Os*

Holandeses no Brasil, pp. 47–48. Recife: Instituto do Açucar e do Alcool, 1942. BBM.

Moerbeeck, Jan Andries. "Motivos porque a companhia das Indias Ocidentais deve tentar tirar ao rei da Espanha a terra do Brasil." 1624. Reprinted in *Os Holandeses no Brasil*, pp. 29–43. Recife: Instituto do Açucar e do Alcool, 1942. BBM.

Nieuhof, Johan. *Memorável viagem marítima e terrestre ao Brasil*. Edited by José Honário Rodrigues. Translated by Moacir Nascimento Vasconcelos. 1681. Reprint, São Paulo: Editora da Universidade de São Paulo, 1981.

N. N. *A Little True Forraine Newes* [. . .]. London, 1642. EEBO.

Pudsey, Cuthbert. *Journal of a Residence in Brazil*. Vol. 3. Edited by Nelson Papavero and Dante Martins Teixeira. Petrópolis: Editora Index, 2000.

Richshoffer, Ambrosio. *Diario de um soldado da companhia das Indias Occidentais (1629–1632)*. Translated by Alfredo de Carvalho. Recife: Instituto Archeologico e Geographico Pernambucano, 1897. BBM.

Rodrigues, Mathias. "Relacam verdadeira e breve [. . .]." Lisbon, 1630. BA.

Santa Rita Durão, Frei Jose. *Caramaru: poema épico do descubrimento de Bahia*. Rio de Janeiro: Fundação Biblioteca Nacional, 1781.

Santiago, Diogo Lopes. *História da guerra de Pernambuco e feitos memoráveis do mestre de campo João Fernandes Vieira, herói digno de eterna memoria*. Recife: Fundarpe, 1984.

Séyner, António. "Historia del levantamiento de Portugal." Zaragoça, 1644. General Reference Collection DRT, BL.

Skinner John. *A true relation of the late cruell and barbarous tortures and execution, done vpon the English at Amboyna in the East Indies, by the Hollanders there residing*. London, 1624. EEBO.

Slaves Voyages. "Trans-Atlantic Slave Trade—Database." 2013. https://www.slavevoyages.org/voyage/database.

Spilbergen, Joris. *The East and West Indian Mirror: Being an Account of Joris van Spilbergen's Voyage Round the World (1614–1617), and the Australian Navigations of Jacob Le Maire*. London: Haykluyt Society, 1906.

Vasconcelos, Luis Mendes de. *Arte military* [. . .]. Alenquer: Vicente Alvarez, 1612.

Verdonck, Adrian, and Ambrosio Carvalho. "Descripcão das capitanias de Pernambuco, Itamaraca, Parahyba, e Rio Grande." *Revista do Instituto Archeologico e Geographico Pernambucano* 55 (1901): 215–32. https://babel.hathitrust.org/cgi/pt?id=coo.31924092247943&view=1up&seq=230.

Vieira, António. António Vieira to D. João, 1644. Manuscritos da Livraria, ANTT.

Vieira, António. "Carta Ânua da província do Brasil." In *Cartas do padre Antonio Vieira*. Coimbra: Imprensa da Universidade, 1925.

Vieira, António. "Sermão de Nossa Senhora de Penha de França." In *O Chrysostomo Portuguez*, Vol. 3, edited by Antonio Honorati, pp. 170–83. Lisbon: Matteus Moreira, 1878.

Vieira, António. "Papel que fez o padre Antonio Vieira a favor de entrega de Pernambuco aos Holandeses." In *Escritos históricos e políticos*. São Paulo: Martins Fontes, 1995.

Vieira, António. "Sermão pelo bom successo das armas de Portugal contra as de Hollanda."

In *O Chrysostomo Portuguez* [. . .], pp. 4:41–53. Lisbon: Editora de Mattos Moreira, 1881.

Unpublished Primary Sources

"Carta dos holandeses, oferecendo o perdão a todos os rebeldes que se renderem a seu domínio e respostas dos brasileiros [. . .]," April 7, 1648. Mss. II-31, 28, 003, BNDB.
Charles Boxer. Assorted writings on seventeenth-century Brazil. Box 11, Mss. III, Boxer Collection, LL.
Charles Boxer. Notebooks, 58 volumes (1946–1974), Boxer Collection, LL.
Charles Boxer. Boxer to José Honório Rodrigues. Mss. II, Boxer Collection, LL.
"Holandeses na Bahia," June 3, 1638. BNDB.
Inventaris van de collectie verspreide West-Indische stukken (1614–1875), Archieven-Zoeken, West-Indische Compagnie Brazil Nationaal Archief, The Hague.
Maurits, Johan. Maurits to rectors of Leiden. Dutch West India Company Brazil records (1624–1670), Brevoort Collection, Mss. Collection 377, Manuscripts and Archives Division, NYPL.
Negócios de Portugal, Fundo/Coleção 59, Arquivo Nacional, Rio de Janeiro.
Offícios de Conde Maurício de Nassau (1637–1643). Documentos para a história do Brasil colligidos na Holanda pelo escarregado de negócio Joaquim Caetano da Silva. Arquivo Nacional, Rio de Janeiro.
Valesio, Francesco. *Fernambuch citta principale nel Regno del Brasil acquistato dalli Signori Statti delli Paesi Bassi l'Anno 1630 adi 2. di Marzo*. Prints and Photographs Division, LOC.
Vargas, Dom Thomas Tamaio de. "Restavracion de la civdad del Salvador, Baìa de Todos-Sanctos en la provincia del Brasil por las armas de Don Philippe IV El Grande Rei Catholico de las Españas i Índias," 1628. Ricardo Brennand Institute, Recife.

Secondary Sources

Abreu, Capistrano. *Chapters in Brazil's Colonial History*. Translated by Arthur Brakel. New York: Oxford University Press, 1998.
Abreu-Ferreira, Darlene. "Fishmongers and Shipowners: Women in Maritime Communities of Early Modern Portugal." *Sixteenth Century Journal* 31, no. 1 (September 2001): 7–23.
Abreu-Ferreira, Darlene. "Women, Law and Legal Intervention in Early Modern Portugal." *Continuity and Change* 33, no. 3 (2018): 293–313.
Abreu-Ferreira, Darlene. "Women's Property, Women's Lives: A Look at Early Modern Portugal." *Portuguese Studies Review* 13, no. 1 (2007): 211–28.

Abreu-Ferreira, Darlene. "Work and Identity in Early Modern Portugal: What Did Gender Have to Do With It?" *Journal of Social History* 35, no. 4 (Summer 2002): 859–87.
Albuquerque, Cleonor Xavier. *A remuneração de serviços da guerra Holandesa*. Recife: Universidade Federal de Pernambuco Imprensa Universitária, 1968.
Albuquerque, Marcos, Veleda Lucena, and Rubia Nogueira. "O Forte Real do Bom Jesus: um marco da resistência à invasão Holandesa." In *VI seminário regional de cidades fortificadas e primeiro encontro técnico de gestores de fortificações*, pp. 1–19. Santa Catarina: Universidade Federal de Santa Catarina, 2010.
Alden, Dauril. "Some Reflections on Antonio Vieira: Seventeenth-Century Troubleshooter and Troublemaker." *Luso-Brazilian Review* 40, no. 1 (2003): 7–16.
Alden, Dauril. *The Making of an Enterprise: The Society of Jesus in Portugal, Its Empire, and Beyond, 1540–1750*. Stanford: Stanford University Press, 1995.
Alencastro, Luiz Felipe de. *The Trade in the Living: The Formation of Brazil in the South Atlantic, Sixteenth to Seventeenth Centuries*. Translated by Gavin Adams and Luiz Felipe de Alencastro. Albany: State University of New York Press, 2018.
Almeida Teles, Maria Amélia de. *Breve história do feminismo no Brasil e outros ensaios*. São Paulo: Editora Alameda, 2017.
Alpers, Svetlana. *The Art of Describing: Dutch Art in the Seventeenth Century*. Chicago: University of Chicago Press, 1984.
Anastácio, Vanda. "Notes on the Querelle Des Femmes in Eighteenth-Century Portugal." *Portuguese Studies* 31, no. 1 (2015): 50–63.
Anderson, Carrie. "Mapping Colonial Interdependencies in Dutch Brazil: European Linen and *Brasilianen* Identity." *Artl@s* 7, no. 2 (Fall 2018): 56–70.
Antúnes, Catia. "Free Agents and Formal Institutions in the Portuguese Empire: Towards a Framework of Analysis." *Portuguese Studies* 28, no. 2 (2012): 173–85.
Araujo-Jorge, A. G. de. "História diplomática do Brasil Frances no século XVI; história diplomática do Brasil Hollandez durante o século XVII." In *Proceedings of the Second Pan-American Scientific Conference*: 796–832. Washington, DC: Government Printing Office, 1917.
Asher, G. M. *A Bibliographical and Historical Essay on the Dutch Books and Pamphlets Relating to New-Netherlands and to the Dutch West India Company and to Its Possessions in Brazil/Angola/etc*. 1854. Reprint, Amsterdam: N. Israel, 1960.
Associacão dos Amigos do Torre do Tombo, "Conselho da Fazenda." http://www.aatt.org/site/index.php?op=Nucleo&id=207.
Behrens, Ricardo. *Salvador e a invasão Holandesa de 1624–1625*. Salvador: Editora Pontocom, 2013. http://www.editorapontocom.com.br/livro/16/16-ricardo-behrens-salvador.pdf.
Benton, Lauren. *A Search for Sovereignty: Law and Geography in European Empires, 1400–1900*. Cambridge: Cambridge University Press, 2009.
Bezerra, Cláudio. *Tejucupapo; história, teatro, cinema*. Recife: Edições Bagaço, 2004.
Bleiberg, Germán, Maureen Ihrie, and Janet Pérez, eds. *Dictionary of the Literature of the Iberian Peninsula*. Vol. 1. Westport, CT: Greenwood Press, 1993.

Bordo Michael D., and Roberto Cortés-Conde, eds. *Transferring Wealth and Power from the Old to the New World: Monetary and Fiscal Institutions in the 17th through the 19th Centuries.* New York: Cambridge University Press, 2001.

Borschberg, Peter. "The Seizure of the Sta. Catarina Revisited: The Portuguese Empire in Asia, VOC Politics and the Origins of the Dutch-Johor Alliance (1602–c.1616)." *Journal of Southeast Asian Studies* 33, no. 1 (February 2002): 31–62.

Borucki, Alex, David Eltis, and David Wheat. "Atlantic History and the Slave Trade to Spanish America." *American Historical Review* 120, no. 2 (2015): 433–61.

Boxer, Charles. "The Carreira da India, 1650–1750." *Mariner's Mirror* 46, no. 1 (1960): 35–54.

Boxer, Charles. *The Dutch in Brazil, 1624–1654.* 1957. Reprint, Hamden: Clarendon Press, 1973.

Boxer, Charles. *Four Centuries of Portuguese Expansion, 1415–1825: A Succinct Survey.* Berkeley: University of California Press, 1972.

Boxer, Charles. "Padre António Vieira, S. J., and the Institution of the Brazil Company in 1649." *Hispanic American Historical Review* 29, no. 4 (November 1949): 474–97.

Boxer, Charles. *The Portuguese Seaborne Empire, 1415–1825.* New York: A. A. Knopf, 1969.

Boxer, Charles. *Salvador de Sá and the Struggle for Brazil and Angola, 1602–1686.* Westport, CT: Greenwood Press, 1975.

Brandão, Marcílio. "Tejucupapo—um filme sobre mulheres guerreiras." YouTube, November 27, 2019. https://www.youtube.com/watch?v=Tg6aHFAbAH0&ab_channel=DhyogoRodrygues.

Brandon, Pepijn, and Karwan Fatah-Black. "'For the Reputation and Respectability of the State': Trade, the Imperial State, Unfree Labor, and Empire in the Dutch Atlantic." In *Building the Atlantic Empires: Unfree Labor and Imperial States in the Political Economy of Capitalism, ca. 1500–1914*, edited by John Donoghue and Evelyn P. Jennings, pp. 84–108. Leiden: Brill, 2015.

Breen, Benjamin, and Jorge Cañizares-Esguerra. "Hybrid Atlantics: Future Directions for the History of the Atlantic World." *History Compass* 11, no. 8 (August 2013): 597–609.

Brienen, R. P. "George Marcgraf (1610–c.1644): A German Cartographer, Astronomer, and Naturalist-Illustrator in Colonial Dutch Brazil." *Itinerario* 25, no. 10 (March 2001): 85–122.

Brienen, Rebecca Parker. "Albert Eckhout and Frans Post: Two Dutch Artists in Colonial Brazil." In *Brazil, Body and Soul*, edited by Edward J. Sullivan, pp. 62–74. New York: Guggenheim Museum Publications, 2001.

Brienen, Rebecca Parker. "From Brazil to Europe: the Zoological Drawings of Albert Eckhout and Georg Marcgraf." In *Early Modern Zoology: The Construction of Animals in Science, Literature and the Visual Arts*, Vol. 1, edited by Karel A. E. Enkel and Paulus Johanes Smith, pp. 273–314. Leiden: Brill, 2007.

Brooks, Mary Elizabeth. "Military Defeat to Immortality: The Birth of Sebastianism." *Luso-Brazilian Review* 1, no. 2 (1964): 41–49.

Caminietzki, Carlos Ziller, and Gianrricardo Grassi Pastore. "O fogo e o tinto." *Topoi* 6, no. 11 (2005): 261–88.

Campos, Danielly. "Nova escadaria Mariz Ortiz, reformada por detentos, é entregue nesta quarta." Prefeitura de Vitória. August 1, 2018. https://www.vitoria.es.gov.br/noticia/nova-escadaria-mariz-ortiz-reformada-por-detentos-e-entregue-nesta-quarta-26711.

Cañizares-Esguerra, Jorge. "Preliminary Material." In *Theorising the Ibero-American Atlantic*, edited by Harald E. Braun and Lisa Vollendorf, i–xii. Leiden: Brill, 2013.

Cardoso, Alírio. "The Conquest of Maranhão and Atlantic Disputes in the Geopolitics of the Iberian Union (1596–1626)." *Revista Brasileira de história* 31, no. 61.

Carrega, Jorge. *Breve história socioeconômica de Faro*. Faro: União de Freguesias de Faro, 2018.

Chaunu, Pierre. "Brésil et Atlantique au XVII siècle." *Annales* 16, no. 6 (1961): 1176–1207.

Cleveland, Kimberly. "Mapping the Landscaped, Brazilian Body in Albert Eckhout's 'Ethnographic Types' Series: Or, Whose Africans Are These, Anyways?" Unpublished master's degree paper, Indiana University, 2003.

Coates, Timothy. *Convicts and Orphans: Forced and State-Sponsored Colonizers in the Portuguese Empire, 1550–1755*. Stanford: Stanford University Press, 2001.

Cohen, Thomas. "Millenarian Themes in the Writings of Antonio Vieira." *Luso-Brazilian Review* 28, no. 1 (1991): 23–46.

Collins, John Joseph. *Daniel: With an Introduction to Apocalyptic Literature*. Grand Rapids, MI: W. B. Eerdmans, 1984.

Cooper, Frederick. *Colonialism in Question: Theory, Knowledge, History*. Berkeley: University of California Press, 2005.

Corrêa do Lago, Bia, ed. *Frans Post e o Brasil Holandês na coleção do instituto Ricardo Brennand*. Recife: Ricardo Brennand, 2003.

Corrêa do Lago, Pedro, and Bia Corrêa do Lago. *Frans Post, 1612–1680: Catalogue Raisonné*. Rio de Janeiro: Capivara, 2006.

Corrêa do Lago, Pedro, and Bia Corrêa do Lago. *Frans Post, 1612–1680: Catalogue Raisonné*. Milan: 5 Continents, 2007.

Coroacy, Vivaldo. "O Rio de Janeiro no século 17." In *Coleção Rio 4 séculos*, Vol. 6. Rio de Janeiro: Editora Rio de Janeiro, 1964.

Costa, Fernando Dores. "Interpreting the Portuguese War of Restoration (1641–1668) in a European Context." *E-Journal of Portuguese History* 3, no. 1 (Summer 2005): 1–14.

Costa, Fernando Dores. "O conselho de guerra como lugar de poder: a delimitação da sua autoridade." *Análise Social* 44, no. 191 (2009): 379–414.

Costas, Leonor Freire. "Merchant Groups in the 17th-Century Brazilian Sugar Trade: Reappraising Old Topics with New Research Insights." *E-Journal of Portuguese History* 2, no. 1 (Summer 2004).

Costas, Leonor Freire. *O transporte no Atlântico e a companhia geral do comércio do Brasil, 1580–1663*. Vol. 2, *Apêndices*. Lisbon: Comissão Nacional para Comemoracões dos Descobrimentos Portugueses, 2002.

Costas, Leonor Freire. "Pernambuco e a companhia geral do comércio do Brasil." *Penélope* 23 (2000): 41–65.

Costas, Leonor Freire, Pedro Lains, and Susana Münch Miranda. *Economic History of Portugal 1143–2010*. Cambridge: Cambridge University Press, 2016.

Costa, Maria Leonor. "Redes Mercantis na Companhia Geral do Comércio do Brasil." Paper presented at the IV Congresso Brasileiro de História Econômica e 5ª Conferência Internacional de História de Empresas. São Paulo, 2001. https://www.abphe.org.br/arquivos/maria-leonor-costa.pdf.

Craigwood, Joanna. "The Place of the Literary in European Diplomacy: Origin Myths in Ambassadorial Handbooks." In *Cultures of Diplomacy and Literary Writing in the Early Modern World*, edited by Joanna Craigwood and Tracy Sowerby, pp 33–36. Oxford: Oxford University Press, 2019.

Crosby, Alfred. *The Measure of Reality: Quantification in Western Europe, 1200–1500*. Cambridge: Cambridge University Press, 1997.

Cunha, Mafalda Soares da. "Elites e mudança política: a caso de a conspiração de 1641." In *Brasil-Portugal: sociedades, culturas e formas de governar no mundo Português (séculos XVI–XVIII)*, pp. 325–43. Sao Paulo: Annablume, 2006.

Diggs, Irene. "Zumbi and the Republic of Os Palmares." *Phylon* 14, no. 1 (1953): 62–70.

Disney, A. R. *A History of Portugal and the Portuguese Empire: From Beginnings to 1807*. Cambridge: Cambridge University Press, 2009.

Draper, G. I. A. D. "Grotius' Place in the Development of Legal Ideas about War." In *Hugo Grotius and International Relations*, edited by Hedley Bull, Benedict Kingsbury, and Adam Roberts, pp. 177–208. Oxford, Oxford University Press, 2003.

Drummond, Adriano Lima. "Um rei encoberto debaixo dum santo: sebastianismo no 'sermão a São Sebastião,' de Padre Antônio Vieira." *Revisita do Centro de Estudos Portugueses* 28, no. 40 (December 2008): 53–77.

Donoghue, John, and Evelyn P. Jennings. *Building the Atlantic Empires: Unfree Labor and Imperial States in the Political Economy of Capitalism, ca. 1500–1914*. Leiden: Brill, 2012.

Doré, Andréa. "A Ásia no papel forte do Padre Antônio Vieira." *Revista Diálogos Mediterrânicos* 12 (June 2017): 51–66.

Dutra, Francis A. "Duarte Coelho Pereira, First Lord-Proprietor of Pernambuco: The Beginning of a Dynasty." *Americas* 29, no. 4 (1973): 415–41.

Dutra, Francis A. "A Hard-Fought Struggle for Recognition: Manuel Gonçalves Doria, First Afro-Brazilian to Become a Knight of Santiago." *Americas* 56, no. 1 (1999): 91–113.

Dutra, Francis A. "The Vieira Family and the Order of Christ." *Luso-Brazilian Review* 40, no. 1 (2003): 17–31.

Duve, Thomas. "Spatial Perceptions, Juridical Practices, and Early International Legal Thought Around 1500: From Tordesillas to Saragossa." In *System, Order, and International Law: The Early History of International Legal Thought from Machiavelli to Hegel*, edited by Stefan Kadelbach, Thomas Kleinlein, and David Roth-Isigkeit, pp. 418–42. Oxford: Oxford University Press, 2017.

Ebben, Maurits. "José Gonsalves de Mello: Nederlanders in Brazilië, 1624–1654," *Itineráro* 26 no. 2 (July 2002): 32–33.

Ebert, Christopher. *Between Empires: Brazilian Sugar in the Early Atlantic Economy, 1550–1630*. Leiden: Brill, 2008.

Elliott, J. H. *Imperial Spain: 1469–1716.* New York: Penguin, 2002.
Elliott, J. H. "Self-Perception and Decline in Early Seventeenth-Century Spain." *Past & Present* 74 (February 1977): 41–61.
Edmundson, George. "The Dutch Power in Brazil (1624–1654): Part I—The Struggle for Bahia (1624–1627)." *English Historical Review* 11, no. 42 (April 1896): 231–59.
Emmer, Pieter C. "The Dutch Atlantic, 1600–1800: Expansion Without Empire." *Itinerario* 23, no. 2 (June 1999): 48–69.
Esteves, Maria Luísa. "Para o estudo das relações comerciais de Angola com as Índias de Castela e Génova no período da restauração, (1640–1668)." *Studia* 51 (1992): 29–60.
Fernández Duro, Cesáreo. *Armada Española desde la unión de los reinos de Castilla y de León.* Madrid, 1895.
Ferrão, C., and J. P. Soares, eds. *Dutch Brazil: The "Thierbuch" and "Autobiography" of Zacharias Wagener.* Translated by D. H. Treece and R. Trewinnard. Vol. 2. Rio de Janeiro: Editora Index, 1997.
Ferry, R. J. "Encomienda, African Slavery, and Agriculture in Seventeenth-Century Caracas." *Hispanic American Historical Review* 61, no. 4 (1981): 609–35.
Flynn, Dennis O., and Arturo Giráldez. "Born with a 'Silver Spoon': The Origin of World Trade in 1571." *Journal of World History* 6, no. 2 (1995): 201–21.
Fraga, Joanne, and Thiago Krause. *1640: Portugal, Uma Retrospectiva.* Lisbon: Público, 2019.
França, Gerson. "Maria Ortiz: A lenda, a verdade e a tradição." *História Capixaba*, November 25, 2016.
Frazão, Dilva. "Anna Paes: Proprietária de engenho na época colonial brasileira." E-biografia, 2024. https://www.ebiografia.com/anna_paes/.
Gadelha, Regina Maria A. Fonseca. "Conquista e ocupação da Amazônia: A fronteira norte do Brasil." *Estudos Avançados* 16, no. 45 (August 2002): 63–80. https://dx.doi.org/10.1590/S0103-40142002000200005.
Galvão, Ingrid. "Heroínas de Tejucupapo." *Blogger*, December 10, 2008. https://heroinasdetejucupapo.blogspot.com/2008/12/epopia-das-heronas-de-tejucupapo.html?m=1.
Games, Alison. "Anglo-Dutch Connections and Overseas Enterprises: A Global Perspective on Lion Gardiner's World." *Early American Studies* 9, no. 2 (Spring 2011): 435–61.
Garcia, Belinda Mora. "The Aeneid of Brazil: Caramaru." PhD dissertation, University of Texas, 2012. https://repositories.lib.utexas.edu/handle/2152/ETD-UT-2012-05-5387.
Gaspar, Lúcia. "Anna Paes." Pesquisa Escolar. August 2009. http://basilio.fundaj.gov.br/pesquisaescolar/index.php?option=com_content&view=article&id=331&Itemid=1.
Gesteira, Heloisa Meireles. "O recife holandês: história natural e colonizacão Neerlandesa (1624–1654)." *Revista da Sociedade Brasileira de História da Ciência* 2, no. 1 (2004): 6–21.
Givens, Bryan. *Judging Maria de Macedo: A Female Visionary and the Inquisition in Early Modern Portugal.* Baton Rouge: Louisiana University Press, 2011.
Givens, Bryan. "The St. Paul of Sebastianism: Tracing the Millenarian Legacy of Dom Joao de Castro." *Portuguese Studies Review* 17, no. 1 (2012): 83–103.

Gouvea, Fernando da Cruz. *Mauricio de Nassu e o Brasil holandês: correspondência com os Estados Gerais*. Recife: UFPE, 1998.
Gray, Erik. "'Save Where . . .' The Trope of Exceptionality." *English Literary History* 77, no. 3 (Fall 2010): 645–63.
Groesen, Michiel van. *Amsterdam's Atlantic: Print Culture and the Making of Dutch Brazil*. Philadelphia: University of Pennsylvania Press, 2016.
Groesen, Michiel van. "Lessons Learned: The Second Dutch Conquest of Brazil and the Memory of the First." *Colonial Latin American Review* 20, no. 2 (2011): 167–93.
Groesen, Michiel van, ed. *The Legacy of Dutch Brazil*. New York: Cambridge University Press, 2014.
GV/News. "Escadaria Mariz Ortiz é Reformada Por Detentos." January 10, 2018. https://gvnews.com.br/escadaria-mariz-ortiz-e-reformada-por-detentos.
Halbwachs, Maurice. *On Collective Memory*. Translated by Lewis A. Coser. Chicago: University of Chicago Press, 1992.
Hamer, Deborah. "'Our Dutchmen Run After Them Very Much': Cross-Cultural Sex in New Netherland and the Dutch Global Empire." In *Crossings and Encounters: Race, Gender, and Sexuality in the Atlantic World*, edited by R. Prieto, Stephen R. Berry, and Sandra Slater, pp. 13–29. Columbia: University of South Carolina Press, 2020.
Hanke, Lewis. "The Portuguese in Spanish America, with Special Reference to the Villa Imperial de Potosi." *Revista de Historia de América* 51 (June 1961): 1–48.
Harmsen, A. J. E. "Barlaeus' Description of the Dutch Colony in Brazil." In *Travel Fact and Fiction: Studies on Fiction, Literary Tradition, Scholarly Discovery and Observation in Travel Writing*, edited by Zweder von Martels, pp. 158–69. Leiden: E. J. Brill, 1994.
Havik, Philip J., and Malyn Newitt, eds. *Creole Societies in the Portuguese Empire*. Cambridge: Cambridge Scholars Publishing, 2015.
Hefaeli, Evan. "Breaking the Christian Atlantic: the Legacy of Dutch Tolerance in Brazil." In *The Legacy of Dutch Brazil*, edited by Michiel van Groesen, pp. 124–45. New York: Cambridge University Press, 2014.
Hemming, John. *Ouro vermelho: a conquista dos Índios Brasileiros*. São Paulo: EDUSP, 2007.
Herculano, Alexandre, ed. "A Padeira d'Aljubarrota." *O Panorama: jornal litterário e instructivo da Sociedade Propagadora dos Conhecimentos Úteis* 3, no. 90 (December 1839): 413–14.
Hermann, Jacqueline. "As metamorfoses da espera: messianismo Judaico, Cristãos-Novos Sebastianismo no Brasil colonial." In *Judeus no Brasil: ensaios sobre inquisição, imigração e identidade*, edited by Keila Grinberg. Rio de Janeiro: Civilização Brasileira, 2005.
Hermann, Jacqueline. *1580–1600: O sonho da salvação*. São Paulo: Companhia das Letras, 2000.
Hermann, Jacqueline. *No reino do desejado*. São Paulo: Companhia das Letras, 1998.
Hermann, Jacqueline. "Um rei indesejado: notas sobre a trajetória política de D. Antônio, Prior do Crato." *Revista Brasileira de História* 30, no. 59 (June 2010).

Hespanha, António Manuel. "Revoltas e revoluções: a resistência das elites provinciais," *Análise Social* 28, no. 120 (1993): 81–103.
Hobsbawm, Eric. "The General Crisis of the European Economy in the 17th Century." *Past and Present Society* 5, no. 1 (1954): 33–53.
Hochstrasser, Julie. "Visual Impact: The Long Legacy of the Artists of Dutch Brazil." In *The Legacy of Dutch Brazil*, edited by Michiel van Groesen, pp. 240–83. Cambridge: Cambridge University Press, 2014.
Israel, Jonathan. *Conflicts of Empires: Spain, the Low Countries and the Struggle for World Supremacy*. London: Hambledon Press, 1997.
Israel, Jonathan. "The Diplomatic Career of Jeronimo Nunes da Costa: An Episode in Dutch–Portuguese Relations of the Seventeenth Century." *BMGN—Low Countries Historical Review* 99, no. 2 (1983): 167–90.
Israel, Jonathan I. *Diasporas Within a Diaspora: Jews, Crypto-Jews, and the World of Maritime Empires 1540–1740*. Leiden: Brill, 2002.
Israel, Jonathan. "Duarte Nunes da Costa (Jacob Curiel) of Hamburg, Sephardi Nobleman and Communal Leader (1585–1664)." *Studia Rosenthaliana* 21, no. 1 (1987): 14–34.
Israel, Jonathan. *Dutch Primacy in World Trade, 1585–1740*. Oxford: Oxford Publishing, 1989.
Israel, Jonathan. *The Dutch Republic: Its Rise, Greatness and Fall: 1477–1806*. Oxford: Oxford University Press, 1995.
Israel, Jonathan. *The Dutch Republic and the Hispanic World, 1601–1661*. Oxford: Clarendon Press, 1982.
Israel, Jonathan. *Empires and Entrepots: The Dutch, the Spanish Monarchy and the Jews, 1585–1713*. London: Hambledon Press, 1990.
Israel, Jonathan, and Stuart B. Schwartz. *The Expansion of Tolerance: Religion in Dutch Brazil (1624–1654)*. Amsterdam: Amsterdam University Press, 2007.
Ittersum, Martine Julia van. *Profit and Principle: Hugo Grotius, Natural Rights Theories and the Rise of Dutch Power in the East Indies, 1595–1615*. Leiden: Brill, 2006.
Jardine, Lisa. *Going Dutch: How England Plundered Holland's Glory*. New York: Brill, 2008.
Jordán, Maria V. "The Empire of the Future and the Chosen People: Father António Vieira and the Prophetic Tradition in the Hispanic World." Special issue, *António Vieira and the Luso-Brazilian Baroque: Luso-Brazilian Review* 40, no. 1 (2003): 45–58.
Kagan, Richard L. *Clio and the Crown: The Politics of History in Medieval and Early Modern Spain*. Baltimore: Johns Hopkins University Press, 2009.
Kagan, Richard L., and Philip Morgan. *Atlantic Diasporas: Jews, Conversos, and Crypto-Jews in the Age of Mercantilism, 1500–1800*. Baltimore: Johns Hopkins University Press, 2009.
Kent, R. K. "An African State in Brazil." *Journal of African History* 6, no. 2 (1965): 161–75.
Klein, Kerwin Lee. "On the Emergence of Memory in Historical Discourse," *Representations* 69 (2000): 127–50.

Klooster, Wim. *The Dutch Moment: War, Trade, and Settlement in the Seventeenth-Century Atlantic World*. Ithaca: Cornell University Press, 2016.

Lay, Stephen. *The Reconquest Kings of Portugal*. London: Palgrave Macmillan, 2009.

Lenk, Wolfgang. *Guerra e pacto colonial: a Bahia contra o Brasil Holandês, 1624–1654*. São Paulo: Alameda Casa Editorial, 2013.

Lima Rodrigues, Lucia, and Russel Craig. "Recovery amid Destruction: Manoel da Maya and the Lisbon Earthquake of 1755." *Libraries and the Cultural Record* 43, no. 4 (January 2008): 397–410.

Lima, Luís Filipe Silvério. "Prophetical Hopes, New World Experiences and Imperial Expectations: Menasseh Ben Israel, Antonio Vieira, Fifth Monarchy Men, and the Millenarian Connections in the 17thc Atlantic." *Anais de Historia de Alem Mar* 17 (2010): 359–408.

Litrel, Suzanne. "A 'True Liberation': Braudel, *The Mediterranean*, and Stories of Dutch Brazil." *World History Bulletin* 33, no. 2 (Fall 2017): 32–35.

Livermore, H. V. *History of Portugal*. Cambridge: Cambridge University Press, 1947.

Lockhart, James, and Stuart Schwartz. *Early Latin America: A History of Colonial Spanish America and Brazil*. Cambridge: Cambridge University Press, 1983.

Lucan, Marcus Annaeus. *The Civil War* (Pharsalia). Translated by J. D. Duff. Cambridge: Harvard University Press, 1969.

MacKay, Ruth. *The Baker Who Pretended to Be King of Portugal*. Chicago: University of Chicago Press, 2012.

MacKay, Ruth. "The Tragedy of Alcazarquivir: The Collapse of Kingship, Empire and Narrative." *Bulletin for Spanish and Portuguese Historical Studies* 40, no. 1 (2015). https://doi.org/10.26431/0739-182X.1196.

Magalhães, Pablo Antonio Iglesias. "A relacion de la vitoria que alcanzaron las armas Catolicas en la Baia de Todos Santos, do Bispo D. Juan de Palafox y Mendoza." *Topoi* 12, no. 23 (December 2011): 43–65.

Magalhães, Pablo Antonio Iglesias. "A jornada dos vassalos, por D. Jerônimo de Ataíde em 1625." *Revista do Instituto Histórico e Geográfico Brasileiro* 471 (June 2016): 219–80.

Maravall, José Antonio. *Culture of the Baroque: Analysis of a Historical Structure*. Manchester: Manchester University Press, 1986.

Marcena, Adriano. *Mexendo o pirão: importância sociocultural da farinha de manioca no Brasil Holandês, 1637–1646*. Recife: Funcultura, 2012.

Marcocci, Giuseppe. "Conscience and Empire: Politics and Moral Theology in the Early Modern Portuguese World." *Journal of Early Modern History* 18, no. 5 (2014): 473–94.

Marley, David F. *Wars of the Americas: A Chronology of Armed Conflict in the New World, 1492 to the Present*. Oxford: ABC-CLIO, 1998.

Mattos, Hebe. "'Black Troops' and Hierarchies of Color in the Portuguese Atlantic World: The Case of Henrique Dias and His Black Regiment." *Luso-Brazilian Review* 45, no. 1 (2008): 6–29.

Mattos, Hebe. "Da guerra preta às hierarquias de cor no Atlântico Português." São Leopoldo: Rio Grande do Sul, 2007.

McAllister, Lyle N. *Spain and Portugal in the New World: 1492–1700*. Oxford: Oxford University Press, 1994.
McCloskey, Pat. "Saint Anthony Novena Day One: A Man of Many Talents." *Franciscan Media*. June 5, 2019. https://www.franciscanmedia.org/franciscan-spirit-blog/saint-anthony-novena-day-one-man-of-many-talents.
McGarty, Craig, Vincent Y. Yzerbyt, and Russell Spears. *Stereotypes as Explanations: The Formation of Meaningful Beliefs about Social Groups*. Cambridge: Cambridge University Press, 2002.
McGinness, Anne B. "Negotiating the Confessional Divide Between Dutch Brazil and the Republic: The Case of Manoel de Moraes." In *Encounters Between Jesuits and Protestants in Asia and the Americas*, edited by Jorge Cañizares-Esguerra, Robert A. Maryks, and Ronnie Po-chia Hsia, pp. 228–52. Leiden: Brill, 2018.
Mello, Evaldo Cabral de. *O Brasil holandês*. São Paulo: Penguin-Companhia, 2010.
Mello, Evaldo Cabral de. *Olinda restaurada: guerra e acuçar no nordeste, 1630–1654*. São Paulo: USP, 1975.
Mello, Evaldo Cabral de. *Rubro veio: o imaginário da restauração Pernambucana*. Rio de Janeiro: Editora Nova Fronteira, 1986.
Mello, José Antônio Gonsalves de. *Filipe Bandeira de Melo: tenente de mestre de campo general do estado do Brasil*. Recife: Universidade do Recife, 1954.
Mello, José Antônio Gonsalves de. *Gente da nação: cristão-novos e judeus em Pernambuco, 1542–1654*. Recife: Fundação Joaquim Nabuco, Editora Massangana, 1989.
Mello, José Antônio Gonsalves de. *Restauradores de Pernambuco: biografias de figuras do século XVII que defenderam e consolidaram a unidade brasileira*. Recife: Imprensa Universitária, 1967.
Mello, José Antônio Gonsalves de. *Tempo dos flamengos: influência da ocupação Holandesa na vida e na cultura do Norte do Brasil*. 4th ed. Rio de Janeiro: UniverCidade Editora, 2001.
Mendes da Luz, Francisco Paulo. *O Conselho da India*. Divisão de Publicações e Biblioteca, Lisbon: Agência Geral do Ultramar, 1952. BNP.
Mendes, Margarida Vieira. "Baroque Literature Revisited and Revised." In *A Revisionary History of Portuguese Literature*, edited by Miguel Tamen and Helena Buescu, pp. 58–78. London: Garland Publishing, 1999.
Metcalf, Alida. *Go-Betweens and the Colonization of Brazil: 1500–1600*. Austin: University of Texas Press, 2008.
Meuwese, Mark. *Brothers in Arms, Partners in Trade: Dutch–Indigenous Alliances in the Atlantic World, 1595–1674*. Leiden: Brill, 2012.
Meznar, Joan E., Thomas Cohen, and Stuart B. Schwartz. "António Vieira: Word and Power in the Portuguese Baroque." *Luso-Brazilian Review* 40, no. 1 (Summer 2003): 116–22.
Miranda, Bruno Romero Ferreira. "'Doentes e incapazes para marchar': Vida e morte no companhia neêrlandesa das Índias Ocidentais no nordeste do Brasil, 1630–1654." *História, Ciências, Saúde-Manguinhos* 22, no. 2 (2015): 337–53.
Miranda, Susana Münch, and João Paulo Salvado. "Struggling for Brazil: Dutch,

Portuguese and Spaniards in the 1640 Naval Battle of Paraíba." *Tijdschrift Voor Zeegeschiedenis* 34, no. 1 (2015): 51–64.

Moises, Massaud. *A literatura portuguesa através dos textos*. 29th ed. São Paulo: Editora Cultrix, 2000.

Montcher, Fabien. "Early Modern Bibliopolitics: From a Seventeenth-Century Roman-Iberian Perspective." *Pacific Coast Philology* 52, no. 2 (2017): 206–18.

Montcher, Fabien. *Mercenaries of Knowledge: Vicente Nogueira, the Republic of Letters, and the Making of Late Renaissance Politics*. Cambridge: Cambridge University Press, 2023.

Moreira, Rosemeri. "Heroínas, gênero e Guerras: mulheres em periódicos militares (1942–1945)." *Antíteses* 13, no. 25 (June 2020): 207–41.

Myrup, Erik Lars. "Kings, Colonies, and Councillors: Brazil and the Making of Portugal's Overseas Council, 1642–1833." *Americas* 67, no. 2 (2010): 185–218.

Myrup, Erik Lars. *Power and Corruption in the Early Modern World*. Baton Rouge: Louisiana State University Press, 2015.

Muldoon, James. "Papal Responsibility for the Infidel: Another Look at Alexander VI's 'Inter Caetera.'" *Catholic Historical Review* 64, no. 2 (April 1978): 168–84.

Nascimento, George Silva do. "Evocação Pernambucana: O rubro veio de Evaldo Cabral de Mello." *Tempos Históricos* 17 (2013):107–25.

Newitt, Malyn. *A History of Portuguese Overseas Expansion, 1400–1668*. London: Routledge, 2005.

Newson, Linda, and Susie Minchin. *From Capture to Slave*. Leiden: Brill, 2017.

Noorlander, Danny. *Heaven's Wrath: The Protestant Reformation and the Dutch West India Company in the Atlantic World*. Ithaca: Cornell University Press, 2019.

Nora, Pierre. "Between Memory and History: Les Lieux de Mémoire." Translated by Marc Roudebush. *Representations* 26 (1989): 7–25.

Novinsky, Anita. *Cristãos Novos na Bahia*. Sao Paulo: Editora Perspectiva, 1972.

O'Donnell, Thomas J. "Portugal: A Double Centenary." *Studies: An Irish Quarterly Review* 30, no. 118 (1941).

Olival, Fernanda. "Portugal in the Sixteenth and Seventeenth Centuries." *E-Journal of Portuguese History* 8, no. 2 (Winter 2008).

Oliveira, Carla Mary S., Mozart Vergetti de Menezes, and Regina Célia Gonçalves, eds. *Ensaios sobre a América portuguesa*. Recife: Editora Universitária/UFPB, 2009.

Olsen, H. Eric. *The Calabrian Charlatan, 1598–1603: Messianic Nationalism in Early Modern Europe*. New York: Palgrave-Macmillan, 2003.

O'Malley, Gregory E., and Alex Borucki. "Patterns in Intercolonial Slave Trade." *Revista Tempo* 23, no. 2 (May–August 2017): 313–38.

Oostindie, Gert. "Historical Memory and National Canons." *Dutch Colonialism, Migration, and Cultural Heritage*. Leiden: Brill, 2008.

Ormrod, David. *The Rise of Commercial Empires England and the Netherlands in the Age of Mercantilism, 1650–1770*. Cambridge: Cambridge University Press, 2003.

Orso, Steven. "Why Maíno? A Note on the Recovery of Bahia." *Notes in the History of Art* 10, no. 2 (Winter 1991): 26–31.

Ozment, Steven, ed. *Three Behaim Boys: Growing Up in Early Modern Germany: A Chronicle of Their Lives*. New Haven: Yale University Press, 1990.

Padrón, Ricardo. "Mapping Plus Ultra: Cartography, Space, and Hispanic Modernity." *Representations* 79, no. 1 (Summer 2002): 28–60.

Parker, Charles. *Global Calvinism: Conversion and Commerce in the Dutch Empire, 1600–1800*. New Haven: Yale University Press, 2022.

Parker, Geoffrey. *The Army of Flanders and the Spanish Road, 1567–1659*. 2nd ed. Cambridge: Cambridge University Press, 2004.

Parker, Geoffrey. "The 'Military Revolution,' 1560–1660—A Myth?" *Journal of Modern History* 48, no. 2 (1976): 196–214.

Pereira Fagundes, Igor. "Felipe Camarão, um cavaleiro a serviço del rei: memória, história e identidade nas Pernambucanas, século XVII." *Revista 7 Mares*, no. 5 (October 2015).

Phaf-Reinberger, Ineke. "Science and Art in the 'Dutch Period' in Northeast Brazil: The Representation of Cannibals and Africans as Allies Overseas." *Circumscribere* 2 (2009): 37–47.

Pijning, Ernst. "Paradise Regained: Historiography on the Dutch Occupation of Northeastern Brazil, 1630–1654." *Itinerario* 26 no. 2 (2002): 120–25.

Pimentel, Alberto. *Historia do culto de nossa senhora em Portugal*. Guimarães: Libanio, 1900. https://archive.org/details/historiadocultodoopime.

Pinto, Paolo Jorge de Sousa. "Captains, Sultanas and Liaisons Dangereuses." In *Iberians in the Singapore-Melaka Area and Adjacent Regions: 16th to 18th centuries*, edited by Peter Borschberg, pp. 131–46. Wiesbaden: Harrassowitz, 2004.

Piterburg, Gabriel, Teofilo Ruz, and Geoffrey Symcox. *Braudel Revisited: The Mediterranean World 1600–1800*. Toronto: University of Toronto Press, 2010.

Poley, Jared. *The Devil's Riches: A Modern History of Greed*. New York: Berghahn, 2016.

Polzonetti, Pierpaolo. "Tartini and the Tongue of Saint Anthony Source." *Journal of the American Musicological Society* 67, no. 2 (Summer 2014): 429–86.

Poska, Allison. "The Case Against Agentic Gender Norms for Women in Early Modern Europe." *Gender & History* 30, no. 2: 354–65.

Prestage, Edgar. "O papel da diplomacia na luta entre Portugueses e Holandeses pela posse do Brasil (1641–1661)." Vols. 1–3. London: Revista dos Estudos Históricos, 1926.

Prior, David. "After the Revolution: An Alternative Future for Atlantic History" *History Compass* 12, no. 3 (March 2014): 300–9.

Protschky, Susie. "Defining Masculinities." In *Governing Masculinities in the Early Modern Period: Regulating Selves and Others*, edited by Susan Broomhall and Jacqueline Van Gent. Burlington, VT: Farnham, Surrey, 2011.

Raminelli, Ronaldo. "Nobreza e principais da terra—América Portuguesa, séculos XVII e XVIII." *Topoi* 18, no. 38 (May–August 2018): 217–40.

Raminelli, Ronaldo. *Viagens ultramarinas: Monarcas, vassalos e governo à distância*. São Paulo: Alameda, 2008.

Rogers, Thomas D. *The Deepest Wounds: A Labour and Environmental History of Sugar in Northeast Brazil*. Chapel Hill: University of North Carolina Press, 2010.

Rosenthal, Earl. "Plus Ultra, Non Plus Ultra, and the Columnar Device of Emperor Charles V." *Journal of the Warburg and Courtauld Institutes* 34 (1971): 204–28.
Rosenthal, Olympia. "As órfãs d'el rei: Racialized Sex and the Politicization of Life in Manuel da Nóbrega's Letters from Brazil." *Journal of Lusophone Studies* 1, no. 2 (2016): 72–97.
Rubright, Marjorie. *Doppelgänger Dilemmas: Anglo-Dutch Relations in Early Modern English Literature and Culture*. Philadelphia: University of Pennsylvania Press, 2014.
Russell, Nicholas. "Collective Memory before and after Halbwachs." *French Review* 79, no. 4 (March 2006): 792–804.
Russell-Wood, A. J. R. "Men Under Stress: The Social Environment of the Carreira da India, 1550–1750." Lisbon: Instituto de Investigacão Cientíífica Tropical, 1985.
Russell-Wood, A. J. R. *The Portuguese Empire, 1415–1808: A World on the Move*. Baltimore: John Hopkins University Press, 1998.
Russell-Wood, A. J. R. "Women and Society in Colonial Brazil." *Journal of Latin American Studies* 9, no. 1 (May 1977): 1–34.
Sadlier, Darlene. *Brazil Imagined: 1500–Present*. New York: EBSCO, 2008.
Salas Almela, Luis. *The Conspiracy of the Ninth Duke of Medina Sidonia (1641): An Aristocrat in the Crisis of the Spanish Empire*. Translated by Ruth MacKay. Leiden: Brill, 2013.
Santis, Ana Julia G. de. "A imagen de D. Sebastião em 'O Conquistador' e 'Rei Luis de Souza.'" UNIMEP. 2008. http://www.unimep.br/phpg/mostraacademica/anais/6mostra/4/299.
Saraiva, A. J. "Antonio Vieira, Menasseh Ben Israel et le Cinquième Empire." *Studia Rosenthaliana* 6, no. 1 (1972): 25–57.
Saraiva, A. J. *Historia e utopia: estudos sobre vieira*. Translated by Maria de Santa Cruz. Lisbon: Ministerio da Educacão, 1992.
Schalkwijk, Frans Leonard. *The Reformed Church in Dutch Brazil (1630–1654)*. Zoetermeer: Boekencentrum, 1998.
Schmidt, Benjamin. "The Dutch Atlantic: From Provincialism to Globalism." In *Atlantic History: A Critical Approach*, edited by Jack P. Greene and Philip Morgan, pp. 163–87. Oxford: Oxford University Press, 2009.
Schmidt, Benjamin. "The Dutch Atlantic and the Dubious Case of Frans Post." In *Dutch Atlantic Connections, 1680–1800: Linking Empires, Bridging Borders*, edited by Gert Oostindie and Jessica V. Roitman, 249–72. Leiden: Brill, 2014.
Schmidt, Benjamin. *Innocence Abroad: The Dutch Imagination and the New World, 1570–1670*. Cambridge: Cambridge University Press, 2001.
Schneider, Alberto Luiz, "Ventura e desventura dos judeus portugueses no nordeste do Brasil." *Revista de História* 166 (January–June 2012): 313–21.
Schwartz, Stuart B. "Prata, açúcar e escravos: de como o império restaurou Portugal." *Tempo* 24 (2008): 201–23.
Schwartz, Stuart B. *Sugar Plantations in the Formation of Brazilian Society: Bahia, 1550–1835*. Cambridge: Cambridge University Press, 1985.
Schwartz, Stuart B. "A Commonwealth within Itself: The Early Brazilian Sugar Industry,

1550–1670." In *Tropical Babylons: Sugar and the Making of the Atlantic World, 1450–1680*, edited by Stuart B. Schwartz. Chapel Hill: University of North Carolina Press, 2004.

Schwartz, Stuart B. "The Voyage of the Vassals: Royal Power, Noble Obligations, and Merchant Capital Before the Portuguese Restoration of Independence, 1624–1640." *American Historical Review* 96, no. 3 (1991): 735–62.

Schwartz, Stuart B., ed. *Early Brazil: A Documentary Collection*. Cambridge: Cambridge University Press, 2010.

Schwartz, Stuart B., ed. *Tropical Babylons: Sugar and the Making of the Atlantic World, 1450–1680*. Chapel Hill: University of North Carolina Press, 2004.

Scott, Alison. *Literature and the Idea of Luxury in Early Modern England*. Burlington, VT: Ashgate.

Sewell, William H. "Historical Events as Transformations of Structures: Inventing Revolution at the Bastille." *Theory and Society* 25, no. 6 (1996): 841–81.

Shatzman, Aaron M. *The Old World, the New World, and the Creation of the Modern World, 1400–1650: An Interpretive History*. London: Anthem Press, 2013.

Silva, Felipa Ribeiro da. *Dutch and Portuguese in Western Africa: Empires, Merchants and the Atlantic System, 1580–1674*. Leiden: Brill, 2011.

Silva, José Justino de Andrade e. "Instituição da companhia geral para o estado do Brasil." In *Collecção chronologica da legislação Portugueza*. Lisbon: F. X. de Souza, 1856.

Silva, Leonardo Dantas. "João Mauricio de Nassau e os Livros." *Frans Post e o Brasil Holandês*, http://www.institutoricardobrennand.org.br/pinacoteca/fpost/mauricio.htm.

Silva, Maria Angélica da, and Melissa Mota Alcides. "Collecting and Framing the Wilderness: The Garden of Johan Maurits (1604–1679) in North-East Brazil." *Garden History* 30 no. 2 (Winter 2002): 153–76.

Silva, Rafael Ricarte da. "Sesmarias." *Atlas Digital da América Lusa*. http://lhs.unb.br/atlas/Sesmaria.

Soares, Mariza de Carvalho. "Engenho sim, de açúcar não: o engenho de farinha de Frans Post." *Varia Historia* 25, no. 41 (June 2009): 61–83.

Soares da Silva, José. *Memórias para a historia de Portugal*. Vol. 3. Lisboa Occidental, 1730.

Souza Silva, J. Norberto de. *Brasileiras celebres*. Rio de Janeiro: Garnier, 1862. BBM.

Spenlé, Virginia. "'Savagery' and 'Civilization': Dutch Brazil in the Kunst and Wunderkammer." *Journal of the Historians of Netherlandish Art* 3, no. 2 (2011). https//:doi.org/doi:10.5092/jhna.20113.2.3.

Stols, Eddie. "The Expansion of the Sugar Market in Western Europe." In *Tropical Babylons: Sugar and the Making of the Atlantic World, 1450–1680*, pp. 237–88. Chapel Hill: University of North Carolina Press, 2004.

Suárez, José I. "Portugal's Saudodismo Movement: An Esthetics of Sebastianism." *Luso-Brazilian Review* 28, no. 1 (Summer 1991): 129–40.

Subrahmanyam, Sanjay. *The Portuguese Empire in Asia: A Political and Economic History*. Oxford: Wiley-Blackwell, 1993.

Sutton, Elizabeth A. *Cartography and Capitalism in the Dutch Golden Age*. Chicago: University of Chicago Press, 2015.

Tähtinen, L. L. "The Intellectual Construction of the Fifth Empire: Legitimating the Braganza Restoration." *History of European Ideas* 38, no. 3 (September 2012): 413–25.
Tavares, Vito. "Dia internacional da mulher: as mulheres que derrotaram soldados holandeses em Pernambuco com água fervente e pimento." BBC News Brasil. March 6, 2020. https://www.bbc.com/portuguese/brasil-51761283.
Torres Megiani, Ana Paula, and Luis Filipe Silvério Lima, eds. *Visions, Prophecies and Divinations: Early Modern Messianism and Millenarianism in Iberian America, Spain and Portugal*. Leiden: Brill, 2016.
Tracy, James. *The Rise of Merchant Empires: Long Distance Trade in the Early Modern Era 1350–1750*. Cambridge: Cambridge University Press, 1990.
Treece, David. "Caramuru the Myth: Conquest and Conciliation." *Ibero-Amerikanisches Archiv Neue Folge* 10, no. 2 (1984): 139–73.
Tutino, John. *Making a New World: Founding Capitalism in the Bájio and Spanish North America*. Durham, NC: Duke University Press, 2011.
Vainfas, Ronaldo. "Saint Anthony in Portuguese America: Saint of the Restoration." In *Colonial Saints: Discovering the Holy in the Americas, 1500–1800*, edited by Allan Greer and Jodi Bilinkoff, pp. 99–114. New York: Routledge, 2003.
Vainfas, Ronaldo. *Traição: um jesuíta a serviço do Brasil Holandês processado pela Inquisição*. São Paulo: Companhia das Letras, 2008.
Valladares, Rafael. *A Independência de Portugal: Guerra e Restauração, 1640–1680*. Lisbon: A Esfera dos Livros, 2006.
Villiers, John. "Trade and Society in the Banda Islands in the Sixteenth Century." *Modern Asian Studies* 15, no. 4 (1981): 723–50.
Voigt, Lisa. "Imperial Celebrations, Local Triumphs: The Rhetoric of Festival Accounts in the Portuguese Empire." *Hispanic Review* 79, no. 1 (2011): 17–41.
Voragine, Jacobus de. *The Golden Legend or Lives of the Saints*. Fordham University, 2025. https://sourcebooks.fordham.edu/basis/goldenlegend/GoldenLegend-Volume2.asp.
Wiesebron, Marianne L. "As muitas facetas da sociedade durante a occupacão neerlandesa do Brasil." *Iberoamericana* 6, no. 24 (December 2006): 7–26.
Wiesner-Hanks, Merry. *Challenging Women's Agency and Activism in Early Modernity*. Amsterdam: Amsterdam University Press, 2016.
Wilson, Eric. *The Savage Republic: De Indis of Hugo Grotius, Republicanism, and Dutch Hegemony Within the Early Modern World-System (1600–1619)*. Leiden: Martinus Nijhoff Publishers, 2008.
Wiznitzer, Arnold. *Jews in Colonial Brazil*. New York: Columbia University Press, 1960.
Wiznitzer, Arnold. "The Jews in the Sugar Industry of Colonial Brazil." *Jewish Social Studies* 18, no. 3 (July 1956): 189–98.
Wright, I. A. "The Dutch and Cuba." *Hispanic American Historical Review* 1, no. 4: 597–634.

Index

Page numbers in italic text indicate figures.

açucarocracia (sugarocracy), 18. *See also* sugar economy
Afro-descended people: alliances with Portuguese, 73–74; blood purity and, 78, 100; *crioulos* and, 109; Henriques and, 73, 99, 109; identity formation and, 4; Infantaria Natural and, 122; mocambos and, 72; *mouros* and, 63; political loyalty and, 71, 73; runaways and, 71–72, 109, 185n2; sugar production and, 72–73. *See also* Dias, Henrique; guerrilla resistance; slavery and slave trade
aguardente, 110
Albernaz, João Teixeira, 52–53
Albuquerque, Brites de, 86
Albuquerque, Matias de: conquest of Pernambuco and, 61, 63, 70, 104, 107–8, 138; Dias and, 73, 98; invasion of Salvador and, 42–43; Pernambuco posting of, 183n65; recapture of Salvador and, 45–46, 49; Spain and, 152; wartime burials and, 70
Albuquerque Coelho, Duarte de, 3, 91–92, 95, 117, 126
aldeias (agricultural villages), 19, 41, 124, 197n36
al-Malik, Abd, 22
Almeida, Brites de (baker of Aljubarrota), 82–83, 101
Almeida, Jerômina de, 92–93
Almeida, João de, 144–45
Almoravids, 13
Amsterdam Jewish community, 162–63
Angola, 129–31, 137–38, 141–45, 147
António (Prior of Crato), 24
Armada Real do Mar Oceano, 166
Arminianism, 37
artisans of Lisbon. *See* House of Twenty-Four (Casa dos Vinte e Quatro)
artistic representation of Brazil, 67–68, 70, 87–88
asiento, 134, 136–37. *See also* slavery and slave trade
Ataide, António de, 47
Ataide, Jerônimo de, 47, 52, 184n89
Atlas of Brazil (Albernaz), 52–53
Atlantic islands: loyalty to Dom João IV, 141, 151; military recruitment and, 105, 110–11, 122, 127; treaties and, 15
Auto da Lusitânia (Vicente), 17
Azores, 110–11, 122, 141. *See also* Atlantic islands

backlands of Brazil (*sertão*): elite women and, 87, 88; reconquest of Salvador and, 7, 40–42, 44; recruitment evasion and, 104; Siege of Bahia and, 115; silver mines and, 17; Tarairu and, 189n77. *See also* aldeias (agricultural villages); guerrilla resistance; mocambos (runaway settlements)
Bagnuolo, Count of 108, 116–19

Bahia, 18–19, 29, 35, 38–39, 75. *See also* Bay of All Saints; invasion of Salvador de Bahia (1624); Luso–Dutch war; reconquest of Salvador de Bahia (1625); Siege of Bahia (1638)
baker of Aljubarrota, 82–83, 101
Bandarra, António Gonçalves de, 20–21, 23–24. See also *Trovas* (Bandarra)
bandeirantes (backwoodsmen), 19, 188n58
Barlaeus, Caspar van, 74, 77
Barros, António Cardoso de, 29
"Batavian land" (Salvador de Bahia), 41, 182nn44–45
Battle of Alcácer-Quiber, 22–23, 169
Battle of Aljubarrota, 82
Battle of Guararapes (first), 158, 166
Battle of Guararapes (second), 158, 163–64, 166
Battle of Ourique, 13–14, 19, 20
Battle of Paraíba, 65
Battle of Porto Calvo, 97, 98
Battle of Tamandaré, 143
Battle of Tejucupapo, 97–98, 100–101, 192n3
Bautista Maíno, Juan, 53–54
Bay of All Saints, 54, 60, 117. *See also* Bahia; invasion of Salvador de Bahia (1625); reconquest of Salvador de Bahia (1625); Salvador de Bahia; Siege of Bahia (1638)
Behaim, Stephan, 113, 187n37
bibliopolitics, 155–56
blood purity, 44–45, 46–47, 97–100
Board of Conscience and Orders (Mesa da Consciência e Ordens), 98–99, 106, 133, 195–96n13
Book of Daniel, 177–78n63
Botelho, Diogo, 36
Braganza, House of, 154, 203n48. *See also* João IV, King of Portugal (former Duke of Braganza)
Brandão, Francisco, 83, 101, 192n10

brasilienses, 68–70, 190n83. *See also* Tupinambá
Brazil: artistic representation of, 67–68, 70, 87–88; donatários and, 17; Dutch control of the northeast, 57–58; early threat of WIC to, 31–32; exploration in, 16–17; fortifications and, 29, 30, 32; Portuguese diplomacy and, 154; reconquest of Angola and, 143; Restoration of Portugal and, 121, 130, 139–40; role in Spanish imperial system, 38–39; sugar economy and, 17, 18–19. *See also* Dutch Brazil; inter-captaincy coordination; Luso–Dutch war
Brazil General Company, 8, 151, 164–67
Brazilian scholars, 6
brazilwood, 16–17
Brevísima relacíon (Las Casas), 31
Buenos Aires, 130, 138, 142
Bulhões, Fernando Martins de. *See* St. Anthony (Santo Antônio)

Cabo Verde. *See* Atlantic islands
Cabral, Pedro, 16–17
Calabar, Domingo Fernandes, 64–65, 66, 77–78
Calado, Manoel: account of, 3, 174n14; Calabar and, 65, 187–88n44; conquest of Pernambuco and, 61–62, 187n32; Dias Ferreira and, 76; Henrique Dias and, 99; women of Tejucupapo and, 81
Camarão, Clara, 95–96
Camarão, Felipe, 4, 7, 45, 67, 70, 158
Camarão, Maria, 81
Camões, Luis de, 21–22, 32
Caracas, 137
Caramaru (Santa Rita Durão), 1–2
Carreira da Índia, 15–16, 196n14
Carta Ânua (Vieira), 3, 42–43, 54–55
Cartagena de Indias, 135, 202n40
cartographic instruments, 14–15

Carvalho, Antônio, 103, 114
Casa Forte (Paes sugar mill), 89–91, 158
Castro, João de, 12, 24–26, 27, 29, 33
Catalan revolt, 121
Catizone, Marco Tulio, 25
chronicles of martial women, 94–97, 101–2
commissioned art (Maurits), 67–68, 70
conceptismo, 58, 186n6
conquest of Pernambuco, 60–65, 72, 107–8, 114
Conselho Ultramarino (Overseas Council), 8, 121–22, 133, 142–43, 152
conspiracy of 1641, 151, 203n48
conversos. *See* Jews; New Christians (*conversos*)
Correia, Diogo Álvares, 173n1
corsairs, 29–30
Council of Indies (Conselho da Índia), 106, 133
Council of Treasury (Conselho da Fazenda), 107, 133, 196n15
Council of War (Conselho da Guerra), 121, 133, 151–53
Couto, Domingos Loreto, 96
cowrie shells (zimbo), 147–48
crioulos (term), 109
cross-cultural alliances. *See* guerrilla resistance; interfaith coordination and Brazil General Company; Luso-Brazilian identity; Luso-Brazilians
Cunha, Paulo da, 93, 97

desertion, 63, 187n37
De With, Gijsbert, 89–90
Dias, Baltasar, 94
Dias, Henrique, 4, 7, 73, 97–100, 109, 171, 197n13
Dias Ferreira, Gaspar, 76–77, 90, 160
Dias Pimentel, Francisco, 135
diplomacy: bibliopolitics and, 155–56; Pernambucan uprising and, 158–59; post-restoration, 154–55; Vieira and, 161–62
Discurso da vida (Castro), 25, 33
"divided" men, 75–76
Divine War of Liberation, 8, 79, 94, 143, 145, 157–61
dowries, 85
drama, 17–18
Dussen, Adrian van der, 87, 114
Dutch archives, 5
Dutch Brazil: administration of Iberian union and, 107; beginnings of, 35; commissioned art and, 78–79; as imperial moment, 4; Jewish communities and, 195n2; Luso-Brazilian documents and, 3–4; Luso-Brazilian identity and, 59–60, 172; Portuguese myth and, 3–4; scholarship on, 5–6. *See also* Dutch West India Company (WIC); Grand Design; Luso–Dutch war
Dutch East India Company (VOC), 2–3, 27–28
Dutch–Portuguese war. *See* Luso–Dutch war
Dutch–Spanish relations, 29–31, 60–61, 163. *See also* Luso–Dutch war
Dutch West India Company (WIC): alliance with Indigenous people, 189n77; Angola and, 144–45, 151; archives of, 186n10; Caribbean and, 60; chartering and development of, 31, 37–38; claims in Brazil, 1, 2; concerns with Iberian-held Bahia, 114; conquest of Pernambuco and, 60–61; desertion and, 187n37; fall of Bahia and, 35; governor-general of Brazil and, 67; Grand Design and, 38–39; Indigenous alliances with, 68–70; "liberation" of the Portuguese and, 38, 41, 70, 107; marriage of local women and, 89; orange grove incident and,
Dutch West India Company (*continued*)

103; peace treaty violations and, 156; Pernambucan uprising and, 157–60; Pernambuco casualties and, 195n3; Portuguese resistance to, 42–43; provisioning and, 104–5, 112–13; raiding practices of, 60; Restoration of Portugal and, 139; settlement options for soldiers in, 195n2; Siege of Bahia and, 115–20; targeting of Brazil, 3; trafficking and, 72; trials of, 5; West Africa and, 137; withdrawal from Portuguese America, 9; zimbo trade and, 147. *See also* Dutch Brazil; Luso–Dutch war; Maurits van Nassau-Siegen, Johan; United Provinces

Eckhout, Albert, 59, 68, 70, 71, 125
Edict of Expulsion, 75
Eighty Years War, 37, 51
elite women, 84–85, 87–88. *See also* noblewomen (Luso-Brazilian)
Elmina, 19, 72, 137
engenhos (sugar mills), 18, 87, 89–90
Estado da Índia, 16, 29
exploration and imperial expansion, 14–19

faith, 57–59, 78. *See also* interfaith coordination and Brazil General Company; mythological discourse (Portuguese)
farinha (manioc flour), 125–26, 200–201n136, 200n134
female resistance, 81–83, 94–97, 101–2
fidalgueira (aristocracy), 44, 46–47, 55
flour of war, 125–26, 200–201n136, 200n134. *See also* manioc
food insecurity and war, 103–5, 111–13, 126
Forte Real do Bom Jesus, 64–65, 103, 111–14, 126
Fort Frederick Hendrick, 78–79
fortifications in Brazil, 29, 30, 32, 188n53
Forty Conspirators, 121, 129, 131–32. *See also* Restoration of Portugal

France, 155
Freire, Francisco Brito, 95
Furtado, Diogo de Mendonça, 32, 39–40, 42

Galicia, 175n12
Gama, Vasco da, 16, 32
gold, 4
Grand Design: ambitions of, 181n23; implementation of, 31, 110; invasion of Salvador and, 36, 38–42; Mina and, 115; New Christians and Jews in, 74–75. *See also* Dutch West India Company (WIC); Luso–Dutch war
Grotius, Hugo, 2–3, 28–29, 37, 175n10, 179n94
guerrilla resistance: Afro-Brazilian and Indigenous motivations for, 73–74, 78; battles of Guararapes and, 163, 164; Divine War of Liberation and, 8; Dutch conquest of Pernambuco and, 7, 45, 104, 108; effectiveness of, 2, 118–20, 166–67; networks and, 5; Pernambucan uprising and, 119–20, 143, 157–60; provisioning and recruitment for, 104–5, 109–10, 123–24, 126–27; Salvador and, 41–43, 49; Siege of Bahia and, 55, 78, 115; Vieira and, 59; WIC and, 114. *See also* Luso-Brazilian identity; Luso-Brazilians; Luso–Dutch war; *individual engagements*

Habsburg war, 26
Hague, The, 149, 158, 171
Heeren XIX, 67, 118. *See also* Dutch West India Company (WIC)
Henriques, 73, 99, 99. 109, 109. *See also* Dias, Henrique
Henriques, Afonso, 13–14, 19
Heyn, Piet, 60, 94, 186n11

High Court, 133
Hoogstraten, Samuel van, 189n71
Hope of Israel, The (Israel), 162–63
Hopes of Portugal, The (Vieira), 170
House of Twenty-Four (Casa dos Vinte e Quatro), 48, 132
human trafficking. *See* slavery and slave trade

Iberian union: access to ports and, 195n8; Bahia and, 7; consequences for Portugal of, 11, 26; dissolution of, 8; Forty Conspirators and, 121, 129, 131–32; internal conflict and, 55–56; Portuguese overseas colonies and, 7, 106–7; post-restoration chronicles and, 50–51; provisioning and, 111–12; royal galleon visit and, 106; slave trade and, 136–37; succession crisis and, 2, 11, 24, 33, 175n3; taxation and grain revolts in, 120–21; trans-imperial exchanges and, 134. *See also* rescue armadas; Restoration of Portugal; silver economy and human trafficking
identity formation. *See* Luso-Brazilian identity
Ilha da Santa Cruz (Brazil), 16. *See also* Brazil
Indigenous people: aldeias and, 19, 41, 124, 197n36; alliances with WIC, 5, 62–63, 189n79; alliance with Jesuits, 7, 55; Dutch occupation and, 4; enslavement of, 19, 65, 188n58; female resistance and, 95–96; identity formation and, 4; "liberation" of, 31, 37–38; political loyalty and, 68–71; Portuguese grouping of, 189n77; reconquest of Salvador de Bahia and, 49; resistance to Dutch occupation and, 41–43, 45, 170; WIC and, 189n79; women and, 95–97, 171, 173n1.

See also Camarão, Felipe; guerrilla resistance; manioc; *individual Indigenous groups*
Infantaria Natural, 122
inheritance law, 86, 98, 99–100, 122–23
Ink Wars, 50
inter-captaincy coordination, 8, 43, 55, 120, 140, 142–43
interfaith coordination and Brazil General Company, 161–67
invasion of Salvador de Bahia (1624), 35–36, 38–40
Israel, Menasseh Ben (Manuel Dias Soeiro), 156, 162–63, 207n67
Itaparica, 41

Jesuits, 18–19, 40–41, 45, 55, 65–66
Jesus, Rafael de, 81–82
Jews: blood purity and, 44, 98; cross-cultural alliances and, 59; emigration to Brazil and, 16, 74–76, 191n118, 195n2; interfaith coordination and, 156, 161–65, 167; Judaizing and, 75, 178n75, 207n64; trade and, 26. *See also* synagogues in Brazil
João II, King of Portugal, 15
João III, King of Portugal, 17, 18
João IV, King of Portugal (former Duke of Braganza), 99, 121–22, 129–33, 140, 154, 162–64, 172
Journey of the Vassals (Guerreiro), 50–51. *See also* rescue armadas; rescue armada to Bahia ("journey of the vassals")
just war, 2–3, 7, 28

Lancaster, James, 18, 177n40
land grants, 86–87
landscapes (*landschap*), 59
Las Casas, Bartolomé de, 31
Lei Mental, 47
letrados, 133, 153

Lévy, Aaron (António de Montesinos), 162
Lisbon, 30–31, 46–48, 106, 111–12, 195n8
Lobo, Rodrigo, 135
Loronha, Fernão de, 16–17
Lusiads, The (Camões), 21–22
Luso-Brazilian identity: Dutch threat and, 36, 49; formation of, 4–9, 59, 101; Jesuit–Indigenous alliance and, 55; legacy of Dutch challenge and, 170–72; manioc and, 127. *See also* guerrilla resistance
Luso-Brazilians: "Divine War of Liberation" and, 79; Dutch conquest of Pernambuco and, 108; Dutch occupation and, 3; Maurits-commissioned art and, 68; military–morador tensions and, 117; motivations for alliances and, 73–74; Pernambucan uprising and, 157–58; provisioning and, 104–5, 117–20, 123–24, 126–27; reconquest of Angola and, 144–45; reconquest of Salvador and, 50, 55; transatlantic Lusophone consciousness, 7; zimbo trade and, 147–48. *See also* guerrilla resistance; Luso-Brazilian identity; women, Luso-Brazilian
Luso–Dutch war: 1624 invasion of Salvador in, 35–40; 1638 siege of Bahia in, 55, 57, 70–71, 73–74, 76, 114–20; Angola and, 141–42, 144–45, 148; attacks on Portuguese posts in, 7; Battle of Tejucupapo in, 97–98, 100–101, 192n3; battles of Guararapes in, 158, 163–64, 166; Brazil General Company and, 166; conquest of Pernambuco in, 60–65, 72, 107–8, 114; Divine War of Liberation and, 8, 79, 94, 143, 145, 157–61; embargoing of ships and, 113; food insecurity and, 103–5, 111–13, 126; fortifications in Brazil and, 29, 30, 32, 188n53; Iberian union and, 26; interfaith coordination and, 161–62; Luso victory in, 167; orange grove incident in, 103; overview of, 2–3, 8, 27; Papel Forte and, 163; Pernambucan uprising in, 157–60; Portuguese attempts at truce in, 149–51; Portuguese diplomacy in, 154–55; resistance and reconquest in Salvador and, 44–47, 49, 55; Restoration of Portugal and, 121, 130–31, 138, 139; Sebastianism and, 12; significance of multi-ethnic victory and, 170–72; treason and, 63–66, 77, 92–93, 159–60; West Africa and, 110. *See also* Dutch West India Company (WIC); Grand Design; guerrilla resistance; provisioning; recruitment; rescue armadas; individual battles

Madeira, 141. *See also* Atlantic islands
Malícia das Mulheres (Dias), 94
mameluco (term), 187–88n44
manioc, 105, 123, 124–27, 200–201n136, 200n134
Manuel, King of Portugal, 16
mappa mundiae, 14
Mare Liberum (Grotius), 7, 28–29, 179n94
Margaret of Savoy (Duquesa de Mântua), 121, 132
Marquis de Niza, 155–56, 166
martial service and status improvement, 97–99, 104–5
martial women, 82–84, 94, 100–102
Mascarenhas, Fernando de (Conde de Torre), 136
Mascarenhas, Jorge de (Marquis de Montalvão), 109, 130, 133, 136, 138–39, 153, 203n49
Matos, Baltazar Rodrigues, 161–62
Maurits van Nassau-Siegen, Johan: 1638

invasion of Bahia and, 55; Ana Paes and, 89; appraisal of, 5–6; Dias Ferreira and, 76–77; as governor-general of Brazil, 67; on guerrilla resistance, 118–19; Portuguese Bahia and, 115–16; Restoration of Portugal and, 139; scholar-aesthetes and, 59; West Africa and, 137. *See also* Dutch West India Company (WIC)
Mello, Evaldo Cabral de, 6
Mello, José Antônio Gonsalves de, 6
Memórias diárias (Albuquerque Coelho), 3
Mendez, Jeronyma, 95
Mesa da Consciência e Ordens (Board of Conscience and Orders), 98–99, 106, 133, 195–96n13
messianic inspiration, 20–21. *See also* mythological discourse (Portuguese); Sebastianism
military orders, 98, 104–5
mocambos (runaway settlements), 72, 190n93
Moerbeeck, Jan Andries, 38, 107
moradores, 57, 79, 125
Moraes, Manoel de, 45, 65–66, 77–78, 188–89n62
Moreno, Martim Soares, 30
motherhood and mother-martyrs, 91–92, 95
Moura, Francisco de, 45
mouros (term), 63
mulato (term), 187–88n44
Muslims, 13–14
mythological discourse (Portuguese), 12, 15, 32–33, 170. *See also* Sebastianism

navigational technologies, 14–15
Neves, Clara, 90
New Christians (also conversos), 16, 21, 26, 74–76, 156, 161–62, 178n75
New Holland, 76, 191n116
news of Portuguese restoration, 138–41

nobility of blood. *See* blood purity
noblewomen (Luso-Brazilian), 85, 91, 93. *See also* elite women
Nogueira, Vicente, 156
Noronha, Fernão, 16, 75
North Africa, 21–23, 204n62
Nova Lusitania (Freire), 95
Nunes, Gregório, 75
Nunes da Costa, Duarte, 26
Nunes da Costa, Jerônimo, 26, 162, 165

O castrioto Lusitano (Jesus), 81–82
Olinda, 39, 61–64. *See also* conquest of Pernambuco; Forte Real do Bom Jesus; Pernambucan uprising; Pernambuco
Olivares, Count-Duke of (Gaspar de Guzmán), 107, 120, 131, 134
Order of Our Lady of Penha de França, 169
Orellana, Juan de, 52
orphan girls, 85–86
Ortiz, Maria, 94, 101, 193n55, 194n83
Os Lusíadas (Camões), 21–22, 32–33
O valeroso Lucideno (Calado), 3
Overseas Council (Conselho Ultramarino), 8, 121–22, 133, 142–43, 152

Paes, Ana, 89–91, 93
Paiva, Jerônimo Serrão de, 143
Palmares, 72, 190n93
Papel Forte (Vieira), 163
Paraguaçu, 171, 173n1
Pernambucan uprising, 157–60
Pernambuco: decline of, 174n20; Dutch conquest of, 7, 60–65, 72, 107–8, 114; Forte Real do Bom Jesus and, 64–65, 111–13, 126; Grand Design and, 38–39; New Christians and Jews in, 74–76; Papel Forte and, 163; sugar economy and, 18–19; uprising in, 157–60. *See also* guerrilla resistance; Luso–Dutch war

Peru. *See* peruleiros; Potosí; silver economy and human trafficking
peruleiros, 130, 134–36, 138, 142, 147–48
Philip II, King of Spain (Philip I of Portugal), 2, 11–12, 24, 26, 29, 106
Philip III, King of Spain (Philip II of Portugal), 36
Philip IV, King of Spain (Philip III of Portugal), 30–32, 39, 46, 99, 107
piracy, 29–30
Plante, Franciscus, 189n73
planters, 19, 126, 141–43, 147–48. *See also* manioc; provisioning; slavery and slave trade; sugar economy
portolan charts, 14
Portugal: administration in, 133; consequences of Iberian Union for, 11; conspiracy of 1641 and, 151, 203n48; Cortes meeting at Tomar and, 24, 26, 195n8; efforts to recruit allies against Spain, 150; exploration and, 14–16; Forty Conspirators and, 121, 129, 131–32; founding of, 13–14; mythological discourse and, 12, 32–33; Restoration of, 120–21, 129–33; social status and, 44; succession crisis and, 2, 11, 24, 33, 175n3. *See also* Luso–Dutch war; Portuguese Empire; Sebastianism
Portuguese Empire: Brazil and restoration of, 4; colonial holdings in, *146*; coordination within, 8; Estado da Índia and, 16; exploration and trade in, 15–17; identity formation and, 4; internal threats to, 3, 151; Jesuits and, 18; post-restoration, 135–36, 164; reach of, 19–20; royal family housing in Brazil and, 4; VOC assaults on, 2–3. *See also* Luso–Dutch war; Portugal; *individual colonies and captaincies*
Portuguese Inquisition, 21, 75
Post, Frans, 59, 73, 78–79

post-restoration chronicles, 49–54
Poti, Pieter, 69
Potiguar, 44, 68–71, 189n77
Potosí, 17, 129-30, 134, 138–42, 201n2
Prester John, 15
print and Portuguese diplomacy, 155
privateering, 28
prophecy, 2, 8, 12, 15, 21, 54, 163–64. *See also* mythological discourse (Portuguese); Sebastianism
provisioners, 104–5
provisioning: Brazil General Company and, 164–65; embargoes and, 113; guerrilla resistance and, 123–24, 126–27; Luso-Brazilian opportunities for, 104–5; manioc for, 123–27; Siege of Bahia and, 114–15, 117, 118–20; transatlantic voyages and, 111–12, 123; WIC soldiers and, 112–13
Pudsey, Cuthbert, 87, 89, 90–91

quilombo, 190n93, 190n97

Recife, 18, 61–62, 96, 112–13, 138, 143, 157–60, 196n21. *See also* conquest of Pernambuco; Forte Real do Bom Jesus; Luso–Dutch war; Pernambucan uprising; Pernambuco
reconquest of Angola, 130, 142–45
reconquest of Salvador de Bahia (1625), 49, 55. *See also* post-restoration chronicles; rescue armada to Bahia ("journey of the vassals")
recruitment: African-descended troops and, 109–10; Azores and, 122; Casa dos Vinte e Quatro and, 48; Dutch practices of, 111; experienced soldiers and, 45; fidalgueira and, 46–48; Infantaria Natural and, 122; Luso–Dutch war and alternative methods of, 108–9; motivations for, 104; needs of, 8; non-Brazilian,

110; rescue armada to Bahia and, 41, 46–49, 55–56, 108; Spanish practices of, 108, 122. *See also* rescue armadas
Recuperación de Bahía (Maíno), 53–54
refugees, 35, 41–43
rescue armadas: failures of later, 104; Iberian power and, 107; Luso-Spanish-Neapolitan (1631), 108; Mascarenhas and, 202n32; Overseas Council and, 152–53; provisioning for, 111–12; Siege of Bahia and, 116
rescue armada to Bahia ("journey of the vassals"), 41, 46–49, 55–56, 108
resistance efforts in Bahia, 44–47, 49, 55. *See also* guerrilla resistance; rescue armadas
Restoration of Portugal, 8, 120–21, 129–31, 132–33
Rio de Janeiro, 122, 142–43, 201n2, 202–3n45. *See also* silver economy and human trafficking
Rio de la Plata, 136, 138, 148, 201n2.
runaways, 71–72, 109, 185n2. *See also* Afro-descended people; mocambos (runaway settlements)

Sá, Salvador de, 44, 49, 130, 133–36, 139–48 *passim*, 163–64
Salvador de Bahia: 1624 invasion of, 35–36, 38–41; 1625 reconquest of, 49, 55; 1638 siege of, 55, 57, 70–71, 73–74, 76, 114–20; Luso–Brazilian resistance and, 42–43; rescue armada to, 41, 46–49, 55–56, 108; resistance efforts in, 44–47, 49, 55; risk and, 38; role of, 32. *See also* Luso–Dutch war
Santa Catarina (ship), 27–28
Santa Rita Durão, José de, 1
Santiago, Diogo Lopes de, 81, 96–97
Santo Antônio. *See* St. Anthony (Santo Antônio)
São Paulo of Luanda, 72, 137. *See also* Angola
São Paulo/São Vicente, 18, 140, 174n20, 203n57
saudade, 4–5
Sebastian, King of Portugal, 2, 7, 11, 20–24, 32–33
Sebastianism: as crime, 75; development of, 20; *Discurso de vida* and, 32–33; guerrilla resistance and, 166; literature and, 24–27; Portuguese identity and, 7, 12; Restoration of Portugal and, 140; Vieira sermon and, 171–72. *See also* mythological discourse (Portuguese); Vieira, António
Sequeira, Manoel de Rego, 52
sertão. *See* backlands of Brazil (sertão)
sesmarias, 29–30, 86, 192n21
Siege of Bahia (1638), 55, 57, 70–71, 73–74, 76, 114–20
Silva, José Soares da, 101
Silva, Luiza Maria da, 100–101
Silva, Pedro da, 118
silver economy and human trafficking, 129, 134–38, 142–43, 145, 147–48, 201n2. *See also* Potosí; slavery and slave trade
Simões, António, 169
slavery and slave trade: Almeida and, 204n80; bare feet and, 191n128; Dutch Grand design and, 129–30; human trafficking in, 72, 136; Indigenous people and, 19; movement of captives in, 202–3n45; Portuguese women and, 87–88; role of New Christians and Jews in, 74, 76; silver economy and, 129, 134–38, 142–43, 145, 147, 201n2; St. Anthony and, 185n2; sugar economy and, 12, 19, 164, 200–201n136; WIC and, 69–70, 72–73
social status, 44–45, 74, 78, 97–99, 104–5

Sousa, Gaspar de, 39
Sousa, Maria de, 92
Sousa Coutinho, Francisco de, 149, 154–55, 158–61, 166
Sousa Guerra, Mariana de (Condessa do Vimieiro), 204n58
Souto, Sebastião, 65, 116
Spanish Empire: exploration treaties and, 15; Iberian Union and, 11, 24, 26; loss of Portugal, 134; news of Restoration of Portugal in, 134–35; Portuguese officials and, 135; slave trade in, 136–37; trade embargoes and, 30; union of crowns and, 2. *See also* Iberian union
spice trade, 15–16, 27
St. Anthony (Santo Antônio), 57, 60, 185n4, 185nn1–2
St. Michael, 145
succession crisis, 2, 11, 24, 33, 175n3. *See also* Iberian union
sugar economy, 4, 8, 17–19, 72–73, 126. *See also* Brazil General Company; slavery and slave trade
synagogues in Brazil, 76. *See also* Jews

Tamandaré, 143
Tapuya, 68, 189n77
Tarairu, 189n77
taxes and taxation, 52, 74, 76, 120, 130–32, 196n26
Teixeira, Marcos, 40, 42, 45
Tejucupapo, 81–82, 97–98, 100, 192n3
Teles da Silva, António, 142, 143, 152, 157–58, 159, 166
Tempo dos flamengos (Mello), 6
Temudo, Andre Pereira, 62
Toledo Osorio, Fadrique de, 53–54
Tourlon, Charles, 89
trade: embargoes and, 30; Estado da Índia and, 16; exploration and, 15–16; human trafficking and silver, 129, 134–38, 142–43, 145, 147, 201n2;

Iberian union and, 26; Luso–Dutch, 29, 31; *Mare Liberum* and, 28–29; piracy threats to Brazilian, 29–30. *See also* provisioning; slavery and slave trade
treason, 63–66, 77, 92–93, 159–60
Treaty of Alcaçovas, 15
Treaty of Tordesillas, 15, 176n30
Treaty of Tui, 13, 175n12
Tribe of Reuben, 162–63
Trovas (Bandarra), 4, 20–21, 23–25, 27, 75, 155–56
Tupi dictionary, 66
Tupinambá, 43–44, 68–70, 124–26, 189n77
Twelve-Year Truce, 3, 29–30, 31, 37, 186n13
"types of Brazil" (Eckhout), 59, 67

Ugarthe, Catarina, 202n26
Unión de Armas, 108
United Provinces: Brazilian war tax and, 38; domestic issues and, 37; Dutch archives and, 5; Dutch East India Company (VOC) and, 2–3, 27–28; "imperial moment" for, 4; Indigenous people and, 62, 69; recruitment and, 111; relations with Spain, 29–31, 60–61, 160, 163; stability of, 27; territory in 1643, 57–58. *See also* Dutch Brazil; Dutch West India Company (WIC); Luso–Dutch war

Valdoveço, Pedro de, 100
Van Dorth, Johan, 36, 43, 182n45
Van Oldebarneveldt, Johan, 37, 194n94
Vargas, Tamayo de, 51
Vasconcelos, Miguel de, 121, 132
Verdonck, Adrian, 63–64
Viana do Castelo, 197n52
Vicente, Gil, 17
Vieira, António: Brazil General Company and, 164, 166; Carta Ânua of,

3, 7, 41–45, 49, 54–55; interfaith coordination and, 161–63; Israel and, 207n67; João IV and, 140–41; legacy of Luso–Dutch war and, 171–72; mythological discourse and, 3–4; Penha de França sermon and, 169–70; Rio de la Plata and, 138; Salvador sermon and, 57–59, 78; *Trovas* and, 75; on the Tupinambá, 68

Vieira, João Fernandes, 147, 151, 157–59

VOC. *See* Dutch East India Company (VOC)

"voyage of the vassals." *See* rescue armada to Bahia ("journey of the vassals")

Waerdenburch, Colonel, 61, 63, 70

Wagner, Zacharias, 87–88

war flour (farinha da guerra), 105. *See also* manioc

West Africa, 19, 72, 110, 130, 137. *See also* Angola

wheat, 111–12

white gold. *See* sugar economy

WIC. *See* Dutch West India Company (WIC)

"wild nations of people" (Eckhout), 68

William of Orange, 31

women, Luso-Brazilian: chronicles of resistance and, 94–97, 101–2; elite, 87–88; land holding and, 85–87; legacy of, 7, 84; legal status and protections for, 84–85; mother-martyrs and, 91–92, 95; power and agency of, 90–91, 93; records and, 101; resistance and, 100–102; Tejucupapo and, 81, 96–98, 100, 192n3; treason and, 92–93; WIC marriages and, 89

women of Tejucupapo, 81, 97–98, 100, 192n3

zimbo (cowrie shells), 147–48

www.ingramcontent.com/pod-product-compliance
Lightning Source LLC
Chambersburg PA
CBHW020646230426
43665CB00008B/339